UNCTAD/ITE/IIT/6

**UNITED NATIONS CONFERENCE ON TRADE AND DEVELOPMENT**

*Handbook on*
# Foreign Direct Investment by Small and Medium-sized Entreprises
*Lessons from Asia*

**UNITED NATIONS**
New York and Geneva, 1998

## Note

UNCTAD serves as the focal point within the United Nations Secretariat for all matters related to foreign direct investment and transnational corporations. In the past, the Programme on Transnational Corporations was carried out by the United Nations Centre on Transnational Corporations (1975-1992) and the Transnational Corporations and Management Division of the United Nations Department of Economic and Social Development (1992-1993). In 1993, the Programme was transferred to the United Nations Conference on Trade and Development. UNCTAD seeks to further the understanding of the nature of transnational corporations and their contribution to development and to create an enabling environment for international investment and enterprise development. UNCTAD's work is carried out through intergovernmental deliberations, technical assistance activities, seminars, workshops and conferences.

The term "country" as used in this study also refers, as appropriate, to territories or areas; the designations employed and the presentation of the material do not imply the expression of any opinion whatsoever on the part of the Secretariat of the United Nations concerning the legal status of any country, territory, city or area or of its authorities, or concerning the delimitation of its frontiers or boundaries. In addition, the designations of country groups are intended solely for statistical or analytical convenience and do not necessarily express a judgement about the stage of development reached by a particular country or area in the development process.

The following symbols have been used in the tables:

Two dots (..) indicate that data are not available or are not separately reported. Rows in tables have been omitted in those cases where no data are available for any of the elements in the row;

A dash (-) indicates that the item is equal to zero or its value is negligible;

A blank in a table indicates that the item is not applicable;

A slash (/) between dates representing years, e.g., 1994/95, indicates a financial year;

Use of a hyphen (-) between dates representing years, e.g., 1994-1995, signifies the full period involved, including the beginning and end years.

Reference to "dollars" ($) means United States dollars, unless otherwise indicated.

Annual rates of growth or change, unless otherwise stated, refer to annual compound rates.

Details and percentages in tables do not necessarily add up to totals, because of rounding.

The material contained in this study may be freely quoted with appropriate acknowledgement.

UNITED NATIONS PUBLICATION

Sales No. E.98.II.D.4

ISBN 92-1-112425-5

# PREFACE

Foreign direct investment by small and medium-sized enterprises (SMEs) has grown noticeably since the mid-1980s. Driven by, among other factors, the need to be present abroad to access markets and resources in order to maintain their competitiveness in a rapidly liberalizing and globalizing world economy, small and medium-sized transnational corporations are increasingly internationalizing their production activities. Foreign direct investment by SMEs thus complements that by large transnational corporations as a potential avenue for the transfer of productive resources and technology that can enhance the growth and competitiveness of developing countries.

In order to understand this phenomenon better, UNCTAD has for some time been conducting research into foreign direct investment by SMEs and the international activities of these enterprises. Earlier findings of this research were set out in a study entitled *Small and Medium-sized Transnational Corporations: Role, Impact and Policy Implications*, published in 1993. That study was prepared on the basis of a questionnaire survey of SME investors originating in developed countries and of their foreign affiliates operating in developing countries. It found that small and medium-sized transnational corporations can contribute positively to development, and concluded that the positive role they can play should be taken into account in the national economic policies of both host and home countries.

SMEs that engage in foreign direct investment are an important part of the entrepreneurial engine that drives development and growth. In many developing countries, however, the SME sector is insufficiently developed in terms of the core of dynamic and fast-growing SMEs that contribute significantly to development. Foreign direct investment by SMEs has the potential to strengthen the SME sectors of home as well as host countries, contributing to the health and dynamism of their economies. The potential in this regard is high, as more than 95 per cent of all firms are small or medium-sized.

Increasing the awareness and understanding in developing countries of this insufficiently tapped source of investment can thus usefully contribute to their development, including the development of their own SMEs. Carefully designed policies are, however, needed to encourage foreign direct investment by and in SMEs. A number of countries have considerable experience as regards SME development generally, as well of policies to attract investment by such enterprises and to expand and strengthen its role in development. An understanding of this experience would be useful in formulating policies and programmes with respect to attracting and benefiting from foreign direct investment by SMEs.

This *Handbook* contains the results of a questionnaire survey and case studies conducted in selected developing economies in Asia. The survey targeted SMEs that are outward investors in selected home economies, as well as others that are recipients of inward foreign direct investment in selected host countries; the case studies provided further insights into the experiences of selected host and home countries. The *Handbook* also draws on the discussions at the *International Conference on SMEs-FDI-Development: Attracting SMEs and Promoting Development in Developing Asia*, organized by UNCTAD in cooperation with China's Ministry of Foreign Trade and Economic Cooperation, and held in Kunming, China, from 29 to 31 October 1997. The empirical work focused on Asia, since developing Asia has a larger potential to mobilize foreign direct investment by SMEs than any other developing region. Furthermore, a number of countries in the region have considerable experience as regards policies to attract foreign direct investment by SMEs and to strengthen its role in development. Understanding this experience can be of assistance to other countries within and outside the region in formulating policies and programmes with respect to foreign direct investment by SMEs.

This *Handbook* starts with an analysis of the role and behaviour of SMEs and foreign direct investment by them in Asian developing countries, the problems and obstacles facing investment by these enterprises, strategies adopted by them, and the impact of foreign direct investment by SME investors (as well as large investors) on recipient SMEs and economies in the region (Part One). It then examines policies relating to SMEs and foreign direct investment by them in Asian countries that have successfully developed their economies with the efficient use of such enterprises, and attempts to draw lessons as regards the removal of obstacles to, and facilitating foreign direct investment by, SMEs (Part Two). The *Handbook* then provides a framework for assessing policy options with respect to their benefits and costs, and outlines practical steps to help governments formulate and implement measures to attract flows of investments and technology from foreign SMEs to host countries and to maximize their contribution to the fulfilment of their development needs and objectives; it also examines avenues for international cooperation in this respect (Part Three). As Part Three has been designed to be used, if necessary, as a stand-alone document for policy makers, executives from SMEs and others who may not have the time to consult the entire volume, it revisits -- and develops further -- a number of the themes addressed in Part Two.

The *Handbook* was mainly drafted by Chris Hall, and finalized by Masataka Fujita and Padma Mallampally, under the overall direction of Karl P. Sauvant. A number of national consultants for the project prepared inputs that made a significant contribution to the *Handbook*; they include Lolita Belandres, Tain-Jy Chen, Yoon-Bae Ouh, Aung Myint, Laurent Schwab and Wong Marn Heong. Research assistance was provided by Antonella Convertino and Antonella Pradelli. Production of the *Handbook* was carried out by Jenifer Tacardon. Formal copy-editing was done by Graham Grayston. The *Handbook* was desktop-published by Teresita Sabico, and the cover was designed by Diego Oyarzun-Reyes.

Financial assistance from the UNDP/Japan Human Resources Development Fund towards research for this *Handbook*, and its preparation and printing, is gratefully acknowledged.

Rubens Ricupero
Secretary-General of UNCTAD

Geneva, April 1998

# Contents

## PART  TWO
## POLICY LESSONS:  TAKING ADVANTAGE OF
## THE POTENTIAL FOR FDI BY AND IN SMEs

Page

**Page**

# PART THREE
## TECHNICAL COOPERATION MANUAL:
## PRACTICAL MEASURES TO ASSIST SME INVESTORS

**Page**

**Page**

## Boxes

## Tables

**Page**

# PART ONE

# THE CONTRIBUTION OF SMEs AND SME FDI TO DEVELOPMENT IN ASIA

# INTRODUCTION AND OVERVIEW

Small and medium-sized enterprises (SMEs) are an integral part of all economies. In Asia, these enterprises have played an important role in the economic development of some countries. Foreign direct investment (FDI) is now recognized as an important engine of economic development. SMEs in Asia are taking an increasingly active approach to the opportunities provided by FDI and international production by transnational corporations (TNCs). However, FDI by SMEs and in SMEs is still a small part of FDI flows in Asia; at most it makes up only about 10 per cent or less of FDI inflows in many Asian countries and 10-20 per cent of FDI outflows for major Asian investors (e.g., the Republic of Korea). Nevertheless, an improved understanding of FDI by and in SMEs in Asia is important, for two reasons:

- Although SME FDI is not large at present, the potential is there for it to increase quite significantly, in both absolute and relative terms. This could make an important contribution to economic growth, especially via an "entrepreneurial engine" of fast-growing firms.

- Some developing economies in Asia face a structural imbalance in terms of both the distribution and the economic role of enterprises by size. Their SME sectors are underdeveloped, thus impairing the longer-term sustainability of their economic growth and international competitiveness. These economies need to ensure that their SME sectors develop apace, and do not get left behind. FDI in SMEs, and by SMEs, and the cross-border production activities associated with it, could offer an attractive means of achieving this.

For developing countries to take advantage of the potential of SMEs, and of SME FDI to contribute to economic development, it is necessary to understand the relationship between SMEs and development as well as the role of, and factors influencing, SME FDI in developing countries. Part One of this *Handbook* attempts to do this by focusing on the following aspects of SMEs and SME FDI in Asia.

- *The processes by which SMEs contribute to development.* Chapter I examines two types of engines for growth: a conventional production function engine, and a less conventional "entrepreneurial engine". Two important points emerge. One is that in many developing countries in Asia SMEs are underrepresented; SMEs make up less of the economy than might be expected, and thus their contribution is muted. This "missing middle" seems to have arisen because of an emphasis on larger firms and larger projects. The second point is that much economic growth, especially in terms of employment, is concentrated in a relatively few growth-oriented SMEs, or the "entrepreneurial engine". SME FDI could offer an effective means for governments both to help overcome the problems of the "missing middle", and to take advantage of the "entrepreneurial engine".

- *The patterns and trends of SME FDI in Asia.* Chapter II summarizes the evidence. Information on SME FDI is difficult to obtain, but available evidence suggests that while FDI has grown rapidly in recent years, especially in developing Asia, the growth of SME FDI has been more volatile, but about the same on average; it has not increased as a proportion of total value. Small "package" inward FDI (generally involving amounts of less than $1 million) typically accounts for over 50 per cent of cases of FDI, but only about 10 per cent by value. Policy initiatives need to focus on ways to increase the relative importance of SME FDI.

- *The reasons why SMEs invest across borders.* Chapter III summarizes the factors that motivate SMEs to invest abroad, and the factors that assist or impede them. Not surprisingly, SMEs invest abroad for many of the same reasons as large firms do: because of pull factors (larger markets and growth opportunities), push factors (rising costs at home), management capabilities (having the skills and knowledge to internationalize successfully), and chance (being in the right place at the right time, being invited to supply an overseas customer, etc.). However, for SME FDI, competitive strength in management and chance factors are apparently the most important; according to survey data collected for this study, about three-quarters of smaller firms regard management factors, and 71 per cent regard chance factors, as important or very important to their international development. Push factors are regarded as the least important, being considered "not important" by about one-quarter of firms surveyed. Relative to large firms, more SMEs tend to regard all of the factors considered as important, except for two factors: rising costs in the home market and lower costs of production in countries abroad. The implication for developing countries seeking to attract SME FDI is that they cannot simply rely on firms being pushed out of their home countries by higher costs. Instead they need to develop a more structured portfolio of programmes that address these reasons. Barriers created by governments or allowed by them to persist, such as regulatory impediments or corruption, where government policy or practice itself needs to be reviewed, pose the largest impediments to SME FDI. This suggests that it is in the re-engineering of government that the greatest challenges and opportunities lie.

- *The strategies adopted by SMEs investing across borders.* Chapter IV summarizes the evidence on the importance of different factors in SME FDI strategies. The factors regarded by most respondents as important to their strategic business development are improving the quality of services or products, training of local managers, good relations with government, and training of local unskilled staff. However, SME respondents are less likely than large firm respondents to see those factors as important. The exception is increasing exports or foreign earnings, which SME respondents are 1.3 times more likely than large-firm respondents to see as important. In addition, if the degree of importance of these factors is taken into account and only the respondents that see a factor as *very* important are considered, a somewhat different picture emerges: SMEs are more likely to see most of the factors considered as *very* important relative to larger investors. For example, SME respondents are:

- three times more likely to see training of unskilled staff as being very important to their strategic success;
- more than twice as likely to see the introduction or improvement of products or services as very important; and
- more than 50 per cent more likely to see training of local managers and the increasing of foreign earnings as very important.

The implication is that FDI by SMEs can be conducive to development, and that SME investors are thus an attractive target for development-oriented economies.

- *The potential for using SME FDI better as an engine of development.* Chapter V examines the potential for increasing SME FDI in some specific economies in Asia. Here, Myanmar and Viet Nam are examined as examples of less developed economies in Asia.

There are, inevitably, some definitional issues related to SMEs and FDI to be considered in any study on SMEs, FDI and SME FDI. These are discussed in box 1. Table 1 lists the various definitions of SMEs adopted by selected countries in Asia.

---

**Box 1. Definitional issues**

**What is an SME?**

There is no precise definition of an SME. For statistical and policy purposes, most countries use either an employment measure or a monetary measure (capitalization, sales etc.) of size, or both. Definitions vary widely (see table 1). Under most statistical definitions, an SME can be as large as 500 employees or as small as zero employees, or anywhere in between. The only really common characteristic of SMEs is that they are "not large"; that is, whether a firm is really an SME or not is a question of relative size. SMEs are not homogeneous, and so in terms of size it is useful to distinguish a range, as follows:

| Micro or very small | Small | Medium | Large |
|---|---|---|---|
| 0 - 19 employees | 20 - 100 employees | 101 - 500 employees | 501+ employees |

Although an enterprise at the upper end of this categorization of SMEs, with 500 employees, may be considered to be of quite a significant size relative to other firms in a developing economy, as far as SMEs engaged in FDI — or small and medium-sized TNCs — are concerned, this size is not so large. That environment is, moreover, increasingly relevant to all economies, including developing ones.

/...

---

**(Box 1, cont'd.)**

There is also the issue of groups of firms, including those within the cross-border organizational systems of TNCs: if two SMEs (e.g., a parent firm and an affiliate) of 300 employees each are linked through FDI, is the FDI involved SME FDI, and is the resulting group a large firm or an SME? The answer is that this would be SME FDI (because investment is from an SME to an SME), but that the resulting firm taken as a whole would be a large firm. However, as it turns out, it does not matter much whether a firm has 300 or 600 employees. The approach adopted in this study is a pragmatic one. The question is "does size matter?", and not so much "is it an SME or not according to a particular definition (in terms of the number of employees)?". The effect of size (including that of groupings) can be evaluated through empirical work, but it does not depend on whether a firm is categorized as an SME or not an SME.

Finally, there is the issue of the industry: an SME in services is often regarded as being smaller than that an SME manufacturing, and definitions sometimes reflect this (see table 1). The distinction between services and manufacturing is, however, becoming rather blurred, especially amongst internationalized SMEs. Again, the issue is one of size and its effects, but rather of whether a firm is considered to be an SME or not.

**What is FDI?**

FDI is defined as an investment involving a long-term relationship and reflecting a lasting interest of and control by an entity resident in one economy in an enterprise resident in an economy other than that of foreign direct investor (UNCTAD, 1997). FDI flows are thus usually measured by the flows of capital from one location to another for the purpose of investing in or developing a business in which the foreign investor has a long-term interest. This usually entails transfer of technology, skills, organization and managerial resources, access to markets, and so forth.

As just mentioned, FDI involves an element of control: the International Monetary Fund (IMF) defines FDI as requiring ownership of at least 10 per cent of the stock (shares) of the foreign affiliate, or some other effective form of control by the parent or investor firm (IMF, 1993; UNCTAD, 1997). Few SMEs have listed stock, and so control is difficult to ascertain in SMEs, especially smaller unlisted SMEs. Also, some SME managers may pride themselves on their independence, so they do not regard themselves as being "controlled" by a foreign investor even if the investor has a significant stake in the recipient SME. Thus, it is difficult to establish empirically whether an investment across borders by an SME and/or to an SME is indeed FDI in a strict sense. The pragmatic approach adopted in this study is to assume that if an SME has received funds (equity or intra-company loans) from abroad, there is a requisite degree of control, and hence it is FDI.

**What is SME FDI?**

SME FDI may be narrowly defined as FDI from an SME in a home country in an SME in a host country. However in this study, some FDI by large firms in SMEs has been included for comparative purposes, and because it has played an important role in the development of some economies in the Asian region. Therefore, for analytical purposes, SME FDI was divided into the following categories by size in terms of employees:

| Type of FDI | Size of foreign investor | Size of recipient/affiliate |
|---|---|---|
| LE-SME FDI | Large (>500) | SME |
| SME - SME FDI | SME (<500) | SME |
| ME - SME FDI | Medium (<500, >100) | SME |
| SE - SME FDI | Small (<100) | SME |

There are virtually no countries in Asia for which statistics give breakdowns of FDI by firm size. The Republic of Korea and Japan are the exceptions (although, for the latter, the only available data are the *number* of cases of

/...

**(Box 1, cont'd.)**

investment). The only statistics which are fairly readily available give the size of the actual or proposed investment. *Prima facie*, it may be expected that smaller investments are more likely to be made by smaller firms. For analytical purposes, a rough proxy is to view investments of less than $1 million as being "small", and likely to come from SMEs, or to be going to SMEs, or both. (In fact, the average size of approved FDI by SMEs based in the Republic of Korea is about $1 million.) However, the only way to ascertain this is actually to survey the firms involved.

**Table 1. Definitions of SMEs in selected countries in Asia**

| Economy | By employment | By capitalization/assets or sales |
|---|---|---|
| China | Varies with industry; usually less than 100 employees | .. |
| Indonesia | .. | Capitalization/assets: Rp 200 million (excluding land and buildings)[a]<br>Sales: Rp 1 billion[a] |
| Japan | Manufacturing, mining, transport, construction: <301<br>Wholesaling: <101<br>Retailing: <51 | <¥100 million in manufacturing, mining, transport, construction.<br><¥30 million in wholesaling<br><¥10 million in retailing, other services |
| Korea, Republic of | Manufacturing, mining, transport: <301<br>Construction: <201<br>Commerce and other services: <21 | .. |
| Myanmar[b] | Cottage: 1-9<br>Small: 10-50<br>Medium: 51-100<br>Large: <101 | Small:<br>  <K1 million investment<br>  <K2.5 million production<br>Medium:<br>  <K5 million investment<br>  <K10 million production<br>Some definitions also depend on the horsepower-level of energy use. |
| Philippines | Cottage: 1-9<br>Small: 10-99<br>Medium: 100-199 | Assets:<br>  Micro: <P150,000<br>  Cottage: P150,000-1.5 million<br>  Small: P1.5 - 15 million<br>  Medium: P15 - 60 million |
| Singapore | <100 | <S$ 12 million in manufacturing, service and commerce |
| Taiwan Province of China | .. | Mining, manufacturing and construction:<br><NT$40 million in invested capital<br>Manufacturing and construction:<br><NT $120 million in sales<br>Other industries, such as services:<br><NT 40 million in sales |
| Viet Nam[c] | Micro: <5<br>Small: 5-50<br>Medium: 51-300 | Capital:<br>  Micro: < VND 100 million<br>  Small: VND 100 - 300 million<br>  Medium: VND 300 million - 1 billion |

*Source*: UNCTAD, based on APEC, 1994 and national sources.

[a] Firms with assets/sales of more than these amounts are large and medium enterprises (Law No. 9 of 1995 on Small Business).

[b] Refers to private industrial enterprises only, as defined in the Private Industrial Enterprise Law 1990. There is no official definition of SMEs.

[c] No official definition of SMEs.

# CHAPTER 1

# THE ROLE OF SMES IN ASIAN DEVELOPMENT

SMEs constitute an important part of the economies of most countries, contributing substantially to employment and production. They can also make a major dynamic contribution to growth and development. Internationalized SMEs, in particular, offer a significant potential source of growth and development for developing countries. For example, research (UNCTAD, 1993; Fujita, 1998) has demonstrated that smaller TNCs are more likely than larger TNCs to:

- transfer appropriate technology to developing countries;
- have a favourable impact on the trade balance; and
- have more flexible local arrangements, and contribute more to the local economy by using subcontracting to a greater extent.

Understanding the role of SMEs in Asia and their contribution to development, especially the contribution of SMEs engaged in FDI, with a view to strengthening policies and programmes for enhancing that contribution, is fraught with difficulties. The lack of consistent and reliable data makes analysis and comparisons difficult. To understand the picture better it is useful, first of all, to develop a conceptual framework within which some of the available evidence can be seen.

## A. Conceptual framework for analyzing the SME contribution to development

Asian economies have had some of the most successful experiences with economic growth and development. Most of this growth has been driven by factors such as exports, infrastructure investment and entrepreneurial activity. In order to identify ways in which governments can increase SMEs' contribution to growth, and the potential for increasing the contribution by SME FDI, it is necessary to have a better idea of the ways in which SMEs can and do contribute to development. In this context, it is useful to distinguish two main means of contribution:

- *Conventional contributions through the production process.* The SME contribution through the production process can be expected to be roughly in proportion to the role of SMEs in production or value added -- around 40 to 60 per cent of output and value added in the leading Asian economies. The main sources of growth on the supply side are improvements in human capital (through education and training) and improvements in technology and productivity. SMEs play an important role in both. It seems that the less developed the economy, the more important is the contribution by human capital investment, while in more developed economies investment in technology development becomes more important. This suggests a shift of emphasis in the way in which SMEs contribute as economies develop.

- *Contributions through the entrepreneurial engine.* This less conventional contribution suggests that, in developed countries at least, SMEs' contribution to growth is much larger than might be suggested by conventional models, and comes mostly from a relatively small proportion of growth-oriented SMEs. SMEs engaged in FDI are more likely to form part of this core of growth-oriented firms, and this would be important in the design of policies to facilitate FDI for development.

Table I.1 summarizes the main points about the ways in which SMEs contribute to economic development, and the ways in which SME FDI assists in that process. These are then explored in more detail in the discussion that follows.

Although there is a substantial body of research on factors contributing to economic growth, there is little empirical evidence about the contribution of SMEs to growth. In principle, it should be possible to estimate this contribution, but the problem is how to do this in such a way that governments and others have a more reliable basis for evaluating policy options. The following discussion is intended to provide a framework for piecing together the rather fragmentary evidence set out in section B.

## 1. Conventional growth engines

There are two main types of growth engine that are conventionally recognized and estimated: a supply-side growth engine and a demand-side growth engine.

### (a)  Supply side

The supply-side growth engine is made up of two parts: expansion in production capabilities and expansion of savings funds for growth.

#### i.  Production

Although there are some problems in estimating the contribution of different factors to production, the main evidence suggests the following with respect to the two main factors contributing to production growth:

- *Increasing factor inputs*, such as physical capital, human capital and labour. This is estimated to make up about 65 per cent of GDP growth in Asia (World Bank, 1993, p. 48). It can be broken down into three parts:

**Table I.1. Schematic summary of the contribution of SMEs to development**

| Source of contribution | SME and SME FDI contribution |
|---|---|
| **Conventional engine:** | |
| *Supply side - production* | |
| • Increased factor inputs | |
| - Capital investment | SMEs contribute about 40-60 per cent. The SME FDI contribution is usually small, but can probably be increased by several orders of magnitude. |
| - Labour | SMEs have no major impact, but may increase the effective use of the labour force. |
| | SMEs employ over 60 per cent of the workforce, which means that they have a major potential impact on training. |
| - Intangible investment | SME FDI is a major source of technical training and productivity improvement. |
| • Improved productivity | SMEs probably contribute about half. SME FDI is an important source of technology transfer and catch-up. |
| *Supply side - savings for financing investment* | SMEs employ over 60 per cent of the workforce and are an important source of funds. SME FDI is a small but useful source of investment funds. |
| *Demand side* | |
| - Domestic | SME wage payments make up over half of GDP, which means that SME growth is important in domestic demand expansion. |
| - Export | SMEs contribute about 35 per cent or so of exports in the Asian region, making a major contribution to this growth engine. SME FDI is usually export-oriented, increasing the potential for exports. |
| **Entrepreneurial engine:** | Most of the SME contribution to growth is concentrated in a relatively small proportion of fast-growing firms which start up and expand rapidly. |
| Fast-growth firms | SMEs receiving FDI generally have higher growth rates. |
| Adaptability and technology-use | SMEs receiving FDI tend to have a greater propensity to apply technology and training. |
| Flexible exports | SMEs receiving FDI tend to be more willing to increase exports and to internationalize. |

*Source:* UNCTAD.

- *Increased physical capital investment*, by both public and private sectors. Physical investment accounts for about 35 to 50 per cent of predicted growth due to factor expansion.

- *Increased population/labour force.* This factor makes a relatively minor contribution, usually around only 10 per cent of total predicted growth; but sectoral demographic change, particularly as the population moves from low-productivity agriculture to higher-productivity industry and services, can have a much larger contribution.

- *Increased investment in intangible human capital*, again by both the public and private sectors. This is by far the largest contributor to growth, typically accounting for 60 per cent and 80 per cent of predicted growth due to factor expansion. The usual estimates are based on primary and secondary education.[1]

- *Increasing productivity*, either general technological progress or catch-up productivity growth. This is the unexplained or residual component (that is, the difference between predicted growth and actual growth), and is estimated to make up about 35 per cent of GDP growth. Rapid growth can to some extent be explained by catch-up (that is, the economy is below optimum levels in the production function), and as it moves on to the optimum production frontier it gains from both catch-up and steady technological improvement. Estimating the relative importance of these factors, however, is difficult.[2]

### ii. Savings

Supply-side growth in production on the basis of the above factors is only possible if it can be funded. Domestic savings are the main source of funds; they can be complemented by foreign capital inflows. Rates of saving in fast-developing Asian economies have increased rapidly, and are now about double those in other developed countries.

### (b) Demand side

Expansion of demand is essential for supporting continued supply-side growth. This is made up of growth in domestic demand and export demand.

### i. Domestic demand

In most developing Asian economies (China, India and, possibly, Indonesia are exceptions) the size of the economy is small relative to the world economy, and domestic demand is not really adequate to sustain significant growth, or at least growth at the rates that have been common in Asia over the past 20 years. High levels of savings, necessary for supporting investment, also tend to limit domestic demand.

### ii. Export demand

Exports have thus been the main demand-side engine of growth. Export growth rates have been typically about double GDP growth rates. The export share of the fast-growing developing economies in Asia in world exports more than tripled, from around 5 per cent to 18 per cent, in the period 1970-1995.[3]

### (c) The contribution of SMEs

The nature of the contributions by SMEs to the factors driving growth on the supply and demand sides of the conventional growth engine are summarized in table I.1. With SMEs being considered as a group of similar firms, their contributions to growth through these factors can be expected to be comparable to their significance in output and value added. These contributions stem principally from the role of SMEs in investment in physical and human capital on the supply side, and in income generation for domestic demand and exports on the demand side. Moreover, not all SMEs are alike and, as discussed below, growth-oriented, entrepreneurial SMEs play an important role in growth that conventional views of growth may not capture.

## 2. The entrepreneurial engine

The conventional views of growth tend to overlook the dynamic importance of an "entrepreneurial engine" in driving economic growth, and hence the role of SMEs in growth. The key features of the entrepreneurial engine are summarized in table I.2. The figures are indicative only, and relate to a typical developed country. In short:

- Much economic growth and most growth in net jobs come from about 20-25 per cent of firms. These are typically growth-oriented SMEs, though by the time they actually make a tangible contribution, they are usually medium-sized (i.e., with more than 100 employees). These firms tend to last longer than most SMEs, living for at least 8-10 years. In many developing countries this high-growth group of firms is missing or under-represented (the "missing middle").

- Larger firms (with more than 500 employees) make up only 1 per cent or so of firms, but employ more than 30 per cent of the workforce. They do not contribute much to employment growth, because they often focus on improving productivity and efficiency. The growth they achieve is often generated by absorbing fast-growing SMEs, and by making them more efficient. However, in developing countries these large firms are sometimes heavily protected by government arrangements, and thus may be relatively inefficient.

- Smaller, low-growth SMEs make up the bulk of the firms in an economy. Although there are many such firms, they often have a rather short life expectancy (3-5 years). There is considerable turnover, as firms are born or die. This turnover allows a dynamic process of exploring new opportunities. Although the bulk of these firms are "lifestyle" firms, without any real focus on growth, some are successful in opening up growth opportunities, and have the capability to grow. This large group of firms acts as a seedbed for successful growth-oriented firms. In developing countries, many of these firms are in the informal sector, and have difficulty in making the transition to growth because they lack the management skills and financial resources required.

In most developed countries, there is a distinct cyclical pattern to the entrepreneurial engine. In developing countries, the role of the entrepreneurial engine is less well known. SMEs (and especially those operating across borders, including those with FDI) are likely to contribute to growth via an entrepreneurial engine in the ways outlined below.

### (a) Fast-growth firms

About 25 per cent or less of SMEs are growth-oriented (the rest tend to be small "mum and dad" SMEs, which are important structurally, but not dynamically). Only 5 to 10 per cent of SME start-ups will ever really succeed in growing and making a significant contribution to employment and economic growth. In developing countries, this process may be even more difficult, because some of the prerequisites for successful SME growth (management skills, access to finance, efficient communications infrastructure, etc.) are less likely to be present. FDI may be a very important means of creating the conditions for the start-up and success of these fast-growth SMEs, especially where local market conditions limit sustainable financial growth. In developing countries, the role of the entrepreneurial engine has perhaps been overshadowed by more obvious growth drivers such as government infrastructure investment, but it seems likely to be of increasing importance to the newly industrializing economies.

**Table I.2. Summary of the main features of the entrepreneurial engine**

| Item | High-growth firms | Large firms | Low-growth firms |
|---|---|---|---|
| Size of firms | Medium: (21 to 500 employees), but start small | Large: >500 employees | Mostly small: <20 employees |
| Share of employment | 10% | 40%+ | 50% |
| Share of firms | 10% | 1% | 89% |
| Cycle of renewal | 8-10+ years | Indefinite life | 3-5 years |
| Gross employment-growth contribution | About 70% to 100% of new jobs created by 5% of firms | Negative in downturn, positive in upturn ± 20 - 30% | Significant gross job creation, and cyclical absorption |
| Net employment-growth contribution | Major: probably 60% - 70% | Moderate: probably 20% - 30% | Small: probably 0% - 10% but may be larger in developing countries undergoing structural change |

*Source:* Hall, 1996.

### (b) Bringing forth latent domestic demand

Most of the fast-growth firms are not at the leading edge of technology even in developed countries. They grow because they have found market niches or identified a latent demand. In other words, they form a bridge between supply and demand. In developing countries, SMEs may play an important part in adapting suitable products, improving them and bringing them to a local market. SMEs with access to ideas and technologies and skills from abroad may be particularly important. This generates growth in domestic demand that would otherwise not be revealed.

### (c) Creating a flexible and competitive export base

Exports are a major source of growth and, to export, it is necessary to be internationally competitive. The lowering of trade barriers, the liberalization of international financial flows and the shift from naturally endowed comparative advantage to created comparative advantage mean that economies must continually adapt if they are to remain internationally competitive. SMEs and SME FDI assist in two respects:

- First, at an aggregate level, SMEs are arguably better than large firms at adapting to competitive change. They are quickly weeded out if they are unsuccessful, and so resources are less likely to be left in uncompetitive industries. Because they have less political power, they are less likely to be successful in lobbying to monopolize property rights to protect them from competitive forces. However, at an individual level, many SMEs, and especially those in developing countries, are not well placed to adapt to change; they may lack the necessary financial and managerial resources to accommodate themselves to changes. SME FDI may be important in assisting such SMEs to adapt, survive and grow.

- Second, SMEs receiving and engaging in FDI are generally oriented towards exports and internationalization. They thus assist in creating a flexible and competitive export base.

## B. Evidence of the contribution of SMEs and SME FDI to development in Asian economies

Although there have been studies on the contribution of different factor inputs to growth, there have been no analytical studies of the contribution of different size classes of firms to aggregate economic growth in developing countries, including in Asia. What evidence there is about the role of SMEs tends to be rather fragmentary. Evidence about the role of SME FDI is even more limited. The main points in this section are as follows:

- The available evidence suggests that SMEs have played a major role in the development of all the leading (and successful) countries in Asia. Although this contribution differs between countries, SMEs typically contribute between 40 and 60 per cent of GDP (see below).

- Structurally, developing countries may be having difficulty, or face difficulties, in building up a robust and dynamic SME sector; there is often a wmissing middle". Developing countries lack the growth-oriented SMEs (mostly medium-sized) which can make a significant contribution to longer-term economic development.

- SMEs' contribution to growth through conventional growth engines is roughly in proportion to their importance in the economy. Thus, they contribute about 40 to 60 per cent of capital investment (a major source of economic growth), and about the same for productivity growth. The contribution of SMEs through the entrepreneurial engine is more difficult to assess, but it seems certain that the potential contribution via SME FDI is both large and underutilized at present.

- SME FDI appears to make up only about 10 per cent or less of FDI flows. For developing countries seeking to expand their SME sectors and avoid the "missing middle" problem, encouraging SME FDI in both absolute and relative terms is an important policy issue, and which tends to be overlooked.

### 1. The structural contribution and the "missing middle"

According to data for the economies examined for this *Handbook*, SMEs have been an important component of the economic structures in all the leading economies in Asia, and their importance has tended to increase over time, especially in terms of employment. Their contribution in output terms is set out in table I.3, which shows that SMEs (defined as firms with up to 500 employees) contributed 40 per cent (Singapore) to 60 per cent (Taiwan Province of China) of manufacturing output. The contribution of SMEs to employment is more diverse (tables I.4 and I.5), but in general has increased in all the leading Asian economies over the past three decades.  Typically, in the early stages of industrialization or pre-industrialization, SME employment was large; it then dropped, and then increased again.

**Table I.3.  Share of output, employment and number of establishments,
by size-class of enterprise in selected Asian economies**
(Percentage)

| Economy (Employment size) | Micro (<20) | Small (20-100) | Medium (101-500) | Large (>501) | Total number of firms/establishments |
|---|---|---|---|---|---|
| **Leading economies** | | | | | |
| *Japan* (1995)[a] | | | | | 387 726 |
| Establishments | 75 | 21 | 3 | 1 | |
| Output | 10 | 22 | 20 | 49 | |
| Employment | 23 | 31 | 18 | 28 | |
| *Republic of Korea* (1995) | | | | | 1 155 689 |
| Establishments | .. | .. | .. | 1 | |
| Output | .. | .. | .. | 48 | |
| Employment | .. | .. | .. | 32 | |
| *Singapore* (1994)[b] | | | | | 4 013 |
| Establishments | 41 | 42 | 14 | 3 | |
| Output | 3 | 12 | 26 | 59 | |
| Employment | 5 | 26 | 27 | 44 | |
| *Taiwan Province of China* (1991)[c] | | | | | 738 914 |
| Establishments | 96 | 3 | 1 | 0.1 | |
| Output | 25 | 16 | 20 | 39 | |
| Employment | 46 | 18 | 16 | 20 | |
| **Other developing countries** | | | | | |
| *Indonesia* (1990)[d] | | | | | 16 536 |
| Establishments | .. | 72 | 21 | 7 | |
| Output | .. | 8 | 27 | 65 | |
| Employment | .. | 17 | 28 | 55 | |
| *Myanmar* (1994/1995)[e] | | | | | 32 621 |
| Establishments | .. | 86 | 10 | 4 | |
| Output | .. | 42 | 29 | 29 | |
| Employment | .. | 65 | 21 | 14 | |
| *Philippines* (1983) | | | | | 56 047 |
| Establishments | 90 | 8 | 1 | 1.3 | |
| Output | 1 | 13 | 8 | 78 | |
| Employment | 21 | 14 | 8 | 57 | |
| *Viet Nam* (1994)[f] | | | | | 26 000 |
| Establishments | .. | .. | .. | .. | |
| Output | .. | .. | .. | .. | |
| Employment | .. | .. | .. | .. | |

*Source*:  UNCTAD, based on official national sources.

[a]  Manufacturing only.  Medium: up to 300 employees; large: 300 and more.  Not included are establishments with less than 4 employees.  The total number of enterprises that own these establishments is about 82,000.

[b]  Manufacturing only.

[c]  Figures are for the non-agricultural sector.  Micro: firms with less than 30 employees; small: 30-99 employees.

[d]  Manufacturing only.  Applies to registered firms only.  Indonesia does not collect figures on firms with less than 20 employees.

[e]  Refers to private industrial enterprises only, as defined in table 1 in the introduction to Part One.

[f]  There is no official definition of an SME in Viet Nam.  Unofficial estimates suggest there are about 350,000 very small/micro enterprises.  There are about 6,000 state enterprises.

In most developed countries, the importance of SMEs, especially smaller ones employing between 20 and 100 people, as contributors of job growth and output growth has tended to increase over the past ten years (OECD, 1997, p. 19). This group of SMEs is generally in the 20 - 300 employees size category. This segment provides a competitive edge in two ways -- as leading subcontractors and as venture firms in their own right. However, in some Asian developing economies there is evidence of a "missing middle" (box I.1): a shortage of these middle-sized growth-oriented SMEs which make an important contribution to development.

Unfortunately, available statistics by firm size tend to be somewhat limited, and tend to hide this "missing middle" by aggregating all SMEs together. Comparisons between economies are also fraught with difficulties because of different definitions and data series. Nonetheless, evidence suggests that there is a structural imbalance (the missing middle) which has arisen, or is emerging in developing countries, and which blunts their competitive edge. While the leading (developed and developing) economies in Asia could allow their SME sectors to evolve and develop over relatively long periods of time, other developing countries tend to face a more urgent need to ensure that they have internationally competitive and viable SME sectors. This poses a serious challenge to policy makers in developing countries: how to ensure that their SME sectors develop at the same accelerated rate as the rest of their economies. Policies to encourage SME FDI provide an attractive way of addressing the problems associated with a missing middle, and of avoiding the problem in the first place.

**Table I.4. SME contribution to output in manufacturing, 1960s-1990s**

(Percentage of total)

| Economy | 1960s | 1970s | 1980s | 1990s |
|---|---|---|---|---|
| **Leading economies** | | | | |
| Japan[a] | .. | .. | 52 | 52 |
| Republic of Korea[b] | 43 | 34 | 33 | 44 |
| Singapore | 53 | 19 | 18 | 19 |
| Taiwan Province of China[c] | .. | 37 | 46 | 39 |
| **Other developing countries** | | | | |
| Indonesia | .. | .. | 23 | 30 |
| Myanmar | .. | .. | .. | 71[d] |
| Philippines | .. | .. | 24 | .. |
| Viet Nam[e] | .. | .. | .. | 40-70 |

*Source*: UNCTAD, based on official national sources.

[a] Manufacturing only.

[b] Data for 1960s are for 1963-1969.

[c] Figures are for share of sales, not output.

[d] Private industrial enterprises only. For 1994/1995 only.

[e] There is no official definition of an SME in Viet Nam. Figures for the pre-*doi moi* period are not available.

*Note:* For definitions of SMEs in the respective economies, see table 1 in the intoduction to Part One.

**Table I.5. SME contribution to employment in manufacturing, 1960s-1990s**

(Percentage of total)

| Economy | 1960s | 1970s | 1980s | 1990s |
|---|---|---|---|---|
| **Leading economies** | | | | |
| Japan | .. | 70 | 76 | 85 |
| Republic of Korea | 58 | 46 | 61 | 63 |
| Singapore | 55 | 29 | 31 | 35 |
| Taiwan Province of China | 43 | 46 | 63 | 80 |
| **Other developing countries** | | | | |
| Indonesia | .. | .. | 48[a] | 42[b] |
| Myanmar[c] | .. | .. | .. | 86 |
| Philippines | .. | 45 | 47 | .. |
| Viet Nam[d] | .. | .. | .. | 90 |

*Source:* UNCTAD, based on official national sources.

*Note:* For definitions of SMEs in the respective economies, see table 1 in the introduction to Part One.

[a] For 1986-1989.
[b] For 1990-1993.
[c] Private industrial enterprises only.
[d] Most jobs have been created in the private sector since *doi moi*, and most of these have been in SMEs.

---

**Box I.1. The "missing middle"**

What are the characteristics of a "missing middle"? There are four main features:

- Large firms (more than 300-500 employees) account for a disproportionate contribution to GDP, and tend to dominate the economy.

- SMEs tend to be concentrated in the informal, craft and agricultural sectors, where SMEs are mostly small, of relatively low productivity and not growth-oriented.

- Opportunities are limited for firms or entrepreneurs to move from the informal sector into the formal sector and then to grow. An inability to attract finance and a lack of managerial skills are common impediments.

- There is an absence of a core group of dynamic SMEs. Typically, these have between 20 and 300 employees, grow at average rates that are at least double the rate of economic growth, and are more likely to be internationally active.

In Asia, among the countries studied, the phenomenon of the missing middle is most marked in Indonesia and the Philippines. In these economies, over 65 per cent of output is produced by large firms with more than 500 employees. Smaller dynamic firms (with less than 100 employees) make up only about 8 per cent of output in Indonesia and 14 per cent in the Philippines. This can be contrasted with small firms (those with less than 100 employees) contributing one-third of output in Japan, and two-fifths in Taiwan Province of China. Part of the problem of development in both Indonesia and the Philippines is the shortage of smaller local firms with the ability to grow and act as subcontractors to larger international firms. This limits the integration of the economy into a broader regional economy and impedes development. The underrepresentation of this component of an

*/...*

## 2. The contribution of SMEs and SME FDI to the conventional growth engine

Evidence regarding the contribution of SMEs to supply-side growth is fragmentary, and that regarding the contribution of SME FDI to growth is almost non-existent. From a mosaic of evidence, however, it seems that:

- SMEs contribute about 40 to 60 per cent of capital expenditure, in line with their overall contribution to GDP. They are thus a major contributor to economic growth.

- The contribution of SMEs to productivity growth is more complex. Productivity (measured as output per worker) of SMEs is typically half or less than half that of large firms despite the fact that productivity growth of smaller firms is comparable or slightly better than that of large firms. Perhaps as much as half of the productivity contributions to economic growth come from a relatively select group of SMEs -- the entrepreneurial engine discussed earlier.

*(a)* *Supply side*

    *i.* *Production*

### Increased factor inputs

*Capital investment.* Capital investment is estimated to contribute about a third or more of economic growth, and SMEs account for about half or more of it. The role of SMEs in capital

---

**(Box I.1, cont'd.)**

entrepreneurial engine means that growth opportunities are being forgone. This was probably less important to the leading countries as they developed, but for countries developing now in a more internationally competitive world, SMEs provide an important, renewing source of competitive advantage.

In lower-income Asian developing countries such as Myanmar, Bangladesh and Viet Nam, it is difficult to discern a missing middle. Available evidence, however, suggests that current development trends may lead to a structural bias towards larger firms and thus to a missing middle emerging in the next few years unless policy steps are taken to address the issue. Myanmar is the only one of these three countries that has reasonably accurate figures on economic contributions by firm size. These show that smaller firms contribute around 42 per cent of output in the manufacturing sector, and there is no evidence of a missing middle yet. However, this is understandable as most of Myanmar's firms were established in the past decade, and are therefore still small. Myanmar launched reforms in 1988 and is seeking to transform the economy from a low-productivity agricultural economy to a high-productivity agro-based industrial economy. This will require a significant SME base. However, FDI investment is principally directed at larger projects and larger firms. This raises the real possibility that the SME sector will not develop in line with the rest of the economy, and so a missing middle may emerge in much the same way as it has in Indonesia and the Philippines.

In Viet Nam, the economy has gone through major restructuring in recent years. Figures by size of firm are not available, and there is no official statistical definition of SMEs as such. However, the state sector (mostly large firms) produced about 40 per cent of GDP in 1993, relative to the domestic private sector, which produced 55 per cent, and the private foreign sector, which accounted for 6 per cent. As most of the recent growth in Viet Nam has been in smaller companies, there is no evidence as yet of a missing middle or a structural imbalance. However, the country faces the same potential problem as Myanmar; much of the investment and FDI is being directed to larger projects and larger firms.

investment seems to be roughly in proportion to their percentage contribution to GDP, typically about 40 to 60 per cent (see box I.2). As discussed in the next chapter, SME FDI from Asia makes up only about 5 to 10 per cent of total FDI flows, and so SMEs are underrepresented in international investment. As regions and countries become more integrated, the level and proportion of SME FDI may be expected to increase. Thus, although SME FDI is unlikely to reach the level of 40-60 per cent of FDI in a fully integrated economy, it might be possible to increase it substantially both in absolute and in relative terms.

*Increased population/labour force.* SMEs have little effect on population size, but they may have an effect on increasing the effective labour force, for example by making more effective use of women in employment, and giving employment opportunities to rural people (e.g., the Chinese town and village enterprises and ethnic minorities). FDI does not usually flow to activities geared to such purposes, although development assistance could be directed to them.

---

**Box I.2.  Capital investment by SMEs in Asia**

• **Singapore.**  SMEs provide about 40 per cent or so of capital expenditure in manufacturing, in line with their contribution to output of about 40 per cent.  That contribution has remained relatively stable over a ten-year period.

**Singapore: share of capital expenditure in manufacturing by firms according to size**
(Percentage)

| Firm size (employment) | 1980 | 1990 |
|---|---|---|
| Micro  (10-19) | 4 | 3 |
| Small  (20-299) | 17 | 18 |
| Medium (300-500) | 24 | 20 |
| Large  (501+) | 55 | 59 |

*Source*: Singapore, Department of Statistics, *Report on the Census of Industrial Production* (Singapore:  various years).

• **Taiwan Province of China.**  A similar picture emerges: SMEs contribute about 60 per cent of total assets (figures on capital investment are not available), roughly the same as their proportionate contribution to output.

**Taiwan Province of China: share of total assets in manufacturing by firms according to size, 1991**
(Percentage)

| Firm size (employment) | 1991 |
|---|---|
| Micro (<30) | 22 |
| Small (30-99) | 15 |
| Medium (100-499) | 22 |
| Large (500+) | 41 |

*Source*: Taiwan Province of China, *Census of Industry and Commerce 1991* (Taipei, 1993).

/...

*Increased investment in intangible capital.* Intangible investment, especially in human capital, is the single largest contributor to economic growth. As investment in improved education is usually a public sector responsibility, SMEs do not usually have a large impact, especially at early stages of development when education tends to be focused more on primary school and basic literacy issues. However, SMEs do have a fairly large potential impact on the training of people, especially in basic skills, technical skills and business skills. As noted above, SMEs employ the bulk of the workforce, and their contribution to employment has generally increased in recent years. Consequently, they play a significant role in providing training, and make an important contribution. Measuring this contribution is difficult, and there have been no systematic studies at the macro level. At the micro level, research tends to focus more on the needs and problems of SMEs. For SMEs to provide training, they often need training to begin with -- and this usually requires some form of public sector participation. SME FDI is likely to have a significant "trickle down" effect in this regard, especially in supply/subcontractor industries. For example, in Viet Nam a 1994 survey indicated that 78 per cent of SMEs train their employees on the job, and consider this the best and cheapest method.[4] However, over 50 per cent see a need for technical and management training that can be met only outside the firm, and in many cases by a partner abroad.

## Increased productivity

Increased productivity is the second largest explanatory contributor to GDP growth, after investment in intangible human capital. Productivity increases and technology catch-up are critical elements in economic development. At first glance, SMEs do not seem to contribute much to this aspect of GDP growth. On average, most SMEs operate at around one-half to one-third of the productivity per worker of larger firms (UNCTAD, 1993; Fujita, 1998). Furthermore, although the proportion of people employed by SMEs has generally increased in developed countries, the proportion of output produced by SMEs has remained stable. This suggests that SMEs do not make a large contribution to productivity growth or catch-up, and in fact may have actually experienced deteriorating productivity in relative terms. However, this interpretation may be misleading as regards the following three aspects:

---

**(Box I.2, cont'd)**

- **Myanmar.** SMEs (private industrial enterprises only) contribute between 70 and 80 per cent of invested funds, though there has been a tendency for this to decline in recent years, especially in the medium-size class. This is about the same as the contribution of SMEs to output.

  **Myanmar: share of capital investment by firms according to size, 1991/92 - 1995/96**
  (Percentage)

  | Firm size[a] | 1991/2 | 1993/4 | 1995/6 |
  |---|---|---|---|
  | Small | 52 | 55 | 50 |
  | Medium | 26 | 25 | 21 |
  | Large | 21 | 20 | 28 |

  *Source:* Data provided by Myanmar, Directorate of Regional Industrial Cooperation and Industrial Inspection.

  [a] According to investment/production criteria as defined in table 1 in the introduction to Part One.

- **Viet Nam.** Private sector investment made up about 30 per cent of $18 billion investment during the period 1991-1995. There is no breakdown by size of firm, but most of the employment growth has been due to SMEs, and so SMEs probably contributed the bulk of this investment.

---

- First, although the majority of SMEs have relatively low productivity, and low productivity growth, a small proportion are much faster growing than the average, and may possibly contribute significantly to productivity growth and catch-up. It is more likely that firms engaged in, and receiving, FDI will be in this category. In effect, although the average productivity of all SMEs is below that of large firms, the standard deviation (or dispersion) is probably much greater.

- Second, it is becoming more difficult to measure output and productivity improvement in many service industries. Even in the manufacturing sector a service component can be a major part of the value chain, and SME manufacturers often specialize in providing special services, rather than relying just on bulk throughput. Real productivity improvements tend therefore to be disguised in broad average figures.

- Third, as box I.3 shows, SME productivity growth can be quite high, and has outstripped that of large or medium-sized firms at times, even though productivity per worker remains relatively low in comparison with that of larger firms.

  Three country cases are illustrated in box I.3. On balance, it seems that SMEs probably contribute to catch-up and productivity growth roughly in line with their contribution to GDP -- that is, about half of such growth comes from SMEs.

---

**Box I.3. Productivity growth and firm size in Singapore, Republic of Korea and Viet Nam**

- **Singapore**. The pattern of productivity growth by firm size is quite complex. Output per worker rose from S$151,000 to S$275,000 over an eight-year period (1986-1994), indicating an average productivity growth for all firms of 7.8 per cent per annum. The greatest improvement was in the large firm category (with employees of 500 and more), where output per worker increased at an annual rate of 10.3 per cent. Smaller firms are less productive than large ones, and appear to becoming even less so; firms with 10-99 workers had only 62 per cent of the output per worker of large firms in 1986, but this fell to only 42 per cent in 1994. However, some of the best average productivity improvements were in the smaller firms, where productivity grew by 8.7 per cent per annum.

**Singapore: manufacturing productivity growth (changes in output per worker),
by firm size, 1986-1994**

(Thousands of Singaporean dollars and percentage)

| Firm size | 1986 | | 1994 | | Annual growth % per annum |
|---|---|---|---|---|---|
| | Output per worker | Ratio to that of large firms (500+) | Output per worker | Ratio to that of large firms (500+) | |
| 10-19 | 74 | 44 | 144 | 40 | 8.7 |
| 20-29 | 86 | 51 | 138 | 38 | 6.1 |
| 30-39 | 103 | 62 | 138 | 37 | 3.6 |
| 40-59 | 115 | 69 | 151 | 41 | 3.5 |
| 50-69 | 145 | 69 | 193 | 53 | 3.6 |
| 70-99 | 116 | 70 | 154 | 42 | 3.6 |
| 10-99 | 104 | 62 | 155 | 42 | 5.1 |
| 101-500 | 181 | 108 | 244 | 67 | 3.8 |
| 500 + | 167 | 100 | 365 | 100 | 10.3 |
| All firms | 151 | 90 | 275 | 75 | 7.8 |

*Source*: Data provided by Economic Planning Board of Singapore.

*/...*

---

**(Box I.3, cont'd.)**

If value added is used as a gauge of productivity, a similar, if slightly more pronounced, picture emerges. Value added per worker grew by 4.6 per cent per annum over the period, and smaller firms grew almost as fast as very large ones. It is the middle group of medium-sized firms that seems to have slipped behind, with only a 0.9 per cent per annum growth in productivity, and a value added per worker that has fallen from 107 per cent of large firms to only 79 per cent in the eight years from 1986 to 1994.

**Singapore: manufacturing productivity growth (changes in value added per worker), by firm size, 1986-1994**

(Thousands of Singaporean dollars and percentage)

| Firm size | 1986 | | 1994 | | Annual growth % per annum |
|---|---|---|---|---|---|
| | Value added per worker | Ratio to that of large firms (500+) | Value added per worker | Ratio to that of large firms (500+) | |
| 10-99 | 28 | 52 | 39 | 50 | 4.2 |
| 101-500 | 58 | 107 | 62 | 79 | 0.9 |
| 500 + | 54 | 100 | 78 | 100 | 4.8 |
| All firms | 48 | 88 | 69 | 88 | 4.6 |

*Source:* Data provided by Economic Planning Board of Singapore.

• **Republic of Korea.** SME productivity in the Republic of Korea is also about half or less of that of larger firms, and dipped in the mid-1980s, only to increase again in the early 1990s. Productivity growth of SMEs relative to that of large firms was comparable and slightly better in the second half of the 1980, with increases of 15.6 per cent per annum in output per worker for SMEs, compared with 13.6 per cent per annum for large enterprises, and 18.1 per cent per annum in value added per worker, compared with 16.9 per cent for larger enterprises.

**Republic of Korea: productivity changes in manufacturing, 1980, 1985 and 1990**

(Millions of won and percentage)

| Firm size | Output or value added per worker | | | Annual growth per cent per annum 1980/85 | Annual growth per cent per annum 1985/90 |
|---|---|---|---|---|---|
| | 1980 | 1985 | 1990 | | |
| *Output* | | | | | |
| SME | 12 | 20 | 41 | 11.4 | 15.6 |
| Large firms | 24 | 46 | 88 | 13.8 | 13.6 |
| Ratio[a] | 47 | 43 | 46 | .. | .. |
| *Value added* | | | | | |
| SME | 4 | 7 | 16 | 11.8 | 18.1 |
| Large firms | 8 | 16 | 34 | 15.6 | 16.9 |
| Ratio[a] | 55 | 47 | 49 | .. | .. |

*Source:* Data provided by Ministry of Finance and Economy of the Republic of Korea.

[a] Ratio of output/value added for worker in SMEs to output/value added per worker in large firms.

• **Viet Nam.** The 1994 survey indicates that SME equipment is often over 10 years old, and that 72 per cent of SMEs need long-term finance to upgrade their equipment or enlarge their production capacity.[1] Most of the SMEs surveyed by UNCTAD in Viet Nam expect to expand employment by around 32 per cent per annum, compared with about 20 per cent for the larger firms surveyed, investment by 23 per cent (compared with to 17 per cent for larger firms) and sales by 71 per cent (compared with 41 per cent for larger firms). This suggests that the SMEs receiving FDI are growing at well above average national rates and the rates for larger firms.

[1] The survey was carried out by a consulting firm, ECO Ltd., and was based on 55 SMEs.

### ii. Savings

Savings are a prerequisite for investment. Savings levels have been high in Asia, and the ability to maintain high savings levels is often cited as one of the main factors responsible for the success of the dynamic Asian economies. The connection between savings levels and the importance of SMEs is difficult to gauge, mostly because the former depend on so many other factors. However, a healthy SME private sector (as in Japan and Taiwan Province of China) may have an impact on savings levels, provided that reliable financial systems are at work.

Even where reliable financial intermediaries have not yet evolved, SMEs may also be more effective at mobilizing savings for productive uses, especially at local levels. In the absence of financial intermediaries and financial systems, arrangements known as Nanyang societies in some parts of Asia have tended to mobilize savings for local business ventures. These operate as cooperative arrangements where by a group of family and business associates meets regularly to pool funds and invest in promising ventures. Similarly, in Viet Nam, evidence suggests that less than 10 per cent of SMEs use financial intermediaries such as banks as a source of investment funds. Most rely on traditional sources, and borrow directly from friends or families. This creates something of a dual financial system.

SME FDI is also a source of external savings, which can be important in allowing some high-growth SMEs to continue to expand at rates that would otherwise be financially unsustainable, and may thus help to drive the entrepreneurial engine.

### (b) Demand side

To sustain production growth it is necessary to have growth in demand. This can come from domestic sources and export demand. Since SMEs make up around 50 per cent of wage payments, they are an important source of domestic demand. If they grow, so does domestic demand. Export demand growth has been crucial to economic growth in Asia. SMEs have been important in meeting about 35 per cent of export demand.

### i. Domestic demand

SMEs usually employ about half the workforce, and so they are an important source of increased domestic demand. For example, in Taiwan Province of China, SME wages comprise around one-half of national income, and have increased in importance over the past seven years. In Singapore, SMEs have contributed about the same proportion of wage remuneration over the period 1980-1994, smaller firms (less than 100 employees) accounting for about 25 per cent of wage payments.[5]

### ii. Export demand

Precise figures on exports by SMEs are difficult to obtain. On the best estimates available, SMEs in Asia seem to be responsible for about 35 per cent or so of total exports, which makes them important in this regard. In turn, this appears to account for about 12 per cent of regional GDP (table I.6). SMEs in subcontracting or electronics industries are often a major source of exports because of their access to export markets, technology and know-how.

**Table I.6. Estimated contribution of SMEs to exports,[a] 1991/1992**

(Billions of dollars and percentage)

| Economy | Gross domestic product | Exports as percentage of GDP | Share of SMEs in total exports |
|---|---|---|---|
| **Developed countries** | | | |
| Denmark | 122 | 27 | 46[b] |
| Finland | 122 | 19 | 23[b] |
| France | 1 168 | 18 | 26[b] |
| Greece | 66 | 12 | 19 |
| Italy | 1 072 | 15 | 53 |
| Japan | 3 337 | 12 | 13.5 |
| Netherlands | 279 | 47 | 26 |
| Sweden | 280 | 25 | 30 |
| **Asia** | | | |
| China | 435 | 21 | 40 - 60 |
| Indonesia | 128 | 23 | 10.6 |
| Korea, Republic of | 285 | 27 | 40 |
| Malaysia | 60 | 72 | 15 |
| Singapore | 46 | 138 | 16 |
| Taiwan Province of China | 210 | 44 | 56 |
| Thailand | 108 | 29 | 10 |
| Viet Nam | 14 | 7 | 20 |

*Source:* OECD, 1997.

[a] Exports are direct exports by SMEs. This understates the true contribution of SMEs to exports.

[b] Manufacturing only.

## 3. Contribution of SMEs and SME FDI to the entrepreneurial engine

As already discussed, the main contribution of the "entrepreneurial engine" in developing countries is likely to come from a relatively small proportion of fast-growing firms, which are export-oriented and bring products successfully to a local market. To make an accurate assessment of the contribution of fast-growing firms to overall economic growth requires longitudinal data on growth broken down by firm size, and by firms' rate of growth. Such data are not readily available. However, evidence from the UNCTAD survey for this study suggests that SMEs engaged in and SMEs receiving FDI are a potentially important component of the entrepreneurial engine with regard to the following:

- The average growth rates of these SMEs are well in excess of the already high economic growth rates in host countries. Sales growth rates are typically two to three times GDP growth rates.

- These SMEs are more likely than larger investors to regard as very important to their strategic business development the provision of new products and services, improving the quality of those products and services, and adapting technology to local needs.

- They are more likely than larger investors to regard the building up of linkages with overseas firms and the creation of an export capability as important to their strategic success.

- They are likely to see themselves as being well above the market average when it comes to technology, competitiveness, meeting customer needs and innovativeness.

# Notes

1 The reason why the percentage contributions add up to more than 100 per cent relates to the nature of the model that the World Bank used to estimate the contributions. This model includes a dummy which relating to the catch-up period that an economy faces, so that the "contribution" of GDP relative to United States GDP in 1960 is usually negative, in the order of 20 to 30 per cent. Thus, the poorer a country was in 1960 (the greater the catch-up gap), the larger the negative contribution to growth (World Bank, 1993).

2 For example, Singapore was actually falling behind international best practice at 3.5 per cent per annum (World Bank, 1993, p. 57). This result is difficult to accept.

3 Data from the UNCTAD trade database.

4 The survey was carried out by a consulting firm, ECO Ltd., and was based on 55 SMEs.

5 The shares of earnings by SME workers in these two economies are as follows:

**Taiwan Province of China: SME wage payments
as a proportion of national income, 1987-1994**
(Percentage)

| 1987 | 1988 | 1989 | 1990 | 1991 | 1992 | 1993 | 1994 |
|------|------|------|------|------|------|------|------|
| 43 | 44 | 46 | 48 | 49 | 50 | 50 | 50 |

*Source: Census of Industry and Commerce* (Taipei, various issues).

**Singapore: SME remuneration as a proportion
of total remuneration, 1980 and 1994**
(Percentage)

| Firm size | 1980 | 1994 |
|-----------|------|------|
| 0 -99 | 26 | 25 |
| 100 - 499 | 29 | 30 |
| 500+ | 44 | 44 |
| Total | 100 | 100 |

*Source*: Department of Statistics, *Report on the Census of Industrial Productions* (Singapore, various issues).

# CHAPTER II

## SME FDI IN ASIA:  EXTENT, PATTERN
## AND   TRENDS

Information on FDI by SMEs is difficult to obtain.  Some information on FDI at the national, sectoral and industrial levels is collected by the national agencies of many countries as well as international organizations such as UNCTAD.  However, not all countries collect comprehensive data (UNCTAD, 1997).  FDI statistics in Asia, whether on approved or actual investments,[1] are not usually collected by size of firm.  Exceptions in this regard in Asia are Japan and the Republic of Korea.  Thus, identifying SME FDI and measuring its size are not possible.  The only way is to obtain an approximation is to assume that those foreign investors seeking approvals of relatively small amounts of investment, say less than $1 million, are SMEs.  Although this is a reasonable approximation of FDI by SMEs, it is not accurate.  Therefore, in this study, a survey of SMEs making and receiving FDI was also carried out through direct contact, in order to determine more clearly the size of SME FDI.[2]  Both methods are used in this study to gauge the extent of SME FDI.

To understand the extent and pattern of SME FDI it is useful to consider the broader context of overall trends in FDI.  Two main trends are particularly noteworthy:

- The level of world FDI outflows increased at 12 per cent per annum between 1991 and 1996, and by 27 per cent per annum for the period 1986-1990, rates of increase roughly twice the rate of growth of exports of goods and services (UNCTAD, 1997, p. 4).

- FDI is becoming much more closely linked to trade, especially in manufactured goods (UNCTAD, 1996).

A comparison of the latter half of the 1980s with the first half of the 1990s reveals that actual inward FDI has grown rapidly in all the countries considered, both the leading countries (in terms of economic growth and performance) and other developing countries in Asia (table II.1).  Despite this overall growth, however, FDI flows vary from year to year. As a percentage of gross domestic capital formation, FDI inflows show annual variations of as much as 50 per cent (table II.2).

As noted below, only two countries - the Republic of Korea and Japan - keep any form of statistics on outward FDI by size of firm. There are no surveys to identify inward FDI by SMEs. The only way to approximate SME FDI is to obtain FDI data from countries which require registration of foreign investments, and then to break them down by size of investment. Even this, however, does not guarantee that the data relate to investment by SMEs. A small investment may be made by a large firm as part of a bigger project (e.g., the installation of computer equipment in a refinery). Similarly, some SMEs may make large commitments. However, the survey results tended to point to most SME FDI being typically less than $1 million (chapter III).[3]

### Table II.1. Inward FDI flows in selected economies in Asia, 1986-1996

(Millions of dollars)

| Economy | 1990 | 1991 | 1992 | 1993 | 1994 | 1995 | 1996 | Average 1986-1990 | Average 1991-1996 |
|---|---|---|---|---|---|---|---|---|---|
| **Leading economies** | 9 446 | 9 068 | 6 566 | 6 401 | 8 552 | 10 288 | 13 365 | 5 440 | 9 040 |
| Japan | 1 753 | 1 730 | 2 756 | 210 | 888 | 41 | 215 | 321 | 974 |
| Korea, Republic of | 788 | 1 180 | 727 | 588 | 809 | 1 776 | 2 308 | 799 | 1 231 |
| Singapore | 5 575 | 4 887 | 2 204 | 4 686 | 5 480 | 6 912 | 9 440 | 3 333 | 5 601 |
| Taiwan Province of China | 1 330 | 1 271 | 879 | 917 | 1 375 | 1 559 | 1 402 | 987 | 1 234 |
| **Developing countries** | 5 377 | 6 861 | 13 721 | 31 443 | 38 332 | 43 792 | 53 933 | 4 015 | 31 347 |
| Bangladesh | 3 | 1 | 4 | 14 | 11 | 2 | 9 | 2 | 7 |
| China | 3 487 | 4 366 | 11 156 | 27 515 | 33 787 | 35 849 | 42 300 | 2 853 | 25 829 |
| Indonesia | 1 093 | 1 482 | 1 777 | 2 004 | 2 109 | 4 348 | 7 960 | 599 | 3 280 |
| Myanmar | 161 | 238 | 171 | 149 | 91 | 115 | 100 | 42 | 144 |
| Philippines | 530 | 544 | 228 | 1 238 | 1 591 | 1 478 | 1 408 | 493 | 1 081 |
| Viet Nam | 102 | 229 | 385 | 523 | 742 | 2 000 | 2 156 | 45 | 1 006 |

*Source*: UNCTAD, FDI/TNC database.

### Table II.2. Inward FDI flows as a percentage of gross domestic capital formation in selected economies in Asia, 1990-1995

| Economy | 1990 | 1991 | 1992 | 1993 | 1994 | 1995 | Average |
|---|---|---|---|---|---|---|---|
| **Leading economies** | 0.9 | 0.7 | 0.5 | 0.4 | 0.6 | 0.6 | 0.6 |
| Japan | 0.2 | 0.2 | 0.2 | 0.02 | 0.1 | 0.003 | 0.1 |
| Korea, Republic of | 0.8 | 1.0 | 0.6 | 0.5 | 0.6 | 1.1 | 0.8 |
| Singapore | 46.8 | 33.6 | 12.4 | 23.0 | 23.0 | 24.6 | 25.5 |
| Taiwan Province of China | 3.7 | 3.1 | 1.8 | 1.8 | 2.5 | 2.7 | 2.5 |
| **Developing countries** | 2.8 | 3.7 | 6.7 | 15.1 | 17.7 | 19.0 | 11.3 |
| Bangladesh | 0.1 | 0.1 | 0.1 | 0.4 | 0.3 | 0.04 | 0.2 |
| China | 2.6 | 3.3 | 7.8 | 20.0 | 24.5 | 25.7 | 14.0 |
| Indonesia | 2.8 | 3.6 | 3.9 | 3.8 | 3.7 | 6.5 | 4.2 |
| Myanmar | 6.5 | 12.1 | 7.9 | 6.8 | 4.3 | 5.3 | 7.1 |
| Philippines | 5.2 | 6.0 | 2.1 | 9.6 | 10.5 | 9.0 | 7.5 |
| Viet Nam | .. | .. | .. | .. | .. | .. | .. |

*Source:* UNCTAD, FDI/TNC database.

Available figures on "small package" inward FDI of less than $1 million based on FDI approvals indicate that, in terms of cases, small-package FDI makes up a significant proportion of total FDI, ranging from about 15-20 per cent in Myanmar and Viet Nam to over 60 per cent in the Philippines (table II.3). However, in terms of value, small-package FDI does not loom very large in the overall picture: it makes up as little as a half per cent in Viet Nam, and only about 2 per cent in the Philippines. The growth of small package FDI is lower than that of FDI in general. To the extent that small package FDI can be taken as a proxy for SME FDI, this points to investment by SMEs in these countries not being significant, and possibly even declining in significance.

A mixed picture emerges with regard to outward SME FDI. The growth of FDI by SMEs from the Republic of Korea is about the same as that of that country's overall FDI, and the value of SME FDI is about one-fifth of the total, but about 70 per cent of the cases in 1995 (table II.4). The average amount of investment by SMEs was about $600,000. Republic of Korea SME FDI is largely concentrated in Asia; but North America is gaining in importance as a host region for the Republic of Korea SME TNCs, accounting for 15 per cent of total SME FDI from that country (table II.5). More than four-fifths of SME FDI are invested in manufacturing (table II.6) and although SME FDI from that country is becoming diversified, the bulk is in labour-intensive manufacturing activity.

**Table II.3. Trends in inward small-package FDI in selected developing countries in Asia, 1989-1995**

(Millions of dollars and percentage of total approvals)

| Country | 1989 | 1990 | 1991 | 1992 | 1993 | 1994 | 1995 |
|---|---|---|---|---|---|---|---|
| Myanmar[a] | | | | | | | |
| SME FDI ($ million) | 1 | 0.4 | 10 | 6 | 59 | 69 | 136 |
| SME FDI as percentage of total approved FDI | .. | .. | .. | 6 | 15 | 5 | 20 |
| Number of SME FDI cases as percentage of total approved FDI cases | 18 | 15 | 60 | 18 | 11 | 24 | 27 |
| Philippines[b] | | | | | | | |
| SME FDI ($ million) | 35 | 16 | 33 | 36 | 26 | 18 | 16 |
| SME FDI as percentage of total approved FDI | 17 | 8 | 8 | 11 | 7 | 2 | 2 |
| Number of SME FDI cases as percentage of total approved FDI cases | 86 | 83 | 80 | 85 | 73 | 62 | 63 |
| Viet Nam[c] | | | | | | | |
| SME FDI ($ million) | .. | .. | 12 | 13 | 24 | 28 | 29 |
| SME FDI as percentage of total approved FDI | .. | .. | 0.9 | 0.6 | 0.8 | 0.6 | 0.4 |
| Number of SME FDI cases as percentage of total approved FDI cases | .. | .. | 18 | 15 | 22 | 14 | 13 |

*Source:* UNCTAD, based on official national sources.

[a] Figures are for June-to-July year.
[b] Figures are based on approvals for projects of less than P60 million (about $ 2 million).
[c] Figures are estimates based on published information on approved smaller projects.

**Table II.4.  Importance of outward SME FDI stock from the Republic of Korea, 1993-1995[a]**

(Millions of dollars and percentage)

|  | 1993 | 1994 | 1995 |
|---|---|---|---|
| Value |  |  |  |
| All firms | 5 411 | 7 477 | 10 225 |
| SMEs | 1 026 | 1 519 | 2 054 |
| SME share (%) | 19 | 20 | 20 |
| Cases |  |  |  |
| All firms | 2 726 | 4 133 | 5 326 |
| SMEs | 1 603 | 2 722 | 3 593 |
| SME share (%) | 60 | 66 | 67 |

*Source*:  UNCTAD, based on data provided by Ministry of Finance and Economy of the Republic of Korea.

[a]    Figures represent cumulative flows since 1980.


**Table II.5.  SME FDI from the Republic of Korea, by host region, 1993-1995**

(Millions of dollars and number of cases)

| Host region | Flows | | | | | | Stock | |
|---|---|---|---|---|---|---|---|---|
|  | 1993 | | 1994 | | 1995 | | 1995[a] | |
|  | Value | Cases | Value | Cases | Value | Cases | Value | Cases |
| Developed regions | 33.2 | 44 | 76.4 | 106 | 115.0 | 113 | 418.9 | 539 |
| Europe[b] | 7.7 | 10 | 15.4 | 24 | 32.1 | 31 | 64.1 | 100 |
| North America | 22.1 | 29 | 58.7 | 75 | 77.8 | 70 | 314.0 | 379 |
| Oceania[c] | 3.3 | 5 | 2.3 | 7 | 5.2 | 12 | 40.8 | 60 |
| Developing regions | 272.5 | 470 | 413.6 | 1 013 | 420.0 | 758 | 1 635.6 | 3 054 |
| Africa | 0.7 | 3 | 1.6 | 6 | 2.3 | 2 | 11.3 | 25 |
| Latin America and the Caribbean | 9.0 | 13 | 14.2 | 17 | 6.1 | 12 | 112.5 | 140 |
| South, East and South-East Asia[d] | 263.0 | 453 | 397.0 | 989 | 411.0 | 744 | 1 509.0 | 2882 |
| West Asia | 0.3 | 1 | 0.7 | 1 | 0.7 | - | 3.2 | 7 |
| World | 306 | 514 | 490 | 1 119 | 535 | 871 | 2 054 | 3 593 |

*Source:*  UNCTAD, based on the data provided by Ministry of Finance and Economy of the Republic of Korea.

[a]  Cumulative flows since 1980.
[b]  Includes Central and Eastern Europe.
[c]  Includes developing countries in the Pacific.
[d]  Includes Japan.

**Table II.6. SME FDI from the Republic of Korea, by industry, 1993-1995**

(Millions of dollars and number of cases)

| Sector/industry | Flows | | | | | | Stock[a] | |
| | 1993 | | 1994 | | 1995 | | 1995 | |
| | Value | Cases | Value | Cases | Value | Cases | Value | Cases |
|---|---|---|---|---|---|---|---|---|
| Primary | 5.9 | 13 | 3.9 | 22 | -10.2 | 12 | 61.2 | 119 |
| Mining | 0.8 | 3 | 3.3 | 7 | -0.6 | 3 | 10.0 | 18 |
| Forestry | 0.9 | 2 | 0.0 | 1 | 1.6 | 2 | 13.8 | 9 |
| Fishery | 4.2 | 8 | 0.5 | 14 | -11.1 | 7 | 37.8 | 92 |
| Manufacturing | 276.5 | 441 | 409.2 | 909 | 447.1 | 707 | 1 680.0 | 2 804 |
| Services | 23.2 | 60 | 76.9 | 188 | 98.1 | 152 | 313.0 | 670 |
| Construction | 1.6 | 3 | 8.0 | 11 | 29.4 | 20 | 39.7 | 36 |
| Transportation | 0.06 | 2 | 5.1 | 12 | 2.4 | 4 | 14.8 | 30 |
| Storage | 15.0 | 38 | 40.0 | 69 | 25.5 | 45 | 143.3 | 350 |
| Trade | 6.6 | 17 | 23.7 | 96 | 40.9 | 83 | 115.2 | 254 |
| All industries | 306 | 514 | 490 | 1 119 | 535 | 871 | 2 054 | 3 593 |

*Source:* UNCTAD, based on data provided by Ministry of Finance and Economy of the Republic of Korea.

[a] Cumulative flows since 1980.

Japan also collects some information on the number of cases of SME investment abroad. SMEs make up about 50 per cent of cases of FDI. The proportion rose to as high as 60 per cent in 1988 when the yen was rising steeply, and then dropped to around 40 per cent in 1991, increasing again to 55 per cent in 1996 (table II.7).

Surveys by UNCTAD of SME investors in the Republic of Korea, Singapore and Taiwan Province of China for this study indicate that, on average, they plan to increase their FDI by about a quarter in 1997 and would increase this further by one-third per annum if governments took significant positive steps to address problems that they face in investing abroad. Similarly, table II.8 gives the average expected gains in sales and FDI of investors who are already in developing countries under either normal (or status quo) conditions; or "blue sky" conditions, under which the government takes active steps to address the problems faced by SMEs engaged in FDI. The expected gains in FDI are quite modest, even when scaled up to the national level, but they are not unimportant. For example in Myanmar, SME FDI was about $136 million in 1995, and only $8 million more would be expected over and above the "normal" expected increase of 18 per cent per annum. Sales growth for these firms (between 17 and 70 per cent) is generally much higher than the expected GDP growth, and is expected to increase even further (to between 30 and 120 per cent) if governments take steps to address problems faced by firms.

These findings underscore two points:

- Firms engaged in FDI form an important part of the entrepreneurial engine for growth. They typically expect much higher growth rates than national GDP growth. These high growth rates are more likely to be sustainable because of the firms' ability to draw on financial, managerial and technical resources abroad. Thus, these firms, both in host and home countries, could provide an important nucleus for development.

• Although SME FDI has a relatively insignificant impact at present in developing Asia, this is mostly because its size is below its potential. The needs of developing Asia require a rapid expansion of a dynamic, internationally competitive SME sector. FDI could provide an attractive policy option for achieving this. This is something of a new challenge -- the lessons of the leading countries in Asia are not necessarily all that helpful. To understand the potential and the policies required, it is necessary to obtain a better idea of the processes underlying the behaviour and strategies of SMEs and those underlying SME FDI.

**Table II.7.  Japan:  number of new equity investments abroad[a] by SMEs,[b] 1977-1996[c]**

| Year | Equity investments by SMEs[d] | | Equity investments by all firms[d] | | Share of equity investments by SMEs | |
|---|---|---|---|---|---|---|
| | All industries | Manufacturing | All industries | Manufacturing | All industries | Manufacturing |
| 1977 | 342 | 76 | 830 | 203 | 41.2 | 37.4 |
| 1978 | 306 | 112 | 887 | 323 | 34.5 | 34.7 |
| 1979 | 437 | 133 | 990 | 309 | 44.1 | 43.0 |
| 1980 | 326 | 99 | 790 | 260 | 41.3 | 38.1 |
| 1981 | 336 | 108 | 748 | 240 | 44.9 | 45.0 |
| 1982 | 247 | 86 | 765 | 226 | 32.3 | 38.1 |
| 1983 | 306 | 94 | 868 | 246 | 35.3 | 38.2 |
| 1984 | 312 | 109 | 828 | 303 | 37.7 | 36.0 |
| 1985 | 318 | 137 | 1 023 | 363 | 31.1 | 37.7 |
| 1986 | 599 | 279 | 1 419 | .. | 42.2 | .. |
| 1987 | 1 063 | 469 | 2 126 | .. | 50.0 | .. |
| 1988 | 1 625 | 724 | 2 725 | .. | 59.7 | .. |
| 1989 | 1 401 | 535 | 2 602 | .. | 53.8 | .. |
| 1990 | 994 | 381 | 2 249 | .. | 44.2 | .. |
| 1991 | 619 | 281 | 1 556 | .. | 39.8 | .. |
| 1992 | 574 | 291 | 1 397 | .. | 41.1 | .. |
| 1993 | 698 | 432 | 1 530 | .. | 45.6 | .. |
| 1994 | 684 | 520 | 1 203 | .. | 56.4 | .. |
| 1995 | 783 | 573 | 1 498 | .. | 52.3 | .. |
| 1996 | 673 | 458 | 1 228 | .. | 54.8 | .. |

*Source:* Fujita, 1998.

[a]  New equity investments abroad refer to investments in initial capital acquisition (thus excluding additional investments by the same company in the same affiliate) and establishment of new foreign affiliates. Intra-company loan investments, which are an important component of FDI, are not included.

[b]  The definition of an SME in Japan is as follows: in manufacturing, an enterprise with capital of less than 100 million yen and fewer than 300 employees; in wholesale trade, an enterprise with capital of less than 30 million yen and fewer than 100 employees; and in retail trade and other services, an enterprise with capital of less than 10 million yen and fewer than 50 employees.

[c]  Calendar year for SMEs and fiscal year for all firms.

[d]  On approval/notification basis. As notification criteria in terms of investment value have changed from more than 3 million yen to 10 million yen since April 1984, from more than 10 million yen to 30 million yen since July 1989 and from more than 30 million yen to 100 million yen since June 1994, the data before and after 1983, before and after 1988, and before and after 1994, respectively, are not consistent.

**Table II.8. Potential growth of SME FDI by existing investors in the Philippines, Myanmar and Viet Nam**

(Percentage)

| Country | Expected growth of sales of SME affiliates | Growth of sales of SME affiliates under "blue sky conditions" | Expected SME FDI growth (A) | SME FDI growth under "blue sky conditions" (B) | Contribution of "blue sky conditions" SME FDI growth (B) - (A) | Contribution of "blue sky conditions" to SME FDI (Million dollars) |
|---|---|---|---|---|---|---|
| Myanmar | 17 | 30 | 18 | 24 | 6 | 8 |
| Philippines | 24 | 33 | 23 | 26 | 3 | 5 |
| Viet Nam | 71 | 118 | 24 | 48 | 24 | 7 |

*Source:* UNCTAD, based on the questionnaire survey conducted in 1996 (see the annex for a note on the survey methodology).

# Notes

[1] Data on FDI approvals relate to the amounts approved for investment purposes. Data on these are usually collected by boards of investment or other agencies (for example, the Ministry of Finance in the cases of Japan and the Republic of Korea) responsible for monitoring and approving foreign investment. They are often quite detailed, and usually give breakdowns by industry, type of proposed activity, country of origin, addresses of firms involved, etc. Data on realized FDI relate to the amount of funds actually flowing across borders. Data on these are usually collected by central banking authorities, and based on balance-of-payments and financial flows statistics. Although more accurate, these data are usually not detailed, and do not normally give industry breakdowns. As there are also unpredictable lags between approvals and actual investments, the two are not readily comparable. Approval data are usually higher than the value of FDI actually realized. Actual or realized investment is about 40 per cent of that approved in some countries. Flows of funds, whether they are approved or actual, do not necessarily catch the value of the flows of intangible investments, such as expenditure on training or technology. Sometimes data on actual FDI or data on realized FDI -- in particular in stock values -- are also obtained by means of industrial surveys, but these have sampling and other problems.

[2] SME investors from the Republic of Korea, Singapore and Taiwan Province of China and SME recipients in Indonesia, Myanmar, the Philippines and Viet Nam were included in the UNCTAD survey. See the annex for a note on the survey methodology.

[3] Crude estimates may be possible for SME FDI from Taiwan Province of China; most FDI by SMEs, however, is not recorded as it is normally undertaken under individual owners' names. This is because individual income from foreign sources is exempt from personal income tax in this economy. Therefore, the differences between approved outward FDI reported by Taiwan Province of China (Investment Commission) and investment approved by the host country are considered to be close to SME FDI.

# CHAPTER III

## CHARACTERISTICS OF AND FACTORS UNDERLYING SME INVESTMENT IN ASIA

For developing countries seeking to take advantage of SME FDI, it is necessary to have a better understanding of the factors driving SMEs to invest across borders. SME FDI and internationalization are driven by many different factors. This chapter examines the empirical evidence with respect to the nature of SME FDI and the reasons underlying it, with a view to helping identify the relative importance of different factors. The chapter first discusses the general background and factors affecting SME FDI in Asia and then proceeds to examine evidence regarding the specific factors which influence the pattern of SME FDI, including the reasons or motivations for the latter, the problems that impede it, and the factors that assist SME investors.

In general, three key points emerge as regards the reasons for, and strategies with respect to, FDI, including SME FDI (UNCTAD, 1993, 1996):

- FDI is part of a broader process of internationalization. From the point of view of an investing firm, it is usually preceded by a number of other types of international activities: trade, alliances, licensing etc. Strategically, FDI is at the end of a chain of events related to international activities.

- Internationalization (including FDI) is influenced by a host of factors, which can be broadly grouped into four main factors:

    *Push factors*. Factors that make a firm move out of its existing location (e.g., rising costs or adverse exchange-rate movements). Push factors are exemplified, for instance, by Japanese FDI in certain industries which has been driven by rising costs of production at home.

    *Pull factors*. Factors that make markets or locations abroad more attractive (e.g., rapidly expanding markets, markets with large growth potential, or lower costs of production). This is central to theories that see FDI as a replacement for trade or that see FDI as part of corporate expansion. Governments can play an important role in developing a "pull" environment by providing incentives to relocate.

*Management factors.* Successful internationalization is more likely if the management of a firm is committed to international activity and has the time and experience to pursue it.

*Chance.* Chance factors are often important in the process of internationalization, especially for SMEs, and not all internationalization is initiated in a planned way. For example, a firm may be approached by a customer abroad to supply; it may be invited to form an alliance with a partner abroad; or a manager may come across opportunities in a market while on holiday.

- All firms face problems in moving across borders. They also find some assistance. What is a problem for one firm may not be a problem and, indeed, may be of assistance to another. Thus, what constitutes a problem is not always clear-cut.

This chapter seeks to examine the types of FDI in which SMEs are engaged, the purpose of SME FDI, reasons for it, and the assistance received by n as well as the obstacles facing n SMEs engaged in FDI. The empirical results in this section are drawn from prior research as well as surveys in Asian economies carried out specifically for this purpose (see the annex for a note on the survey methodology). The survey research was largely exploratory. However, it supplies some useful insights, and case studies were carried out in order to obtain a deeper understanding. Where appropriate, a distinction is made between inward FDI and outward FDI. The former relates to SMEs in developing countries that have received FDI, either from SMEs or from larger firms. The latter relates to SMEs in leading Asian economies that have invested in SMEs or established SME affiliates abroad.

Several key points emerge from this chapter. Most SMEs transfer to their foreign operations a package of capital and other resources in the form of technology, organization and management know-how and skills; these resource flows go mostly into plant and equipment, into the development of new products or product improvement, and into management training. SME FDI takes place for much the same reasons as FDI by large firms, but there are differences in the degree to which different factors influence large and small investors. Smaller investors are much more likely to be influenced by chance factors (e.g., being approached by a customer from abroad, or seeing an opportunity and taking it) than larger investors. Management factors are more likely to be important for medium-sized and larger investors. Push factors (e.g., rising costs) are relatively less important for SME FDI than are other factors. And the main factors that directly impede SME FDI fall within the responsibility of governments. Corruption heads the list, but regulations, approval procedures, telecommunications deficiencies and unfair competition are all seen as significant concerns and obstacles.

## A. FDI and other resource flows to and from SMEs

FDI involves a flow of resources from a firm based in one country to another (existing or newly established) firm in a foreign country, where that flow creates some form of ownership or management control of the recipient's activities by the investor or parent firm. As discussed earlier, FDI is measured by the flows of capital in the form of equity, intra-company loans and reinvested earnings, and is usually accompanied by a transfer of technology, skills and management practices.

In addition to the flows of the resources received from the parent or investing firm, FDI recipients in host countries may obtain resources from unrelated foreign firms and other sources through loans and contractual arrangements for technology and training. Similarly, SME outward investors may provide recipient SMEs with resources in the form of FDI as well as other types of flows.

## 1. Inward FDI and other resource flows to SMEs

Table III.1 shows the composition of the total number of cases of FDI and other resources received by SMEs located in developing Asia from firms abroad in the preceding five years (1991-1995), according to the survey conducted for this *Handbook*. The bulk of these resources is made up of FDI and skills provided by training, either in cash or in kind; 72 per cent of recipient SMEs received FDI (in the form of equity finance, reinvested earnings or intra-company loans) and 68 per cent received some form of training. SMEs investing in SMEs are, however, much less likely to provide training or technology than are large enterprises that invest in SMEs.

**Table III.1. Resource flows to SMEs in host developing countries in Asia,[a]**
**by size of investing firm, 1991-1995**

(Percentage)[b]

| Size | FDI[c] | Loans from unrelated organizations | Technology | Training | Number of recipient SMEs surveyed[d] |
|---|---|---|---|---|---|
| Total | 72 | 9 | 51 | 68 | 78 |
| SME-SME | 74 | 12 | 38 | 62 | 34 |
| LE-SME | 68 | 9 | 77 | 86 | 22 |
| Ratio[e] | 1.09 | 1.33 | 0.49 | 0.72 | .. |

*Source:* UNCTAD, based on the questionnaire survey conducted by UNCTAD in 1996 (see the annex for a note on the survey methodology).

[a]   Myanmar, Philippines and Viet Nam only.
[b]   Percentage share of total respondent firms that indicated one or more resource flows. Percentage shares do not add up to 100 as the different types of investment and resource flows are not mutually exclusive.
[c]   Includes equity finance, reinvested earnings and/or loans by the investing firm.
[d]   Includes some SMEs whose relationship with parent firms is unknown or whose parent firms are unknown. The number of entries shown in this table applies to the relevant rows in tables III.2 and III.3 as well.
[e]   Ratio of the percentage of SME-SME responses to LE-SME responses. A multiple of more than 1.0 indicates that SME-SME respondents use that resource more frequently than LE-SME respondents, by the size of that multiple.

On average, in 1995, SME investors injected about $1 million in to each recipient SME, while larger firms injected about twice that (table III.2). The distributions are heavily skewed; only one SME-SME equity investment actually exceeded $1 million. Although the value of technology and training is harder to gauge because of their intangible nature, the figures suggest that SME-SME flows in this area are quite valuable (table III.2). The average value of technology received in 1995 by SMEs from foreign SMEs was about $507,000, not far short of that received by SMEs from large firms. The average value of the training received by SMEs from SMEs was about $61,000, compared with about $185,000 from larger firms. The figures support the view that small-size FDI of less than about $1 million is a reasonable approximation of the level of FDI that an SME is likely to make in a host country.

**Table III.2. Resource flows received by SMEs in host developing countries in Asia,[a]
by size of foreign investing firm, 1995**

(Thousands of dollars)

| Item | FDI[b] | Loans from unrelated organizations[c] | Technology | Training |
|---|---|---|---|---|
| SME-SME | | | | |
| Average | 1 006[d] | 800[d] | 507 | 61 |
| Standard deviation | 2 039 | .. | 739 | 94 |
| LE-SME | | | | |
| Average | 2 472 | 350 | 562 | 185 |
| Standard deviation | 3 105 | .. | 652 | 363 |

*Source:* UNCTAD, based on the questionnaire survey conducted by UNCTAD in 1996 (see the annex for a note on the survey methodology).

[a]  Myanmar, Philippines and Viet Nam only.
[b]  Including equity finance, reinvested earnings and/or loans by the investing firm.
[c]  There are only two cases in SME-SME FDI and one case in LE-SME FDI. Standard deviation cannot be calculated.
[d]  Data are biased upwards because of inclusion of irregular cases.

As most FDI is made up of a package of resources, an investor generally combines an equity investment with training and/or transfer of technology. At least one-quarter of firms, and often as many as half received resources in any of the combinations shown in table III.3. However, SME-SME FDI is only about half as likely to involve multiple resource flows as LE-SME FDI, the exception being the combination of FDI plus training. In general, this suggests that there is a better than even chance that a large firm injecting FDI into an SME will bring technology or training (or both) with it.

**Table III.3. Combinations of resource flows received by SMEs
in host developing countries in Asia,[a] 1995**

(Percentage)[b]

| Item | FDI and loans from unrelated organizations | FDI and training | FDI and technology | FDI training and technology |
|---|---|---|---|---|
| Total | 36 | 47 | 42 | 31 |
| SME-SME | 26 | 44 | 29 | 24 |
| LE-SME | 55 | 59 | 68 | 50 |

*Source:* UNCTAD, based on the questionnaire survey conducted by UNCTAD in 1996 (see the annex for a note on the survey methodology).

[a]  Myanmar, Philippines and Viet Nam only.
[b]  Percentage of the number of SMEs in host countries that received a particular combination of resource flows in the total number of SMEs surveyed.

## 2. Outward FDI and other resource flows from SMEs

A similar picture emerges from an analysis of SMEs investing abroad. The bulk of SMEs investing abroad provide FDI, while 13-21 per cent of them provide technology, and 24-29 per cent conduct training (table III.4). The value of outward FDI reported by investing SMEs is somewhat larger than that reported by recipient SMEs because the values are skewed heavily by some large values. However, the FDI funds invested by SMEs are generally less than $1 million, with technology transfer in the order of less than half a million dollars and training valued at less than $100,000 (table III.5).

**Table III.4. Outward resource flows by SMEs from leading economies in Asia, by size[a] of investing firm**

(Percentage)[b]

| Item | FDI[c] | Loans made abroad to non- affiliated firms | Technology | Training |
|---|---|---|---|---|
| Total | 79 | 3 | 18 | 28 |
| Small[d] | 79 | - | 21 | 24 |
| Medium[e] | 77 | 6 | 13 | 29 |

*Source:* UNCTAD, based on the questionnaire survey conducted by UNCTAD in 1996 (see the annex for a note on the survey methodology).

  [a]  Republic of Korea, Singapore and Taiwan Province of China only.
  [b]  Percentage share of total responses.
  [c]  Including equity finance, reinvested earnings and/or loans by the investing firm.
  [d]  Firms with 100 or fewer employees.
  [e]  Firms with 101 to 500 employees.

**Table III.5. Outward resource flows by SMEs from leading economies in Asia[a] in 1995**

(Thousands of dollars)

| Item | FDI[b] | Loans made abroad to non- affiliated firms | Technology | Training |
|---|---|---|---|---|
| Total | | | | |
| Average | 1 936 | - | 363 | 102 |
| Standard deviation | 2 651 | .. | 399 | 102 |
| | | | | |
| Small[c] | | | | |
| Average | 1 429 | - | 450 | 36 |
| Standard deviation | 2 438 | .. | 404 | 37 |
| | | | | |
| Medium[d] | | | | |
| Average | 2 437 | - | - | 182 |
| Standard deviation | 3 076 | .. | .. | 211 |

*Source:* UNCTAD, based on the questionnaire survey conducted by UNCTAD in 1996 (see the annex for a note on the survey methodology).

  [a]  Republic of Korea, Singapore and Taiwan Province of China only.
  [b]  Including equity finance, reinvested earnings and/or loans by the investing firm.
  [c]  Firms with 100 or fewer employees.
  [d]  Firms with 101 to 500 employees.

## B.  What is SME FDI used for?

FDI and other resource flows in SMEs are used in a variety of ways, ranging from financing plant and equipment to investing in technology for process improvement or training of unskilled staff. Data on the use of each of the types of flows discussed above by respondent host country firms in the survey suggest the following (table III.6):

- Most equity and other financial flows by SMEs go to plant and equipment; relatively little goes into buildings or land. About 70 per cent of equity flows go to plant and equipment. SME-SME FDI is more likely to go into buildings, but that is only a small proportion (about 10 per cent of all cases) of SME FDI equity flow use.

- Technology flows are fairly evenly spread across new product and new process technologies, or improvements in processes or products. Relative to LE-SME flows, SME-SME flows are much more likely to occur in product and process improvements and in marketing.

- Most training goes to senior staff, either management or technical staff, according to figures based on the principal use of the expenditures for training. Analysis of data on secondary use (i.e., the second highest priority in use of resources for training) reveals that a higher proportion goes to unskilled staff. SME-SME FDI is much more likely to go to training in marketing and management than is LE-SME FDI.

The implication for developing countries is that foreign SMEs are valuable sources of resources for fixed capital formation, technology and training. Although SMEs are less likely to spend more on technology or training in their host country activities than their larger counterparts, the focus of SME activities in these areas may be more in line with host country characteristics and needs, and hence more beneficial for developing countries.

## C. What are the reasons for SME FDI?

As noted earlier, there are four broad reasons why firms engage in internationalization generally and FDI in particular: push factors (e.g., rising costs or other factors in the home market); pull factors (e.g., attractive markets abroad, incentives and other government measures); management factors (managerial capability, competence and interest); and chance. The specific factors within these broad areas are discussed in greater detail below.

### 1. Inward FDI in SMEs

All of the reasons mentioned above are important, but their relative importance differs a great deal between SMEs and large firms (table III.7). Several key points emerge (table III.7):

- For SME-SME FDI, management and chance factors are the most important. Push factors are the least important.

- For LE-SME FDI, management and pull factors are the most important. Push factors are, again, the least important.

- The comparison ratios show that a larger number of reasons are relatively more important (or very important) for SME-SME FDI as compared with LE-SME FDI. In other words, although SMEs are driven by the same reasons as large firms when they engage in FDI, more SMEs see the reasons as pressing (by multiples of between 1.1 and 1.4).

- Chance factors are significantly more important in the case of SMEs investing in SMEs -- 70 per cent of SME-SME respondents rated chance factors as very important or important, as against only 50 per cent of LE-SME respondents.

### Table III.6. Principal uses of resource flows[a] to SMEs in host developing countries in Asia[b], by size of investing firm

(Percentage)[c]

| FDI[d] | | Loans from unrelated organizations | | Technology | | Training | |
|---|---|---|---|---|---|---|---|
| **SME-SME** | | | | | | | |
| Plant | 68 | Plant | 100 | New product | 31 | Management | 38 |
| Buildings | 12 | Buildings | - | New process | 15 | Marketing | 10 |
| Working capital | 16 | Working capital | - | Product improvement | 23 | Technical | 29 |
| Inventory | - | Inventory | - | Process improvement | 15 | Skilled staff | 5 |
| Technology | 4 | Technology | - | | - | Unskilled staff | 5 |
| **LE-SME** | | | | | | | |
| Plant | 73 | Plant | 50 | New product | 53 | Management | 26 |
| Buildings | 7 | Buildings | 50 | New process | 24 | Marketing | 5 |
| Working capital | 13 | Working capital | - | Product improvement | 12 | Technical | 47 |
| Inventory | - | Inventory | - | Process improvement | 6 | Skilled staff | 11 |
| Technology | 7 | Technology | - | | - | Unskilled staff | 5 |
| **Ratio[e]** | | | | | | | |
| Plant | 0.93 | Plant | 2.00 | New product | 0.58 | Management | 1.45 |
| Buildings | 1.80 | Buildings | .. | New process | 0.65 | Marketing | 1.81 |
| Working capital | 1.20 | Working capital | .. | Product improvement | 1.96 | Technical | 0.60 |
| Inventory | .. | Inventory | .. | Process improvement | 2.62 | Skilled staff | 0.45 |
| Technology | 0.60 | Technology | .. | | | Unskilled staff | 0.90 |

*Source:* UNCTAD, based on the questionnaire survey conducted by UNCTAD in 1996 (see the annex for a note on the survey methodology).

a   The main use to which each respondent put the flows of resources from abroad.
b   Myanmar, Philippines and Viet Nam only.
c   Percentage of total responses with respect to each type of flow that indicate the given use.
d   Including equity finance, reinvested earnings and/or loans by the investing firm.
e   Ratio of the percentage of SME-SME responses to that of LE-SME responses. A multiple of more than 1.0 indicates that a relatively larger proportion of SME-SME respondents indicated that particular use for a given resource, as compared with LE-SME respondents, by the size of that multiple.

- Government pull factors (such as tax concessions, information on opportunities and trade protection) are slightly more important to SME-SME respondents than pull factors generally, and are regarded as very important or important by about 70 per cent of those respondents.

More detailed analysis on the composition of each of the broader summary factors throws further light on the factors underlying FDI in SMEs (table III.8):

- In general, more SME investors regard all of the factors as important (or very important) than do large firms. There are really only two reasons that fewer SME-SME respondents regard as important than their LE-SME counterparts. These are rising production costs at home, and lower costs of production. This seems to point to SME-SME FDI being less likely to be driven by factors related to the "hollowing out" of industries in home countries.

- Lack of access to technology is more than twice as important as a reason for SME-SME FDI as it is for LE-SME FDI, with over 68 per cent of the former citing it as a reason.

**Table III.7. Summary reasons for FDI in SMEs in host developing countries in Asia[a]**
(Percentage)

| Degree of importance | Push | Pull | Government pull | Management | Chance |
|---|---|---|---|---|---|
| **SME-SME FDI** | | | | | |
| No response | 15 | 12 | 12 | 12 | 12 |
| Not applicable | - | 6 | 6 | 3 | 3 |
| Not important | 26 | 18 | 15 | 12 | 15 |
| Important | 44 | 53 | 47 | 41 | 47 |
| Very important | 15 | 12 | 21 | 32 | 24 |
| **LE-SME FDI** | | | | | |
| No response | 27 | 23 | 27 | 32 | 32 |
| Not applicable | 5 | 9 | 5 | - | - |
| Not important | 23 | 9 | 14 | 9 | 18 |
| Important | 45 | 45 | 36 | 36 | 36 |
| Very important | - | 14 | 18 | 23 | 14 |
| **Ratio[b]** | | | | | |
| No response | 0.54 | 0.52 | 0.43 | 0.37 | 0.37 |
| Not applicable | - | 0.65 | 1.29 | - | - |
| Not important | 1.16 | 1.94 | 1.08 | 1.29 | 0.81 |
| Important | 0.97 | 1.16 | 1.29 | 1.13 | 1.29 |
| Very important | - | 0.86 | 1.13 | 1.42 | 1.73 |

*Source:* UNCTAD, based on the questionnaire survey conducted by UNCTAD in 1996 (see the annex for a note on the survey methodology).

[a] Myanmar, Philippines and Viet Nam only.
[b] Ratio of the percentage of SME-SME responses to that of LE-SME responses. A multiple of more than 1.0 indicates that a relatively larger number of SME-SME respondents regard that factor as important than do LE-SME respondents, by the size of that multiple.

This can be viewed in the light of the fact that SME-SME FDI is only half as likely to lead to technology transfer, and only about 38 per cent of SME-SME FDI actually leads to technology transfer (table III.1). This suggests that SMEs are not being as successful as they might wish, and that their contribution to the entrepreneurial engine might be being blunted. Section D below examines some of the possible reasons for this.

• All chance factors are important to SME-SME FDI, but seeing an opportunity (and presumably being in a position to take advantage of it) and being approached by a customer abroad are particularly important. For example, about 80 per cent of SME-SME respondents regard "saw opportunity and took it" as very important or important as a reason for pursuing and maintaining linkages with SMEs abroad. About 70 per cent were approached by a customer from abroad.

## 2. Outward FDI by SMEs

As regards outward SME FDI, a very similar picture emerges judging from the responses of investors surveyed (table III.9). Chance factors are extremely important; indeed, for small enterprises (firms with fewer than 100 employees) investing abroad, they are one of the most important factors. For medium-sized firms investing abroad, management factors become relatively more important, as do government pull factors -- 77 per cent of medium-sized investors regard government incentives as important or very important, as compared with only 43 per cent of small investors.

**Table III.8. Reasons for FDI in SMEs by individual factor in host developing countries in Asia[a]**

(Percentage)[b]

| | Factor | Total | SME-SME | LE- SME | Ratio[c] |
|---|---|---|---|---|---|
| *Push* | Lack of opportunities for growth at home | 44 | 58 | 32 | 1.85 |
| | Lack of access to finance at home | 50 | 59 | 36 | 1.62 |
| | Lack of access to technology at home | 58 | 68 | 32 | 2.13 |
| | Rising production costs in home market | 45 | 44 | 50 | 0.88 |
| | Increased competition in home market | 42 | 47 | 41 | 1.15 |
| | Erosion of home market share | 24 | 29 | 18 | 1.62 |
| | Volatility and risk diversification | 32 | 38 | 18 | 2.10 |
| *Pull* | Access to skilled labour abroad | 38 | 41 | 32 | 1.29 |
| | Access to management skills abroad | 45 | 44 | 32 | 1.39 |
| | Lower costs of production | 51 | 47 | 56 | 0.86 |
| | Market growth opportunities in host country market | 44 | 41 | 36 | 1.13 |
| | Market growth opportunities in third countries | 58 | 56 | 59 | 0.95 |
| | Tax incentives for foreign investment | 54 | 65 | 45 | 1.42 |
| | Access to special materials | 44 | 53 | 36 | 1.46 |
| | Overcoming protective restrictions | 41 | 44 | 41 | 1.08 |
| | Advantage from local market knowledge | 53 | 56 | 41 | 1.37 |
| | Technical or product lead advantages | 58 | 65 | 41 | 1.56 |
| *Management* | International experience of managers | 64 | 71 | 56 | 1.29 |
| | Information about opportunities abroad | 62 | 68 | 45 | 1.49 |
| | Careful planning and market research | 63 | 68 | 50 | 1.35 |
| *Chance* | Chance encounters (e.g., with clients) | 54 | 56 | 41 | 1.37 |
| | Approached by customer from abroad | 59 | 68 | 45 | 1.49 |
| | Approached by partner from abroad | 50 | 59 | 32 | 1.85 |
| | Saw opportunity and took it | 69 | 79 | 56 | 1.49 |

*Source:* UNCTAD, based on the questionnaire survey conducted by UNCTAD in 1996 (see the annex for a note on the survey methodology).

a   Myanmar, Philippines and Viet Nam only.
b   Percentage of each group of respondents that consider a factor important or very important.
c   Ratio of the percentage of SME-SME responses to that of LE-SME responses. A multiple of more than 1.0 indicates that a larger proportion of SME-SME respondents regard that factor as important or very important than LE-SME respondents, by the size of that multiple.

The implications for governments seeking to encourage more SME-SME FDI are the following:

- Given their overriding importance, addressing chance factors could be a very cost-effective way of encouraging FDI. For example, increasing the probability of "chance" encounters, by means of encouraging networking, matchmaking etc., may be the most effective way of initiating SME FDI.

- Government pull factors tend to be of much more importance to medium-sized and larger firms, but are not particularly important to small investors. Smaller investors are much less likely to be able to use investment incentives and if these are to be effective, they must be designed in such a way as to make them accessible to small firms.

- Push factors (e.g., rising costs in home countries) are relatively unimportant, and so it is clear that governments in developing countries cannot simply wait for SMEs in more developed economies to be forced to invest abroad by home country pressures. Instead, host governments must adopt a more active stance if they want to take advantage of the entrepreneurial engine offered by SME investors.

**Table III.9. Summary reasons for SME FDI from leading economies in Asia[a]**

(Percentage)[b]

| | Reason | | | | |
|---|---|---|---|---|---|
| Degree of importance | Push | Pull | Government pull | Management | Chance |
| **All SME FDI** | | | | | |
| No response | 7 | 5 | 8 | 8 | 8 |
| Not applicable | 10 | 3 | 3 | 2 | 5 |
| Not important | 30 | 13 | 15 | 11 | 14 |
| Important | 10 | 38 | 49 | 44 | 35 |
| Very important | 44 | 39 | 25 | 34 | 39 |
| (Very important + important) | (54) | (77) | (74) | (79) | (73) |
| **FDI by small firms** [c] | | | | | |
| No response | 13 | 7 | 10 | 10 | 13 |
| Not applicable | 10 | 10 | 7 | 7 | 7 |
| Not important | 33 | 10 | 40 | 17 | 7 |
| Important | 20 | 53 | 27 | 30 | 37 |
| Very important | 23 | 20 | 17 | 37 | 37 |
| (Very important + important) | (43) | (73) | (43) | (67) | (73) |
| **FDI by medium-sized firms** [d] | | | | | |
| No response | 3 | 3 | 3 | 3 | 3 |
| Not applicable | 6 | - | 3 | - | 3 |
| Not important | 32 | 16 | 16 | 10 | 19 |
| Important | 29 | 52 | 52 | 55 | 42 |
| Very important | 26 | 29 | 26 | 32 | 32 |
| (Very important + important) | (55) | (81) | (77) | (87) | (74) |

*Source:* UNCTAD, based on the questionnaire survey conducted by UNCTAD in 1996 (see the annex for a note on the survey methodology).

[a] Republic of Korea, Singapore and Taiwan Province of China only.

[b] Percentage of respondents giving the particular response as regards importance attached to each reason.

[c] Firms with 100 or fewer employees.

[d] Firms with 101 to 500 employees.

*Note*: Percentage shares for each category of SME investment may not add up to 100 because of rounding.

## D. Problems and assistance: what helps and what hinders SMEs engaged in FDI?

SMEs moving across borders invariably face problems, some of which do not constitute impediments to FDI by large firms (box III.1). However, they also find some assistance. Moreover, what is a problem for one SME may not necessarily be a problem for another. For example, "finding suitable partners" may be an enormous problem for some SMEs, and yet may not be a problem for others. In any event, the policies which might be adopted to overcome these problems will differ according to the type of problems:

•   *Internal problems*, such as management, where policy needs to be directed at the SME itself if the problems are to be overcome. Case studies and interviews clearly show that all internationalized SMEs face these problems, although management is sometimes reluctant to admit to them. Governments can address these problems by providing specific programmes designed to fill gaps, such as management advisory and consultancy programmes and trade missions. However, the survey results tend to show that these initiatives, though welcome, are not regarded as being especially helpful.

- *Market and infrastructure problems*, such as lack of finance and excessive competition. Policy needs to be directed at a more general level such as the operation of markets and infrastructure capabilities. The survey results show that these are major issues which impede FDI. However, they do not pose problems for all firms, and some care needs to be taken to design policies which address problems in the areas where it has most impact.

- *Barriers created or allowed to persist by governments*, such as regulatory impediments or corruption, where government policy or practice itself needs to be reviewed. The survey results clearly show that this is by far the biggest problem area. It is in the re-engineering of government policies and practices that the greatest challenges and opportunities lie.

---

**Box III.1. Obstacles to SME FDI: approval processes, minimum limits and documents**

Some policies, whilst well meaning, tend to inhibit SME FDI unnecessarily. Two examples illustrate this.

*Myanmar*. There is a minimum limit for FDI of $500,000 in manufacturing. This automatically rules out legal investment in many smaller service industries. Another serious impediment is the great difference between official and market exchange rates. The result is that smaller investors do not seek approvals, but simply bring money into the country to exchange on the black market. The regulations have thus not stopped the injection of much-needed capital flowing to smaller SMEs. However, they pose problems in terms of corruption and will pose problems when smaller successful firms grow, and need further capital injections to sustain their growth. Given the poor state of Myanmar's internal capital markets, future access to small-package amounts of foreign capital will be essential for the achievement of growth targets.

*Viet Nam*. Investors are required to submit a study form which requires an analysis of the impact of the proposed investment on employment, exports, local industries, environment etc. Completing the form requires fairly detailed knowledge of local conditions and a capability for economic analysis not usually possessed by SME managers. Preparation of the document can cost upwards of $5,000 to $10,000, which for some SMEs is quite a sizeable part of the first year's expected income. Some SMEs avoid this by registering in the names of local "dummy" companies, which are registered by a compliant local silent partner. Problems arise when the partner ceases to be silent, and claims as his or her property registered in the company name. Another alternative is to operate through representative offices, although under Vietnamese law these are not permitted to trade or book business.

---

## 1. Inward SME FDI

This section gives some idea of the relative importance of the different types of problems facing SME FDI in host countries. Box III.2 illustrates the problems faced by a typical SME investor. In the survey results on SME FDI recipients in developing countries (table III.10), most factors listed were regarded as being both a problem and of assistance. For example, the availability of skilled staff locally is a problem (or major problem) for 44 per cent of SME-SME respondents, but some firms do not face a problem in finding and using skilled staff and, in fact, the existence of the latter is important for these firms. Therefore, this factor is a help or very helpful for 38 per cent. Thus, on balance, only 6 per cent regard it as a problem *per se*. SME-SME respondents were slightly more likely to see the availability of skilled staff as a problem, and less likely to see it as being helpful, as compared with LE-SME respondents.

Although not evident from this table, the pattern of what is a problem and what has been of assistance varies from country to country, and this aspect is analysed further in the case studies in chapter V. The main factors causing problems for SME-SME FDI are as follows: corruption in minor officials, corruption in senior officials, road infrastructure, unfair competition, telecommunications infrastructure, tariffs and quotas, market access restrictions and cultural differences (table III.10). For example, on balance, 56 per cent of SME-SME respondents regard corruption among minor officials as a problem (and 41 per cent hold that view about corruption among senior officials). Virtually no respondents see corruption as being of assistance to them. This is obviously an area in which governments can do something; indeed, with the possible exception of cultural differences, all the factors mentioned are the direct responsibility of governments. In other words, if governments want to encourage more SME-SME FDI, it is directly in their power to address most of the problems that impede it.

---

**Box III.2. Factors inhibiting the growth of SME FDI: the case of Abacus**

Abacus was established in Singapore in 1988 by a consortium of Asian airlines. Its main activity is in the provision of booking services and information to travel agents. Travel agents who are linked to Abacus can offer their clients information and bookings on a range of airlines, hotels and tourist activities. Abacus' revenue is mostly from ticket sales of the main consortium airlines and other associated airlines. The company's central operations are based in Singapore, from where it provides services and manages a series of national marketing companies in 14 other Asian countries. Abacus set up the national marketing companies (NMCs) in host countries on the basis of the expected revenue generation capacity of the respective markets. Abacus employs about 350 people in Singapore, and the national marketing companies established by it typically employ between 40 and 80 people. It provides training to the management of the NMCs and technical support. The NMCs in turn provide training to the travel agents, and assist them with technical support. There are about 6,000 travel agents linked to the Abacus system, and they typically employ 2 to 20 people. Tourism is growing at about 8-9 per cent on average in the region, and Abacus' growth reflects this.

The potential economic impact of the activities of Abacus is quite large, in terms of immediate training of local people in skills ranging from management and electronic systems to quality control and customer services; access to electronic infrastructure (Abacus generally invests in and then leases committed lines and peripherals); and in inbound and outbound tourism. Abacus has recently moved into Indonesia and Viet Nam and is currently considering expansion into Myanmar and the Lao People's Democratic Republic.

The factors that inhibit Abacus in its further expansion in these economies are:

- Telecommunications infrastructure. Abacus needs high-quality data-transmission lines for some of its business, and the agents need to have access to telephones and faxes. Delays in getting phone lines installed and the quality of the service provided are major limits to expansion.

- Regulatory complexity. The bureaucratic approval requirements for commencing business are extremely complex and time-consuming. Because Abacus covers a range of industries (telecommunications, transport, travel and tourism) it is often necessary to go to four or five different ministries (as well as the board of investment and other regulatory agencies) simply to get approval to invest and to set up a NMC. This can take over twelve months, and sometimes more than two years. In some cases these government agencies compete for bureaucratic territory, and do not seek to cooperate in providing services to private-sector investors and potential investors.

- Lack of skilled and trained staff. Abacus overcomes this problem by providing its own training programmes to the NMCs, which in turn provide training to local staff in travel agents. However, staff turnover in these areas is often high, and so a significant investment has to be made in human resource development.

*/...*

---

**(Box III.2, cont'd.)**

- Restrictive government practices, especially where state business is given monopoly rights. This is manifest, for example, in restrictions in Thailand on offering services to travel agents.

- High tariffs on the import of software and sophisticated technical equipment needed to provide services.

- Uncertainty as to the economic and political environment, both of which impact quickly on tourism.

     These problems are more or less faced by all SME investors in Asia. Their degree of seriousness depends, of course, on the type and location of firms' FDI activity.

*Source:* Based on a case study conducted by UNCTAD.

**Table III.10.  Factors contributing to problems or providing assistance
for inward FDI in SMEs in host developing countries in Asia[a]**

(Percentage)

| Factors | SME-SME | | | LE-SME | | | Ratio[b] | | |
|---|---|---|---|---|---|---|---|---|---|
| | h-p | p | h | h-p | p | h | h-p | p | h |
| Skilled staff locally | -6 | 44 | 38 | 5 | 41 | 45 | -1.29 | 1.08 | 0.84 |
| Skilled staff abroad | 21 | 12 | 32 | 32 | 14 | 45 | 0.65 | 0.86 | 0.71 |
| Access to technology | 26 | 21 | 47 | 55 | 14 | 69 | 0.49 | 1.51 | 0.69 |
| Finding suitable distributors | 9 | 24 | 32 | 27 | 14 | 41 | 0.32 | 1.73 | 0.79 |
| Reasonably priced finance | -6 | 35 | 29 | -9 | 41 | 32 | 0.65 | 0.86 | 0.92 |
| Restrictions on market access | -21 | 29 | 9 | -32 | 36 | 5 | 0.65 | 0.81 | 1.94 |
| Tariffs or quotas | -26 | 35 | 9 | -36 | 45 | 9 | 0.73 | 0.78 | 0.97 |
| Unfair competition | -32 | 35 | 3 | -27 | 32 | 5 | 1.19 | 1.11 | 0.65 |
| Distribution systems | -12 | 24 | 12 | -14 | 27 | 14 | 0.86 | 0.86 | 0.86 |
| Business regulations | -15 | 32 | 18 | -36 | 50 | 14 | 0.40 | 0.65 | 1.29 |
| Investment approvals | -15 | 35 | 21 | -18 | 41 | 23 | 0.81 | 0.86 | 0.91 |
| Construction approval | -9 | 24 | 15 | -14 | 32 | 18 | 0.64 | 0.74 | 0.81 |
| Local-content requirements | -3 | 21 | 18 | -9 | 23 | 14 | 0.32 | 0.91 | 1.29 |
| Corruption - minor officials | -56 | 56 | - | -41 | 41 | - | 1.37 | 1.37 | - |
| Corruption - senior officials | -41 | 44 | 3 | -27 | 32 | 5 | 1.51 | 1.39 | 0.65 |
| Telecommunications | -26 | 38 | 12 | -59 | 73 | 14 | 0.45 | 0.53 | 0.86 |
| Roads infrastructure | -41 | 53 | 12 | -59 | 64 | 5 | 0.70 | 0.83 | 2.59 |
| Dispute settlement | -9 | 21 | 12 | -32 | 36 | 5 | 0.28 | 0.57 | 2.59 |
| Legal system | -18 | 32 | 15 | -27 | 36 | 9 | 0.65 | 0.89 | 1.62 |
| Labour restrictions | -18 | 26 | 9 | -18 | 23 | 5 | 0.97 | 1.16 | 1.94 |
| Attitude of workers | 3 | 29 | 32 | 27 | 18 | 45 | 0.11 | 1.62 | 0.71 |
| Cultural differences | -21 | 29 | 9 | -9 | 14 | 5 | 2.26 | 2.16 | 1.94 |
| Market liberalization | 15 | 9 | 24 | 18 | 9 | 27 | 0.81 | 0.97 | 0.86 |
| Business parks | 9 | 12 | 21 | 18 | - | 18 | 0.49 | - | 1.13 |
| Business matching | 3 | 9 | 12 | 5 | 9 | 14 | 0.65 | 0.97 | 0.86 |
| Low-cost labour | 38 | 9 | 47 | 36 | 14 | 50 | 1.05 | 0.65 | 0.94 |
| Government management training | 15 | 3 | 18 | - | - | - | - | - | - |
| Government business advisory | 6 | 6 | 12 | 5 | - | 5 | 1.29 | - | 2.59 |
| Government trade missions | 12 | 3 | 15 | - | - | - | - | - | - |
| Intelligence and information | 9 | 21 | 29 | -5 | 18 | 14 | -1.94 | 1.13 | 2.16 |
| Chambers of commerce | 12 | 12 | 24 | 5 | 5 | 9 | 2.59 | 2.59 | 2.59 |

*Source:* UNCTAD, based on the questionnaire survey conducted by UNCTAD in 1996 (see the annex for a note on the survey methodology).

    [a]  Myanmar, Philippines and Viet Nam only.

    [b]  Ratio of the percentage of SME-SME responses to that of LE-SME responses. A multiple of more than 1.0 indicates that a larger proportion of SME-SME respondents regard that factor as important than of LE-SME respondents, by the size of that multiple.

    *Notes*:  p  = percentage regarding this factor as a problem or major problem.
           h  = percentage regarding this factor as helpful or very helpful.
           h-p = percentage regarding this factor as helpful or very helpful minus percentage regarding this factor as a problem or major problem.

LE-SME FDI is impeded by these factors too, but is also affected significantly by some additional factors. These are also all things that governments can do something about, including, for example, dispute settlement, legal systems, business regulations (box III.3) and restrictions on the use of expatriate workers (box III.4). Relative to larger firms, SME-SME FDI faces more problems with cultural differences, corruption and finding skilled staff locally.

---

**Box III.3.   Regulations impeding expansion**

Orsan is a manufacturer of starch and monosodium glutamate, part of a larger group headquartered in Belgium. Orsan France invested in Viet Nam in 1990, obtaining a licence for a joint-venture arrangement. The capital invested was $2.24 million, with 60 per cent held by the French firm and 40 per cent by the local partner. The Vietnamese affiliate grew rapidly, from 40 employees to 120 employees in 1994 and to 170 employees in 1995. Vietnamese law requires that the local joint-venture partner cannot hold less than 30 per cent of the capital. Orsan wants to continue to expand rapidly in Viet Nam, but the local partner cannot afford to put in more capital, and further dilution is not allowed under the law. The effect of the regulations is to force Orsan either to become a 100 per cent foreign-owned company, or to restrain its growth.

*Source*:   Based on a case study conducted by UNCTAD.

---

**Box III.4.   Work permits and restrictions on expatriate experts and managers**

Training is a major benefit associated with SME FDI, particularly the on-the-job training that comes from foreign managers and technicians working with local staff. Indonesia has a policy of requiring expatriate employees to apply for work permits each year. The permits cost about $3,000 per annum, and are often difficult to obtain without lengthy approval processes. The cost is not much for large TNCs, but many SMEs in the Republic of Korea and Taiwan Province of China find that these charges are a major component of a manager's costs. Thus, this is a factor that discourages SME FDI.

A further problem is that SMEs may seek to circumvent the regulations using other means. For example, one SME, needing a substantial number of technical staff during the start-up phase and frustrated by delays and costs, brought in its own technicians and managers on tourist visas, and then had them working on the factory floor. The local police raided the factory, and arrested the "illegal" workers; and large fines were imposed on the company.

The rationale of these regulations is to protect local jobs from competition from workers abroad, and to encourage technology transfer to local enterprises. In fact, they tend to do the opposite in SMEs.

*Source:*   UNCTAD.

---

The factors that are most helpful to SME-SME FDI are low-cost labour, access to technology from abroad, skilled staff abroad, market liberalization, government training and chambers of commerce (table III.10). The areas where governments can or do have programmes of assistance (management training, business advisory services, trade missions, information and intelligence, business matching, business parks) are generally regarded as helpful, but only by a relatively small percentage of firms, and in most cases, larger firms (LE-SME FDI) do not make use of them at all.

Intelligence and information are seen as helpful by 29 per cent of SME-SME respondents, and as being a problem for about 21 per cent. Anecdotal and case study evidence suggests that there is considerable potential for improvement in this area, at relatively low cost. If the 21 per cent can be shown how to address their needs for intelligence and market information, the balance finding this source helpful could be increased to around 50 per cent, a large percentage in comparison with other items. Similarly, the services of chambers of commerce seem to be under-utilized n they are regarded as helpful, but are mostly used by smaller firms.

About 35 per cent of firms receiving FDI from SMEs regard "availability of reasonably priced finance" as a problem, while 29 per cent regard it as being of assistance. On balance, it is not a particularly serious problem, but it shows that policies to encourage more SME FDI may need to be targeted if they are to be effective. Targeting requires more information about the 35 per cent of firms that have problems, in order to find out why they are having problems.

Approval procedures involving FDI are regarded as helpful by a surprisingly high proportion of respondents. Although these are still seen as problem areas on balance, the problems are not major, and about a quarter of the firms regard these procedures as helpful or very helpful. This suggests that it would not take much effort to make them more helpful ones providing support and promotion.

## 2. Outward SME FDI

A similar picture emerges from the responses of SMEs involved in outward FDI (table III.11). With some differences in ranking, outward SME investors see similar factors as problems, as do recipients of inward FDI from SMEs. However, a relatively higher proportion of outward investors tend to see them as problems, and relatively more medium-sized investors tend to see them as problems, than smaller investors. For example, the main problems cited by outward investors are cultural differences, corruption among senior and minor officials, business regulations, construction approvals, telecommunications infrastructure, road infrastructure and unfair competition. Cultural differences and construction approvals are regarded as problems by relatively more investors than recipients. All of these major problem areas (with the arguable exception of cultural differences) are within the direct responsibility of governments.

As with inward FDI, corruption is a major problem area identified by both small and medium-sized investors; 53 per cent of small investors and 71 per cent of medium-sized investors regard corruption among minor officials as a problem. The figures are slightly higher for corruption among more senior officials. As with recipient firms, access to reasonably priced finance is not a major problem on balance, but it is still a problem for about 37 per cent of small investors and about 45 per cent of medium-sized ones.

The implications for governments seeking to encourage SME-SME FDI seem to be that:

- The most significant impediments to SME FDI come from governments themselves. It is the re-engineering of government policies and practices that will do most to encourage SMEs to invest. If governments wish to attract more SME FDI, they must be serious about addressing issues such as corruption, reviewing and revising unnecessary approval procedures and regulations, and making telecommunications and transport sectors more efficient.

- Providing better market intelligence and information is an area that would benefit SMEs very significantly. Governments have a role to play in this area, but it is more likely that it can be developed in cooperation with chambers of commerce and private sector providers.

**Table III.11. Factors posing problems or providing assistance
for outward FDI by SMEs in leading economies in Asia[a]**

(Percentage)

| Factors | Total | | | Small investors | | | Medium-sized investors | | |
|---|---|---|---|---|---|---|---|---|---|
| | h-p | p | h | h-p | p | h | h-p | p | h |
| Skilled staff locally | -13 | 48 | 34 | -17 | 47 | 30 | -10 | 48 | 39 |
| Skilled staff abroad | -13 | 25 | 11 | -13 | 23 | 10 | -13 | 26 | 13 |
| Access to technology | -8 | 31 | 23 | -17 | 40 | 23 | - | 23 | 23 |
| Finding suitable distributors | -15 | 34 | 20 | -3 | 27 | 23 | -26 | 42 | 16 |
| Reasonably priced finance | -7 | 41 | 34 | 3 | 37 | 40 | -16 | 45 | 29 |
| Restrictions on market access | -20 | 41 | 21 | -3 | 30 | 27 | -35 | 52 | 16 |
| Tariffs or quotas | -44 | 54 | 10 | -37 | 47 | 10 | -52 | 61 | 10 |
| Unfair competition | -44 | 46 | 2 | -40 | 40 | - | -48 | 52 | 3 |
| Distribution systems | -39 | 44 | 5 | -23 | 33 | 10 | -55 | 55 | - |
| Business regulations | -52 | 56 | 3 | -57 | 60 | 3 | -48 | 52 | 3 |
| Investment approvals | -48 | 56 | 8 | -40 | 50 | 10 | -55 | 61 | 6 |
| Construction approval | -46 | 51 | 5 | -53 | 57 | 3 | -39 | 45 | 6 |
| Local-content requirements | -41 | 41 | - | -37 | 37 | - | -45 | 45 | - |
| Corruption - minor officials | -62 | 62 | - | -53 | 53 | - | -71 | 71 | - |
| Corruption - senior officials | -66 | 66 | - | -57 | 57 | - | -74 | 74 | - |
| Telecommunications | -52 | 61 | 8 | -50 | 60 | 10 | -55 | 61 | 6 |
| Roads infrastructure | -49 | 59 | 10 | -43 | 57 | 13 | -55 | 61 | 6 |
| Dispute settlement | -34 | 39 | 5 | -23 | 33 | 10 | -45 | 45 | - |
| Legal system | -46 | 54 | 8 | -30 | 47 | 17 | -61 | 61 | - |
| Labour restrictions | -36 | 41 | 5 | -27 | 37 | 10 | -45 | 45 | - |
| Attitude of workers | -44 | 52 | 8 | -27 | 43 | 17 | -61 | 61 | - |
| Cultural differences | -64 | 64 | - | -60 | 60 | - | -68 | 68 | - |
| Suitable partners | -33 | 43 | 10 | -20 | 37 | 17 | -45 | 48 | 3 |
| Market liberalization | -11 | 30 | 18 | -3 | 30 | 27 | -19 | 29 | 10 |
| Business parks | 2 | 18 | 20 | -7 | 20 | 13 | 10 | 16 | 26 |
| Business matching | -8 | 21 | 13 | -13 | 27 | 13 | -3 | 16 | 13 |
| Low-cost labour | 20 | 8 | 28 | 27 | 3 | 30 | 13 | 13 | 26 |
| Government management training | 16 | 3 | 20 | 17 | 3 | 20 | 16 | 3 | 19 |
| Government business advisory | 15 | 5 | 20 | 10 | 7 | 17 | 19 | 3 | 23 |
| Government trade missions | 15 | 8 | 23 | 17 | 7 | 23 | 13 | 10 | 23 |
| Intelligence and information | 16 | 10 | 26 | 7 | 17 | 23 | 26 | 3 | 29 |
| Chambers of commerce | 8 | 16 | 25 | -3 | 23 | 20 | 19 | 10 | 29 |
| Tax concessions | 23 | 2 | 25 | 17 | 3 | 20 | 29 | - | 29 |
| Cultural connections | 11 | 3 | 15 | 10 | 7 | 17 | 13 | - | 13 |
| TNC affiliation | 18 | 3 | 21 | 20 | 3 | 23 | 16 | 3 | 19 |

*Source:* UNCTAD, based on the questionnaire survey conducted by UNCTAD in 1996 (see the annex for a note on the survey methodology).

[a] Republic of Korea, Singapore and Taiwan Province of China only.

*Notes*: p = percentage regarding this factor as a problem or major problem.

h = percentage regarding this factor as helpful or very helpful.

h-p = percentage regarding this factor as helpful or very helpful minus percentage regarding this factor as a problem or major problem.

• Addressing problems at the level of the firm (e.g., finding suitable partners, management skills, access to finance) requires a better understanding of the client group and the firms most able to benefit from assistance, so that any government participation can be delivered cost-effectively (see box III.5 for an example of trade missions).

---

**Box III.5.  Gateway Pharmaceuticals**

Gateway (Australia) first moved into Viet Nam as an SME with almost zero staff, forming an alliance with a local partner.  In the late 1980s one of its founders noticed that the Vietnamese clients of his pharmacy in Australia were buying non-prescription drugs and shipping them back to relatives in Viet Nam.  Seeing an opportunity, the manager joined a trade mission to Viet Nam, and as a result of the contacts made, obtained licences and began exporting.  Currency restrictions posed problems and required the company to set up counter-trade operations to fund the sale of pharmaceuticals.  Established in 1986, Gateway's affiliate in Viet Nam now handles over 70 types of drugs, including antibiotics, vitamins and cold medicines.  In 1995 its turnover was $9 million, and it has now established a production plant in Ha Tay at a cost of $33 million.

*Source:*  Based on a case study conducted by UNCTAD.

---

# CHAPTER IV

## STRATEGIES ADOPTED BY SMEs
## ENGAGED IN FDI IN ASIA

The decision to invest abroad is not taken lightly and is normally strategically important for firms, especially SMEs. Capital investment abroad, the transfer of technology and expenditure on training can all involve significant expenditure and sunk costs. For policy makers to develop policies that encourage corporate decision makers to invest in their particular location requires an understanding of the more dynamic and strategic aspects of SME FDI. For example, most evidence indicates that SMEs adopt an evolutionary approach to internationalization; thus, FDI is part of a process. Many SMEs test the market in less committed ways (such as using agents or partners) first, before they invest abroad. Encouraging this sort of activity may be an important aspect of encouraging greater FDI in the longer term. SMEs may invest in distribution or market representation first, and others may move to production under licence. Many SMEs do not engage in different forms of international transactions at the same time (e.g., licensing and investing) (Fujita, 1998). They do not invest in technology- or product-development, or independent management development abroad until quite late. Understanding that process is important if policy is to be adapted to facilitating FDI, and to facilitating appropriate FDI.

The key points that emerge from the analysis in this chapter as regards the strategies adopted by internationalizing SMEs in Asia are that:

- The SMEs engaged in FDI have moved to internationalize quickly after their establishment. Many of them have progressed through a series of other international activities (importing, exporting, commissioning an agent, etc.) before engaging in FDI.[1]

- FDI is usually regarded as being important to the firms' success. The factors regarded as being of strategic importance to SMEs are typically factors which are also sympathetic to the requirements of developing countries. SME investors are much more likely than larger investors to regard as "very important" the training of local staff, training of local managers, improving the quality of products and services, providing new products and services, increasing exports, and adapting technology to local needs.

- The predominant strategy with respect to the organizational form used for SME FDI is some form of network or partnership arrangement between two largely independent SMEs. Only about 30 per cent or less of SMEs seem to use a strategy based on establishing affiliates involving significant ownership, and this strategy is used more by larger firms. At least half of the resource flows are between network partners.

- Smaller investors are more likely to make management and strategy decisions in the host country, and are thus more likely to be accessible to and develop linkages with firms in developing countries.

## A. FDI strategy as part of broader internationalization strategy

Internationalization involves a chain of activities (see box IV.1 for some examples). FDI by Asian developing country firms does not usually occur until after the firms have internationalized in other ways. However, the period before internationalization seems to be shorter for SMEs than for larger firms. On average, respondent firms in the developing countries studied had been in operation for 2.8 years before they engaged in any form of international activity (table IV.1). The SMEs investing in SMEs abroad moved more quickly from establishment to international activity than did larger firms, taking only 0.7 years, compared with 3.9 years in the case of the larger firms.

---

**Box IV.1. Examples of the pattern of internationalization of SMEs**

Internationalization is usually a process: typically, a firm will start up and then, some time after that, move to internationalize, usually through imports or exports. Once it has gained some familiarity with international business, it moves to a greater commitment abroad by means of licensing or eventually establishing a plant or office. Some examples are given below:

1. **A light manufacturer in Singapore**
Employees in Singapore in 1995 = 80.
Employees abroad = 30.
Established in 1968.
First international step = export to Sri Lanka in 1985. Now exports to about 20 destinations, including Europe.
Formed alliances/partnerships in China and Indonesia in 1993.
Established local production facility in China in 1994.

2. **A manufacturer of food and beverages in Singapore**
Employees in Singapore = 148.
Established in 1977.
First international step = local agent in Japan in 1977.
Exported to Japan in 1979, then to Malaysia and Indonesia in 1982.
Imported from Japan in 1988, then from India, Philippines and Thailand in 1990, Malaysia and the Republic of Korea in 1991, and a range of other countries subsequently.
Appointed general local agents in South-East Asia in 1982 and in West Asia in 1986, local agent in Malaysia in 1990.
Established a local plant in Malaysia in 1995.

*/...*

---

(Box IV.1, cont'd.)

3.     **A plastics and rubber producer in Taiwan Province of China**
       Employees in Taiwan Province of China = 200.
       Employees abroad = 150.
       Established in 1973.
       First international step = export to Philippines and import from Thailand, Malaysia and Indonesia
            in 1973/1974.
       Local alliances and partnerships formed in Thailand (1991) and Indonesia (1995).
       Transfer of technology and licensing to Thailand (1991), China (1994) and Indonesia (1995).
       Established a local office and plant in China (1991), Thailand (1991) and Indonesia (1996).

       *Source*:   Based on case studies conducted by UNCTAD.

       *Note*:   The names of these firms are not given for reasons of confidentiality.

**Table IV.1.  Average period since establishment and
before the start of internationalization**

| Size of firms | Years since establishment | Years before internationalization |
|---|---|---|
| Total | 8.6 | 2.8 |
| SMEs | 4.0 | 0.7 |
| Large firms | 9.3 | 3.9 |

*Source:*  UNCTAD, based on the questionnaire survey conducted by UNCTAD
in 1996 (see the annex for a note on the survey methodology).

The implications for governments seeking to attract SME FDI are that as SMEs tend to internationalize faster, and as internationalization increases generally, the potential pool of SMEs prepared to invest abroad will grow quickly.  There are thus significant opportunities to capture a share of this growing pool of SME FDI.  Because SME FDI is usually at the end of a chain of other international moves, it is important to encourage other forms of international activity by SMEs (such as trade and licensing).

## B.   Importance of SME FDI to firms' success

FDI is generally regarded by both investors and recipients as important to firms' success.  For example, 69 per cent of respondent SMEs in the Asian developing economies covered by the survey see FDI abroad as being important or very important to the success and development of their company, while 63 per cent of those SMEs receiving FDI see it as important or very important (table IV.2).  This is partly reflected in their expected growth of sales; those recipients of SME FDI regarding FDI as very important to their success expect a sales growth of 40 per cent per annum.  Similarly, those SME investors who see FDI as important tend to expect higher sales growth rates.  The implication is that FDI could be an important and effective means of strategic development for a country's SMEs.

**Table IV.2. Perceived importance of SME FDI to firms' strategic success
in selected developing countries in Asia**

(Percentage)

| Degree of importance | Inward SME FDI[a] | Average expected annual sales growth |
|---|---|---|
| Very important | 43 | 41 |
| Important | 20 | 21 |
| Some importance | 8 | 30 |
| No response | 30 | - |
| Degree of importance | Outward SME FDI[b] | Average expected annual sales growth |
| Very important | 35 | 14 |
| Important | 34 | 13 |
| Some importance | 6 | 6 |
| No response | 25 | 20 |

*Source:* UNCTAD, based on the questionnaire survey conducted by UNCTAD in 1996 (see the annex for a note on the survey methodology).

[a] Figures relate to percentage of respondent FDI-recipient SMEs in Myanmar, the Philippines and Viet Nam.
[b] Figures relate to percentage of respondent outward-investing SMEs from the Republic of Korea, Singapore and Taiwan Province of China.

## C. Factors important to strategic business development

The factors that a firm considers important to its business development underlie the strategy it adopts and the responses it makes to government policy. The factors regarded by more than three quarters of host-country respondents as important or very important for SME FDI are improving the quality of services or products, training of local managers, good relations with governments and training of local unskilled staff (table IV.3).

**Table IV.3. Strategic business-development factors that are important or
very important for FDI in SMEs in host developing countries in Asia[a]**

(Percentage)[b]

| Strategic business-development factor | Total | SME- SME | LE- SME | Ratio[c] |
|---|---|---|---|---|
| Linkages with overseas firms | 71 | 67 | 81 | 0.82 |
| Increasing exports or foreign earnings | 65 | 76 | 52 | 1.44 |
| Increased use of local suppliers | 60 | 61 | 67 | 0.91 |
| Training of local unskilled staff | 75 | 64 | 86 | 0.74 |
| Training of local managers | 81 | 73 | 86 | 0.84 |
| Adapting products to meet local market | 53 | 48 | 67 | 0.73 |
| Providing new products/services | 73 | 73 | 81 | 0.89 |
| Improving quality of product/services | 85 | 88 | 90 | 0.97 |
| Adapting technology to local needs | 62 | 52 | 71 | 0.72 |
| Good relations with government | 79 | 76 | 90 | 0.84 |

*Source:* UNCTAD, based on the questionnaire survey conducted by UNCTAD in 1996 (see the annex for a note on the survey methodology).

[a] Myanmar, Philippines and Viet Nam only.
[b] Percentage of respondents that consider the factor as either important, or very important.
[c] Ratio of the percentage of SME-SME responses to that of LE-SME responses. A multiple of more than 1.0 indicates that relatively more SME-SME respondents regard that factor as important/very important, as compared with LE-SME respondents, by the size of that multiple.

Generally, SME-SME respondents seem less likely to see these factors as important are LE-SME respondents. The exception is increasing exports or foreign earnings, which SME-SME respondents are 1.44 times more likely to see as important or very important. However, when only what the respondents see as *very* important is chosen, the reverse is true. Relatively more SMEs see most of these factors as very important as compared with larger investors. For example, SME-SME respondents are three times more likely to see training of unskilled staff as being very important to their strategic success, more than twice as likely to see the introduction or improvement of products or services as very important, and more than 50 per cent more likely to see training of local managers and the increasing of foreign earnings as very important (table IV.4).

### Table IV.4. Strategic business-development factors for FDI in SMEs in host developing countries in Asia,[a] by degree of importance

(Percentage)b

| Strategic business-development factor | SME-SME | | LE-SME | | Ratio[b] | |
|---|---|---|---|---|---|---|
| | i | vi | i | vi | i | vi |
| Linkages with overseas firms | 24 | 42 | 48 | 33 | 0.51 | 1.27 |
| Increasing exports or foreign earnings | 30 | 45 | 24 | 29 | 1.27 | 1.59 |
| Increased use of local suppliers | 36 | 24 | 38 | 29 | 0.95 | 0.85 |
| Training of local unskilled staff | 27 | 36 | 76 | 10 | 0.36 | 3.82 |
| Training of local managers | 36 | 36 | 62 | 24 | 0.59 | 1.53 |
| Adapting products to local market | 24 | 24 | 38 | 29 | 0.64 | 0.85 |
| Providing new products/services | 42 | 30 | 67 | 14 | 0.64 | 2.12 |
| Improving quality of product/services | 21 | 67 | 57 | 33 | 0.37 | 2.00 |
| Adapting technology to local needs | 24 | 27 | 52 | 19 | 0.46 | 1.43 |
| Good relations with government | 36 | 39 | 38 | 52 | 0.95 | 0.75 |

*Source:* UNCTAD, based on the questionnaire survey conducted by UNCTAD in 1996 (see the annex for a note on the survey methodology).

[a] Myanmar, Philippines and Viet Nam only.

[b] Ratio of the percentage of SME-SME responses to that of LE-SME responses. A multiple of more than 1.0 indicates that more SME-SME respondents regard that factor as important/ very important, as compared with LE-SME respondents, by the size of that multiple.

*Note*: i = percentage of respondents considering the factor important; vi = percentage of respondents considering the factor very important.

The implications for governments seeking to use SME FDI as an engine of growth are that many SME investors' aims are very sympathetic to the needs of governments in developing countries. SME investors are much more likely to see as very important the training of unskilled staff, the training of local managers, the provision of new products, and better-quality products suited to the needs of a local market, and adaptation of technology to local needs. However, SME investors, despite their good intentions and sympathetic aims, may be unable to achieve these aims unless governments in developing countries make serious attempts to address the impediments caused by themselves.

## D. Organizational forms: strategic relations between home and host countries

An investor seeking to engage in FDI has a choice of a range of corporate structures. At the simplest level the choice is either to set up a greenfield organization (i.e., to establish a new organization or subsidiary in the host country), or to find an existing firm and invest in it or become a partner with it. While the former approach tends to be favoured more by larger firms, the latter approach tends to be more favoured by SMEs because it reduces risk and financial commitments. Only about one-third of firms (slightly less for those receiving FDI from SMEs) are wholly owned affiliates of a larger firm abroad. The majority are networked, or in a joint venture with another firm(s) either abroad or both locally and abroad. Despite some equity holding by foreign firms, these firms are slightly more likely to be independently owned or operated.

Table IV.5 shows the relationship between host-country SME FDI recipients and the sources of the flows of FDI and other resources from abroad. SME affiliates are more likely to take the form of networks between an independently owned SME in the host country and a joint venture partner or alliance partner abroad. About half the FDI obtained from SMEs abroad comes from network (group, alliance or joint venture) partners, and about half from parent firms. In SMEs receiving FDI flows from larger firms (LE-SME) the investor is more likely to be a parent than an alliance or joint venture partner.

**Table IV.5. Organizational relations of host-country SMEs in developing countries in Asia,[a] with parent firm or partner providing FDI and other resource flows, by type of flows, 1991-1995**

(Percentage)[b]

| Relationship of source of FDI or other resource flows | SME-SME | | | | LE-SME | | | |
| --- | --- | --- | --- | --- | --- | --- | --- | --- |
| | FDI | Loans from unrelated organizations | Technology | Training | FDI | Loans from unrelated organizations | Technology | Training |
| Parent | 35 | - | 6 | 21 | 41 | - | 45 | 45 |
| Group[b] | 3 | - | 3 | 6 | 5 | - | 9 | 14 |
| Alliance | 6 | - | 9 | 9 | - | - | 5 | 9 |
| Joint venture | 32 | 9 | 9 | 15 | 18 | 9 | 14 | 14 |

*Source:* UNCTAD, based on the questionnaire survey conducted by UNCTAD in 1996 (see the annex for a note on the survey methodology).

[a] Myanmar, Philippines and Viet Nam only.
[b] Another affiliate in the same TNC system or another firm in the same business group.

The implication is that governments seeking to encourage more SME-SME FDI need to encourage the development of networks, and need also to encourage the development of local SMEs with capabilities to form alliances or joint ventures with firms abroad. This organizational arrangement probably makes up more than half of all SME-SME FDI. Encouraging firms abroad to invest and set up local affiliates is also important, especially for larger firms abroad.

## E. Market positioning

In comparison with the other firms in the market, the majority of SME investors see themselves as above or well above the average of firms in the market in such areas as technology, competitiveness, quality, innovation, meeting customer needs, and ability to export. For example, 70 per cent of SME-SME FDI recipients see themselves as above average when it comes to technology: 58 per cent, in competitiveness; 79 per cent, in quality; 53 per cent, in innovation; 71 per cent, in meeting customer needs; and 50 per cent, in ability to export (table IV.6). SMEs receiving FDI from larger firms tend to see themselves as even further advantaged relative to the average firm in the market. The implication is that SMEs receiving FDI are important contributors to improving the average performance in the market, and thus an important contributor to the entrepreneurial engine.

**Table IV.6. Market position of SMEs receiving FDI in host developing countries in Asia[a]**

| Assessment | Technology | Competitiveness | Quality | Innovation | Customer needs | Export capability |
|---|---|---|---|---|---|---|
| Total | | | | | | |
| Average | 23 | 26 | 17 | 33 | 13 | 17 |
| Above | 40 | 42 | 36 | 32 | 46 | 32 |
| Well above | 29 | 19 | 42 | 23 | 31 | 19 |
| SME-SME | | | | | | |
| Average | 26 | 32 | 21 | 41 | 18 | 18 |
| Above | 41 | 47 | 44 | 32 | 50 | 35 |
| Well above | 29 | 9 | 35 | 21 | 21 | 15 |
| LE-SME | | | | | | |
| Average | 27 | 36 | 27 | 41 | 18 | 32 |
| Above | 41 | 36 | 32 | 36 | 45 | 36 |
| Well above | 32 | 18 | 36 | 18 | 32 | 9 |
| Ratio[b] | | | | | | |
| Average | 0.97 | 0.89 | 0.75 | 1.01 | 0.97 | 0.55 |
| Above | 1.01 | 1.29 | 1.39 | 0.89 | 1.10 | 0.97 |
| Well above | 0.92 | 0.49 | 0.97 | 1.13 | 0.65 | 1.62 |

*Source:* UNCTAD, based on the questionnaire survey conducted by UNCTAD in 1996 (see the annex for a note on the survey methodology).

[a] Myanmar, Philippines and Viet Nam only.

[b] Ratio of the percentage of SME-SME responses to that of LE-SME FDI responses. A multiple of more than 1.0 indicates that relatively more SME-SME respondents regard that position as important, as compared with LE-SME respondents, by the size of that multiple.

*Note:* Entries are based on managers' self-assessment of their capabilities.

# F.  Location of key management decisions

The location of where key management decisions relating to strategy, finance, production and product design, marketing and advertising and research and development are made is important for developing countries seeking to attract more FDI from SMEs, because it affects the ability to target the decision maker effectively. It seems that the smaller the investor, the more likely it is that key decisions will be made in host countries.

Strategic and finance decisions relating to operations of affiliates are more likely to be made locally in the host country by smaller firms, and marketing decisions, locally in the host country by larger firms (table IV.7). For example, among the respondent SME-SME FDI recipients, 29 per cent indicated that strategic decisions are all made locally, and 18 per cent that they are mostly made locally, while only 18 per cent said that strategic decisions are made abroad. On balance, decisions are more likely to be made locally than abroad. Decisions on production and research in LE-SME FDI are the two exceptions (where the figures are negative). Overall, SME-SME FDI decisions are more likely to made locally than those in firms with LE-SME FDI.

The implications for policy makers in developing countries seeking to attract SME FDI, and to influence SME decisions, are that smaller investors are more likely to make decisions relating to strategic operations in the host country, and are thus more accessible and more easily targeted. About half or more of SME investors are accessible in this way. For the other half, and particularly larger investors, a more international approach is called for. Either way, it is necessary to understand that decisions about FDI are made in an international context. Investors and potential investors are able to compare the attractiveness of different locations and different government policies and allocate their investment resources accordingly. Unless the governments of countries are able to monitor the relative attractiveness of their location and their policies *vis-à-vis* other competing locations, they will have little influence on strategic investment decisions.

**Table IV.7. Location of management decisions for SMEs receiving FDI in selected host developing countries in Asia[a]**

(Percentage)[b]

| Location of decisions | Strategy | Finance | Production and product design | Marketing and advertising | Research and development |
|---|---|---|---|---|---|
| **SME-SME FDI** | | | | | |
| No response | 3 | 3 | 6 | 6 | 3 |
| All local | 29 | 24 | 21 | 26 | 26 |
| Mostly local | 18 | 24 | 21 | 18 | 15 |
| Equal | 33 | 29 | 18 | 12 | 26 |
| Mostly abroad | 15 | 9 | 15 | 24 | 18 |
| All abroad | 3 | 12 | 21 | 15 | 12 |
| Local minus abroad | 29 | 26 | 6 | 6 | 12 |
| **LE-SME FDI** | | | | | |
| No response | - | - | 5 | 9 | 5 |
| All local | 27 | 18 | 23 | 50 | 14 |
| Mostly local | 9 | 27 | 14 | 14 | 9 |
| Equal | 41 | 32 | 14 | 18 | 45 |
| Mostly abroad | 18 | 14 | 36 | - | 14 |
| All abroad | 5 | 9 | 9 | 9 | 14 |
| Local minus abroad | 14 | 27 | -9 | 55 | -5 |
| **Ratio[c]** | | | | | |
| All local | 1.08 | 1.29 | 0.91 | 0.53 | 1.94 |
| Mostly local | 1.94 | 0.74 | 1.51 | 1.29 | 1.62 |
| Equal | 0.79 | 1.08 | 1.29 | 0.65 | 0.58 |
| Mostly abroad | 1.08 | 0.65 | 0.40 | .. | 1.29 |
| All abroad | 0.65 | 0.96 | 2.26 | 1.62 | 0.86 |

*Source:* UNCTAD, based on the questionnaire survey conducted by UNCTAD in 1996 (see the annex for a note on the survey methodology).

[a] Myanmar, Philippines and Viet Nam only.

[b] Figures relate to the percentage of respondent FDI-recipient SMEs.

[c] These give the ratio of SME-SME to LE-SME FDI responses. A multiple of more than 1.0 indicates that relatively more SME-SME respondents regard that decision as important than LE-SME respondents, by the size of that multiple.

# Note

[1] The survey conducted in 1992-1993 of SME investors based in developed countries indicates that most high-technology SMEs move to invest abroad directly without having had other international activities such as trade and licensing (UNCTAD, 1993; Fujita, 1998).

# CHAPTER V

## THE ROLE OF SME FDI IN ASIA AND ITS CONTRIBUTION TO DEVELOPMENT: TWO CASE STUDIES

### A. Myanmar

As of March 1996, 169 firms had invested in Myanmar, 47 of which could be regarded as SMEs. To put this in perspective, there are some 32,000 SMEs (as defined in terms of small private industrial enterprises) in Myanmar. It is common in the more advanced developing countries in Asia to have about one SME for every 20 people. If Myanmar wishes to reach this level, it needs to expand the number of SMEs by a factor of about 50, from about 32,000 to closer to 1.5 million. If the entrepreneurial engine was started and driven by a relatively small percentage of SMEs, the target might become a little more achievable, but still daunting. If the entrepreneurial engine was focused on about 10 per cent of a population of SMEs, then in Myanmar's case some 100,000 to 200,000 SMEs would be required. This would then set something of a target for SME FDI over the next ten years. A serious critical factor in achieving this target is the need to train managers and skilled technical people. Even 100,000 new SMEs require at least 100,000 (and arguably closer to 200,000) managers with some degree of training and management skills. It is not evident from the national plans that this is regarded as a priority.

The bulk of large-firm FDI in Myanmar has gone into oil and gas production and exploration. While essential, this has not led to much SME development or spin-offs. SME FDI has typically gone into wood products, electronic parts and components, furniture manufacture, soft drinks, hotel- and tourism-related investment, and medium- and high-quality jewellery. Most SME FDI has come from Singapore, which accounted for over 70 per cent of the $280 million cumulative SME FDI by 1995 (see chapter II). The United Kingdom has provided about 7 per cent and Thailand about 5 per cent.

Myanmar has a legacy of good administrative systems and legal systems for property rights that work to its advantage in the development of SMEs. The potential opportunities from its resources are well known. Running counter to this, however, are political and economic problems that deter much-needed SME investment. The greatest economic problem concerns macroeconomic management, particularly administration of the exchange rate. The procedures and the minimum limit ($500,000 for manufacturing and $300,000 for services in 1997) for approving FDI actively discourage SME FDI, especially by smaller service-oriented organizations that could otherwise be extremely important in providing training opportunities and create a competitive environment.

The results of surveys of SMEs in Myanmar as to factors that constitute problems for them or are of assistance to them show that the exchange-rate system is a problem for 75 per cent of respondents, followed by telecommunications (63 per cent) (table V.1). Interestingly, the Mynamar investment-approval processes are often regarded as being of significant assistance.

### Table V.1. Problems facing SME affiliates, and helpful factors, in Myanmar

(Percentage)

| Factors | Balance[a] | Problem | Helpful |
|---|---|---|---|
| Skilled staff in Myanmar | 31 | 19 | 50 |
| Skilled staff abroad | 56 | - | 56 |
| Access to technology | 44 | 13 | 56 |
| Finding distributors | 31 | 13 | 44 |
| Reasonable finance | 25 | 19 | 44 |
| Specific market access | -13 | 31 | 19 |
| Tariffs | 6 | - | 6 |
| Unfair competition | -13 | 19 | 6 |
| Distribution systems | -6 | 19 | 13 |
| Regulations | 6 | 6 | 13 |
| Investment approvals | 25 | 6 | 31 |
| Construction approval | 19 | 6 | 25 |
| Local content required | 6 | 6 | 13 |
| Corruption-minor officials | -13 | 13 | - |
| Corruption-senior officials | -6 | 6 | - |
| Telecommunications | -63 | 69 | 6 |
| Roads | -44 | 56 | 13 |
| Dispute settlement | 6 | - | 6 |
| Legal system | 6 | 6 | 13 |
| Labour restrictions | 6 | - | 6 |
| Attitude of workers | 44 | 6 | 50 |
| Cultural differences | - | 6 | 6 |
| Market liberalization | 13 | - | 13 |
| Business parks | - | 6 | 6 |
| Business matching | - | 6 | 6 |
| Low-cost labour | 50 | - | 50 |
| Government management training | 19 | - | 19 |
| Government business advisory | 13 | - | 13 |
| Government trade missions | 13 | 6 | 19 |
| Intelligence | - | 31 | 31 |
| Chambers of commerce | 31 | 6 | 38 |
| Market development tax concessions | 31 | - | 31 |
| Parallel exchange | -75 | 75 | - |
| Multinational affiliation | 13 | 13 | 25 |
| Finding suitable partners | 13 | 19 | 31 |

*Source:* UNCTAD, based on the questionnaire survey conducted by UNCTAD in 1996 (see the annex for a note on the survey methodology).

[a] Percentage of "helpful" responses minus percentage of "problem" responses.

## B.  Viet Nam

Since *doi moi* was adopted in 1989 the private sector in Viet Nam has grown rapidly, largely through the creation of micro and small-scale household enterprises and the growth of SMEs.  World Bank estimates suggest that value added of private enterprise has grown at 6.5 per cent per annum on average (World Bank, 1993).  However, this has not been as robust as in the public sector, because state enterprises are more capitalized, while private-sector enterprises tend to be smaller, and thus less capitalized, and more recently established.  Foreign investment and trade have not yet directly involved the private sector; the majority of foreign-financed joint ventures still involve state enterprises.  Total investment during 1991-1995 was about $18 billion in 1995 prices, with the state sector accounting for 43 per cent of this.  FDI accounted for about 27 per cent, constituting a major part of total investment.

There is no accepted definition of SMEs in use in Viet Nam.  At the end of 1994 there were 26,500 registered enterprises in Viet Nam, 20,000 of which were private.  Most of these would be SMEs.  Estimates suggest another 713,000 small unregistered household enterprises, all of which would be SMEs,  and about 6,000 cooperatives.   State-owned enterprises have been restructured so that the number has been halved, from 12,296 in 1986 to 6,042 in 1994.  A significant number of state-owned enterprises (about 2,400) are SMEs.

In perspective, Viet Nam should have about 4 million SMEs if it reaches the level comparable to that in leading countries in Asia.  At present, there are only about 20,000 private SMEs, and another 700,000 very small enterprises.  Increasing the number of SMEs, and helping the growth of micro enterprises, are important to long-term sustainable economic development.  On the basis that about 10 per cent of SMEs are growth-oriented and contribute most to the entrepreneurial engine, it is important for Viet Nam to aim at raising the number of SMEs from about 20,000 to closer to 200,000 or more in the next five to ten years.  This requires a significant commitment to providing managerial and technical training.

A cumulative total of about $6 billion (as against about $20 billion approved) in FDI flowed into Viet Nam up to June 1996, most of it coming from Japan, Taiwan Province of China, the Hong Kong Special Administrative Region of the People's Republic of China and Singapore.  Over 70 per cent of FDI projects are joint ventures, 16 per cent are fully foreign-owned and 14 per cent are business-cooperation contracts.  It is not possible to distinguish SME FDI from the rest.  However, survey analysis suggests that SME FDI probably makes up around 10 to 15 per cent or so of cases per year (i.e., less than 50 cases) and less than 2 per cent by value of investment (see chapter II).  If these figures are correct, it would appear that Viet Nam is not exploiting anywhere near the potential offered by SME FDI.

The main problems for SME investors in Viet Nam relate to the legal system, regulations and corruption (table V.2).  One company's experience, described in box V.1, illustrates the impediments faced by SME FDI in the country.

**Table V.2. Problems facing SME affiliates, and helpful factors, in Viet Nam**

(Percentage)

| Problems | Balance[a] | Problem | Helpful |
|---|---|---|---|
| Skilled staff in Viet Nam | -23 | 60 | 37 |
| Skilled staff abroad | 37 | 10 | 47 |
| Access to technology | 10 | 27 | 37 |
| Finding distributors | -13 | 27 | 13 |
| Reasonable finance | -33 | 47 | 13 |
| Specific market access | -47 | 47 | - |
| Tariffs | -53 | 60 | 7 |
| Unfair competition | -37 | 40 | 3 |
| Distribution systems | -27 | 33 | 7 |
| Regulations | -50 | 63 | 13 |
| Investment approvals | -60 | 67 | 7 |
| Construction approval | -47 | 50 | 3 |
| Local content required | -20 | 30 | 10 |
| Corruption-minor officials | -63 | 63 | - |
| Corruption-senior officials | -47 | 50 | 3 |
| Telecommunications | -43 | 53 | 10 |
| Roads | -60 | 63 | 3 |
| Dispute settlement | -30 | 37 | 7 |
| Legal system | -47 | 53 | 7 |
| Labour restrictions | -27 | 30 | 3 |
| Attitude of workers | 17 | 17 | 33 |
| Cultural differences | -23 | 30 | 7 |
| Market liberalization | - | 17 | 17 |
| Business parks | 3 | 13 | 17 |
| Business matching | -10 | 17 | 7 |
| Low-cost labour | 37 | 7 | 43 |
| Government management training | 13 | - | 13 |
| Government business advisory | 10 | 3 | 13 |
| Government trade missions | 7 | - | 7 |
| Intelligence | 7 | 23 | 30 |
| Chambers of commerce | 3 | 13 | 17 |
| Market development tax concessions | -3 | 23 | 20 |
| Exchange rates | 17 | 10 | 27 |
| Multinational affiliation | 27 | 13 | 40 |
| Finding suitable partners | -13 | 33 | 20 |

*Source:* UNCTAD, based on the questionnaire survey conducted by UNCTAD in 1996 (see the annex for a note on the survey methodology).

[a] Percentage of "problem" responses minus percentage of "assistance" responses.

---

**Box V.1. Impediments to SME FDI expansion in Viet Nam**

Company X[a] initially started in entertainment in Singapore, and then diversified into hotels in regional locations, particularly Thailand. It is now pursuing opportunities in tourism and manufacturing in Viet Nam, and seeking other opportunities in Myanmar. The central company in the host country only employs a few people, but the associated tourism operations employ about 50-70. Most of the growth has been financed by joint venture partnerships, usually with local people, although the entrepreneur has bought out partners at various times. To finance the manufacturing venture, funds were sought from the Vietnamese Export-Import Bank, but until now the conditions required by it are too restrictive to justify proceeding with the venture (over 50 per cent of the amount required to be lodged for the investment has to be put up in cash).

The main factors leading to the internationalization of the firm were opportunities, combined to some extent with chance factors. The entrepreneur is European, and was already used to international business, while suitable venture partners were found largely by a chance process. Being in tourism, mostly at a three-to-four star level in small local resorts, the firm passes significant training benefits on to the local communities, and has significant local multipliers.

The main problems that hampered the firm's further expansion in Viet Nam are the following:

• problem of rule by decree. Laws can be interpreted in different ways by local officials, and there is no formal procedure for clarifying what laws and regulations actually mean;

• difficulties with tenure of land and security of assets (whether foreign companies or individuals can hold title in their own right);

• associated problems of holding land and assets through local partners, particularly when a partnership arrangement goes wrong;

• difficulty in enforcing agreements with local partners, contractors or others; and

• potentially arbitrary nature of the licence system used to allow production, especially if licences can be revoked or not renewed. The interview process used to determine the renewal of a licence was seen as bureaucratic, time-wasting and largely useless as regards contributing to local development.

*Source:* Based on a case study conducted by UNCTAD.

[a] The name of the company is not given for reasons of confidentiality.

# PART TWO

# POLICY LESSONS:  TAKING ADVANTAGE OF THE POTENTIAL FOR FDI BY AND IN SMEs

# INTRODUCTION AND OVERVIEW

As discussed in Part One, foreign direct investment (FDI) by small and medium-sized enterprises (SMEs) could play an important role in development, especially in those economies in which dynamic SMEs are underrepresented. What can policy makers do to make better use of SME FDI as an engine of development and growth? What lessons can they learn from those more developed economies in Asia where SMEs play a significant role? What can they do to attract FDI by SMEs and to maximize their contribution to development?

The answer is threefold. Policy makers should consider policies that are:

- generally conducive to the development of growth-oriented, internationally oriented, indigenous SMEs;

- specifically designed to help encourage inward FDI; and

- specifically geared towards reducing the barriers faced by international SMEs, especially those that would seek to invest, transfer technology and provide training to indigenous SMEs.

Chapter VI addresses the question of how best to ensure that policies are generally conducive to the development of growth-oriented, internationally oriented, indigenous SMEs. Chapters VII and VIII address the question of more specific policies related to SME FDI. Chapter VII considers these from the point of view of economies seeking to attract SME FDI, while chapter VIII looks at them from the perspective of countries with SMEs engaged in outward FDI. This is done by drawing on and distilling the lessons of those economies in Asia that have successfully used SMEs in their development.

Although policy with respect to SMEs is traditionally seen largely as a domestic issue, it is increasingly becoming impossible to have an effective SME policy that ignores the increasing internationalization of economies. Most of the developed countries of today could develop their domestic SMEs and SME policies without having to pay much attention to international issues. However, in recent years all the more developed countries in Asia have had to adapt their SME policies to reflect the realities of trade and investment liberalization, and of the more general trends towards globalization. Underlying this study is the fact that the internationalization of SMEs is unavoidable and that policies need to be adapted to this new reality.

SMEs are important to policy makers for reasons related to both the structural and the dynamic aspects of the performance of their economies:

*Structurally*, SMEs are important to policy makers because there are many of them, they employ a large part of the workforce, and they are a significant part of the economy (though this may be underrepresented in some developing countries, reflecting the missing middle). SMEs are thus important politically, socially and in economic terms. As discussed in chapter I, the contribution of SMEs varies depending on the economy; in the Asian region, SMEs typically make up around 95 per cent or more of enterprises, they create between 40 and 80 per cent of employment, between 30 and 60 per cent of GDP, and provide around 35 per cent of direct exports. However, most of these SMEs are not immediately relevant to FDI or FDI-related policy. This does not mean, however, that they are unimportant; there is a substantial domestic policy focus on the large group of domestic SMEs, some of which must increasingly adjust to international competition and meet international standards if they are to survive, and some of which need to be given the opportunity to grow if they are to become attractive partners in international ventures.

*In dynamic terms,* SMEs are important to policy makers because they are a source of both change and growth and because they can provide a buffer against change. They thus provide a key to development, and also provide the flexibility to help overcome the political and social stresses associated with development. However, this dynamic contribution is mostly concentrated in a relatively few SMEs, which constitute the entrepreneurial engine discussed in Part One. As a rough rule of thumb, most of the contribution to economic and employment growth seems to come from only about 10 per cent or so of SMEs (see chapter I). It is these SMEs that provide the dynamic key to economic development, and which are the main focus for policy in this handbook as they are active in FDI, or have the potential to be so. This means focusing on two main target groups:

- those SMEs (and sometimes larger firms) in developed as well as developing countries that are likely to engage in FDI; and

- those indigenous SMEs and entrepreneurs in developing host countries that are able to take advantage of FDI, in particular SME FDI, and the (wholly owned) affiliates of SME TNCs in those countries.

This is illustrated in box 1.

Box 2 provides a "road map" of the policy options discussed in Part Two. It sets out the options available for increasing SME FDI through efforts by host developing countries seeking SME FDI as a means to development; home countries -- more advanced developing countries as well as developed countries -- of SME TNCs; and international agencies.

### Box 1. The policy focus for SME FDI

As already discussed (in chapter I), in economies that are more developed, SMEs make up 99 per cent of the population, and about 10 per cent of these are dynamic fast-growth firms (figures 1 and 2). These fast-growth firms make a more than proportionate contribution to total economic growth. Also, they are the ones most likely to invest across borders, though only some of them will actually do so. The main target for their investment is activities involving growth-oriented counterpart SMEs (or those with the potential to grow) in developing countries; either they seek partner SMEs or they seek personnel who can help manage an SME that they establish.

**Figue 1. SMEs in economic structure, and FDI flows to SMEs in host developing countries**

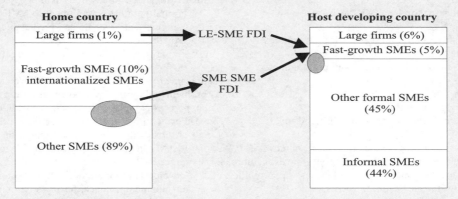

**Figue 2. SMEs as contributors to growth and focus of policy on FDI**

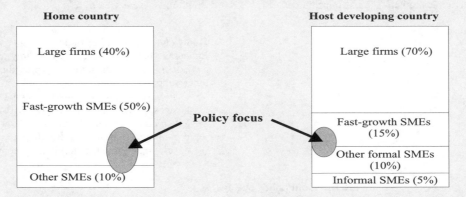

In developing countries, larger firms tend to be more important, and make a much greater contribution to economic growth. The informal sector is much larger, and SMEs tend to be underrepresented (the missing middle). This may ultimately impede economic growth.

The focus of the policies discussed in this handbook is on the relatively small proportion of SMEs that are already internationalized, growth-oriented SMEs, or those SMEs that have the potential to become such enterprises. SME FDI could be an effective way of encouraging the development of an entrepreneurial engine, and thus of longer-term sustainable economic growth in developing countries. The focus has to be on SMEs in home countries and on those in host or recipient countries, simply because much SME FDI is predicated on the existence of suitable partners.

**Box 2.  Increasing SME FDI:  policy options**

Policy targets

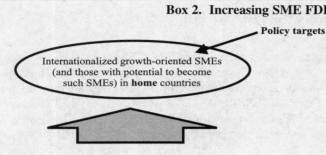

Internationalized growth-oriented SMEs (and those with potential to become such SMEs) in **home** countries

Internationalized growth-oriented SMEs (and those with potential to become such SMEs) in **host** countries

**Host country policy options**
Encourage foreign SMEs to invest by providing:

- Opportunities for foreign SMEs to partner with domestic SMEs.
- Accurate information on investment opportunities.
- Appropriate incentives.
- Access to support infrastructure and programmes.
- Addressing specific impediments.

**Home country policy options**
Encourage more SMEs to internationalize and invest abroad by:
- Adopting support programmes (human resources development, finance etc.) to assist SMEs investing abroad.
- Providing accurate information on business opportunities.
- Encouraging linkages between SMEs.
- Providing appropriate incentives.
- Supporting development of infrastructure (business parks etc.) abroad.
- Liaising with governments, chambers of commerce etc. in host economies to help address impediments to SME FDI.

**Host country policy options**
*Generally* -- encourage development of growth-oriented internationalized SMEs by providing:
- Formal political commitment to SMEs. Commitment to stable and predictable economic growth.
- Framework of laws and property rights.

*Specifically* — help target SMEs to overcome short-term problems inhibiting their potential by providing support programmes which achieve additionality, e.g.:
- Focus on internationalized, growth-oriented SMEs, or those with potential, both domestic and foreign.
- Identify the factors inhibiting the development of target SMEs.
- Develop appropriate programmes (human resources development, finance, business partnering etc.) to help target SMEs overcome problems and inhibiting factors.
- Establish a coordinating agency for delivery of programmes.
- Use cost-effective means of delivery in conjunction with the private sector.

**Home country policy options**
Encourage the development of a healthy internationalized SME sector in host economies by providing technical and other support:
- *Generally* — to assist in developing a conducive business environment for target SMEs.
- *Specifically* — to establish and deliver suitable programmes for target SMEs (human resources development, finance etc.) both in home and in host countries.

**International policy options**
**(for both home and host countries)**
Generally encourage increased flows of trade and investment by SMEs by means of:
- Cooperation on joint support programmes (credit guarantee, training etc.)
- Support for international information systems and global commerce systems.
- Encouraging linkages between SMEs.
- Cooperation on codes for incentives for FDI by SMEs.
- Multilateral cooperation in identifying and reducing barriers to FDI by SMEs.
- Cooperation with respect to monitoring the competitiveness of their programmes to promote/attract SME FDI.

# CHAPTER VI

## GENERAL POLICIES AND PROGRAMMES
## IN ASIAN DEVELOPING COUNTRIES RELATED TO
## SMEs AND THEIR RELEVANCE TO FDI IN AND BY SMEs

This chapter addresses the question of how best to ensure that policies in Asian developing economies are generally conducive to the development of growth-oriented and internationally oriented, indigenous SMEs, including through SME FDI. Although this *Handbook* is primarily concerned with policies specifically aimed at encouraging SME FDI, it is fairly clear from the lessons of the more developed economies that policies with respect to SMEs generally play an important part in developing an international outlook and capability in the SME sector. Policies designed to attract SME FDI cannot be focused solely on SMEs abroad. If the domestic SME sector is not receptive to international SMEs, the economy is a very much less attractive place for foreign SMEs to invest in. At the firm level, the dynamics of SME FDI are such that an internationally oriented, growing SME sector is an important precondition for FDI, simply because much SME FDI is predicated on finding suitable partners in the host country: about half (or more) of all SME FDI relies on the existence of suitable partners in the target economy (chapter III), and difficulties in finding suitable partners are one of the major impediments to SME FDI. If domestic SMEs (or domestic managers) are not attuned to or capable of building reliable partnerships and links with foreign SMEs, SME FDI is much less likely to occur.

Similarly, many foreign SMEs will want to "test the water" first before leaping into a commitment to invest. Much SME FDI from leading economies in Asia is preceded by other forms of international activity (chapter III). The investment of capital tends to come later in the evolutionary process of firms' growth. SMEs are more likely to invest abroad (either by setting up their own affiliates or by building an alliance affiliation with local partners) if they have already had some experience in international activity, especially in the country concerned, although, of course, some SMEs, especially high-technology SMEs, move to the investment stage without other international activity (Fujita, 1998). In any event, if it is difficult for a small foreign firm to do business (e.g., exporting to, importing from, the country) in a country, it will tend to go elsewhere. Opportunities for SME FDI are then reduced.

This means that policy aimed at encouraging the development of a growing and international SME sector is an important foundation for attracting SME FDI. In terms of the schematic diagram in box 1 of the introduction to Part Two, it concerns those developing countries that adopt policies seeking to expand the absolute and relative number of SMEs that are, or have the strong potential to be, growth-oriented and internationalized. As this is, by and large, an underlying aspect of SME policy in most developed economies already, the lessons that can be learned are many.

However, SME policy covers a range of different aspects. Approaches to SMEs and SME policy differ widely in the Asian region. This chapter addresses two main questions:

- What are the general challenges facing policy makers in the area of SMEs, and what lessons can be drawn from the ways in which different policy makers deal with them?

- What is the essence of best-practice SME policy?

SMEs can make a major structural and dynamic contribution to economies, but they are often impeded in doing so. If the general environment is not conducive to business, domestic SMEs are less likely to invest in growth opportunities. Similarly, SMEs from abroad are less likely to invest, and even if they do invest, the spin-off benefits to the local economy will be reduced. Policy initiatives that seek to encourage SME FDI without addressing more fundamental issues are unlikely to produce more than token results.

Consequently, the two main overriding challenges facing governments seeking economic development are to:

- provide a general business environment that is conducive to the development and internationalization of SMEs (and large firms), and that is attractive to investors, both domestic and from abroad; and

- identify specific ways in which they can use their limited resources most effectively to overcome impediments and to release the potential of SMEs, both domestic and from abroad.

Sections A and B of this chapter examine how these two challenges have been addressed by the leading economies in Asia. The lessons from successful countries in meeting them are rather mixed, but the main common points seem to be that they all have:

- pursued a mix of policies and programmes which, as far as possible, provide smaller investors with growth opportunities and with a significant degree of certainty about the future;

- adopted a politically explicit commitment, in the form of a law or strategy document, to the development of SMEs;

- pursued an approach to industrial development that was increasingly open to international transactions; and

- established administrative mechanisms for providing programmes to assist in the development of SMEs, especially growth-oriented SMEs.

What does this mean for best-practice policy? The concept of best practice in policy should not be taken literally -- there is no single policy that is "best" or ideal for all circumstances. However, there are some common elements of policy which seem to be more effective and successful than others. The purpose of examining best-practice characteristics is not to provide prescriptive rules and recipes for policy makers. Rather, it is to assist policy makers by allowing them to compare their policy stance with that successfully adopted elsewhere. Best-practice reference points and indicators can help to identify areas in which a change in policy stance, or a change in priorities, may be beneficial. The main challenges and the key best-practice lessons that can be distilled from the successful countries' experience are summarized in tables VI.1 and VI.2.

**Table VI.1. Environment conducive to the development of SMEs and investment domestically and from abroad**

| Challenge | Best-practice solution |
| --- | --- |
| Strategic policy environment | An explicit political commitment to the development of the SME sector |
| Economic environment for investment | Economic growth with a degree of certainty about the future |
| Socio-legal environment for investment | Stable and predictable framework of laws, e.g., definable and transferable property rights; transparent legal and regulatory systems |

*Source:* UNCTAD.

**Table VI.2. Using limited resources to release the potential of SMEs**

| Challenge | Best-practice solution |
| --- | --- |
| Which SMEs and entrepreneurs should receive most attention? | Focus on those SMEs most likely to grow |
| What should be the role of governments in assisting SMEs? | Focus on those areas where governments can provide additionality. |
| How to accommodate to changing SME needs as the economy develops? | Monitor needs, provide diagnostic services, revise priorities |
| How to meet the wide range of SME needs in a coordinated manner? | Central agency, one-stop shops |
| How to deliver SME programmes in an effective manner? | Cost recovery, cooperation with private sector |

*Source:* UNCTAD.

# A. Providing an environment conducive to business

How can governments in developing countries provide a general business environment that is conducive to the development and internationalization of SMEs (and large firms), and that is attractive to investors, domestic and foreign? This challenge has to be seen in a broader context of economic, social, political, legal and historical dimensions, and these vary from country to country. Different countries have thus addressed this challenge in different ways, and there is no single correct approach to its resolution. For example, Japan has successfully provided a business environment conducive to SME development, but the approach it has adopted to doing so may not be appropriate to developing countries in a more liberalizing and globalizing world. Japan adopted a largely protectionist approach to the development of its industries in the early stages of development. Also, the role of government guidance has been very pronounced in its industrial development. By contrast, the Hong Kong Special Administrative Region of the People's Republic of China and Singapore have successfully adopted a more internationalized approach to developing an environment conducive to business; but, even so, Singapore has a more active and interventionist policy than has the Hong Kong Special Administrative Region of the People's Republic of China.

That an environment which is not conducive to business development impedes economic growth has been clearly shown by the experiences of China prior to the 1978 reforms and Viet Nam pre-*doi moi*. An environment that impedes or discriminates against SMEs can also impede development and international competitiveness; an example is the experience of the Republic of Korea in the late 1970s, prior to the adoption of policies in the early 1980s to promote SMEs. As noted in chapter I, Indonesia and the Philippines both demonstrate some structural bias in terms of an underrepresentation of SMEs; similar imbalances may emerge in Viet Nam, Myanmar and Bangladesh. This underrepresentation -- the "missing middle" -- may well impede future development and create problems in those economies, especially if growth-oriented, internationalized SMEs are not actively encouraged.

Although there are many different approaches, there do appear to be some common lessons to be learned from the experiences of countries in building a business environment conducive to growth-oriented international SMEs. The key components of such an environment and the corresponding best practices were summarized in table VI.1. Although it is difficult to quantify the importance of these elements, or their contribution to growth and development, what seems to be the lesson from the experience of the leading economies in this respect is that the absence of any of these elements has a significant effect on the development of SMEs.

## 1. An explicit political commitment to the development of the SME sector

Major industrial developments and major infrastructure projects inevitably involve governments and strategic planning processes; this has been the case in all the developing countries in Asia. Because of this, government planners and bureaucrats focus their attention on large projects and large firms, which makes it easy to ignore, or to exercise - inadvertently - a bias against, the development of the SME sector.

The challenge facing many developing countries is therefore to provide opportunities for the SME sector to develop, and to ensure that government and bureaucratic processes do not ignore or impede the development of the SME sector. The best-practice solution appears to be that adopted by

Japan, the Republic of Korea, Singapore and the Taiwan Province of China, which have all adopted a clear statement of political commitment to SMEs. This takes the form of either a basic law, which sets out the obligations of the government to SMEs and in terms of SME policy, or a strategy statement, which sets out the broad directions and aspirations of government policy in relation to SMEs. Amongst the leading Asian economies, only the Hong Kong Special Administrative Region of the People's Republic of China has adopted the latter approach, although it also initiated a specific policy approach to SMEs in 1996. However, it has always had a strong and explicit policy commitment to industrial development; and, for the most part, industry and SMEs are synonymous in this economy.

By itself, a basic law or strategy document relating to SMEs means little. In combination with other initiatives and programmes, however, it can help by providing a clear framework for government officials to refer to, and setting the "rules of the game" for them. This, in turn, helps officials and non-government or private organizations to interpret and implement policies, laws and regulations in such a way that SMEs' interests are taken account of, and that they are not unnecessarily disadvantaged (see table VI.3 for country examples).

## 2. Sustainable economic growth

SMEs have made an important contribution to the development of countries in Asia. A major challenge facing policy makers is how to encourage smaller businesses to invest in start-ups and growth. The best-practice lesson from the leading Asian economies is that they have provided smaller investors with growth opportunities and with a degree of certainty about the future. The factors underlying the success of the Asian economies in their achievement of economic growth vary and there is little agreement on the relative importance of different factors (World Bank, 1993, p. 102). How governments stimulate economic growth, and how they provide a business environment with a degree of certainty are beyond the scope of this *Handbook*. The main lesson to be learned is that they should strive to do so in sustainable ways.

Economic growth opens up opportunities for investment, and thus provides a foundation for more economic growth. All the leading economies have had a strong commitment to economic growth, and have maintained sustained economic growth for extended periods. Many of the opportunities for economic growth in Asia have come from encouraging exports and this has relied also on encouraging the export capabilities of SMEs and the internationalization of industry generally.

On the other hand, economic uncertainty inhibits growth. It can be the result of political and social instability, structural changes, exogenous shocks, economic mismanagement, natural disasters and so forth. In all cases, uncertainty manifests itself at the level of the firm, in increased risk and in a risk premium on investment. Risk and uncertainty are important to both large and small firms, but smaller firms tend to have more difficulty with economic uncertainty and risk than larger ones. Smaller firms are less likely to have reserves to fall back on, and have fewer natural hedges in the form of diversification of products or investments. Governments cannot control all aspects of economic uncertainty. Attention to uncertainty is probably more important to the economies now developing than it was to the leaders when they were developing. In a closed economy, an increased risk premium leads to increased costs and a deferring of investment decisions. In a more globalizing world, where capital is relatively mobile and firms are freer to invest where they wish, increasing the risk premium can have a much greater effect on capital investment since a flight of domestic and foreign capital may occur, and as FDI switches to other more attractive destinations.

## Table VI.3. Basic policies with respect to SMEs in leading Asian economies

| Japan | Republic of Korea | Singapore | Taiwan Province of China |
|---|---|---|---|
| Japan passed a basic law with respect to SMEs in 1963. It sets out broad objectives for policy and stipulates specific areas in which the Government should take steps to achieve these objectives. The broad objectives are to promote the growth and development of SMEs in the light of the development of the Japanese economy, and to contribute to the betterment of the economic and social welfare of SME employees. The specific areas where the Government must implement appropriate measures are:<br><br>• modernization of equipment;<br>• improvement of technology;<br>• rationalization of management;<br>• structural upgrading;<br>• rectifying disadvantages;<br>• stimulating demand;<br>• ensuring fair opportunities for business; and<br>• ensuring proper relationships between labour and management. | The Republic of Korea introduced in 1982 a long-term plan for the promotion of SMEs, which set out goals for their development. This was in keeping with the country's constitution, which provides that the Government's responsibilities cover the protection and promotion of small business. There are five basic laws on small business provided in the 1982 legislation: the Basic Small Business Law; the Small Business Promotion Law; the Small Business Cooperative Law; the Small Business Projects Coordination Law; and the Small Business Subcontracting Promotion Law.<br><br>Prior to this, in the 1960s and 1970s, although the importance of SMEs was recognized, actual policy commitment tended to focus more on larger firms. The plan has been revised regularly, the last major revision taking place in 1993. The major thrust of the New Economy Plan (1993) is to encourage competition in domestic and inter-national markets through deregulation and removal of SME protection measures. | In Singapore, the 1988 SME Master Plan sought to:<br><br>• continue to improve and provide a conducive business environment that promotes entrepreneurship and innovation;<br>• increase market efficiency by encouraging information exchange and improving the provision of information about new methods and opportunities;<br>• promote best practices in business through easy access to consultancy, technology adoption and training; and<br>• encourage local enterprises to grow and go international.<br><br>The plan has been implemented by the Economic Development Board, working in conjunction with other agencies. It acts as a reference point for reviewing the effectiveness of programmes and for future initiatives and directions. For example, over the past few years a greater emphasis has been placed on regionalization initiatives. More recently, in 1995 the Productivity and Standards Board took over the responsibility for implementation of much of the plan as it relates to smaller enterprises. | The basic thrust of SME policy in Taiwan Province of China has been encapsulated from time to time in guidance principles issued by the administration. Policies to encourage the start-up and development of SMEs had existed since the 1950s, but these were first brought into coordinated focus by an SME Guidance Unit which was introduced in the 1960s, and which was formalized into an agency in 1981. The guidance principles issued via this agency have formed the cornerstone of a coherent approach to SME policy. These were first issued in 1968, and have been revised at least five times since then to reflect the changing conditions and priorities. In 1991 a Statute for the Development of Medium and Small Business (or Magna Carta for Small Enterprises) was enacted. This provides a more solid legislative foundation for the guidance principles. It also created a Small and Medium Enterprises Development Council, with members from six government agencies, three private sector representatives, and the chairpersons of two public corporations with SME activity. The Council is the body primarily responsible for ensuring that SME policy is coordinated and implemented in line with broader objectives and guidelines. |

## 3. A stable and predictable framework of laws and regulations

The lack of a stable and predictable framework of laws and regulations is often cited by managers of SMEs as one of the greatest impediments to FDI. There are two main ways in which governments can play an important role in this regard: establishing well-defined property rights and ensuring transparent legal and regulatory systems.

*(a)   Well-defined property rights*

Developing countries tend to have large informal sectors. They are made up of many individual entities, often with an agricultural background, few of which may have a formal legal status. These entities constitute an important socio-demographic part of the economy; they support many people. Their contribution to growth is fairly limited, but they provide a large seed-bed from which entrepreneurs and growth-oriented firms can emerge. It is only when these emerging firms can acquire some legal status and well-defined property rights that they can really develop and grow. Smaller businesses in particular usually need physical security (collateral) to raise funds for expansion, and this can be had only where it is possible to directly hold assets such as land and buildings. This is important for encouraging SME FDI, for two main reasons:

- Much SME FDI depends on having access to appropriate local partners, and the informal sector is the source of such partners.

- Even if foreign investors can raise the necessary funds in the absence of well-defined property rights, if they do not have security of ownership, they must seek a higher risk premium, and usually a shorter period in which to recover their investment. The effect is to discourage SME FDI, and for what FDI there is, to encourage more speculative short-term investment.

Similarly, ownership of intangible assets such as licences, patents, technical know-how, copyright, brand names and franchise rights (and protection against having them stolen) is an important aspect of developing a business economy. This is especially the case if technology, knowledge and training from abroad are to be encouraged. Property rights both tangible and intangible are critical to the survival and growth of businesses.

The challenge is therefore to provide a framework of property rights that will facilitate the growth and development of SMEs. It is a common feature of the economies of successful countries that tangible property rights are well defined and accessible (including as regards foreign investors) at a relatively early stage of development, and this seems to be best practice.

Intangible property rights are a more complex and difficult issue, and one which is still not easily resolved even in developed countries. Trade and investment in services are becoming more important, and, with these, the importance of clearly defined and enforceable rights grows. This is especially important for SMEs because they make up a large proportion of the services sector. Almost all countries in the Asian region have made efforts to improve copyright and patent protection, but it will be a long time before there is uniformity, especially in the enforcement of rights. Similarly, the way in which rights are created or recognized can create non-tariff barriers which impede SMEs more, because they raise the fixed costs associated with gaining legally recognized entry to the market. For example, several countries restrict the use of foreign lawyers, and China and Viet Nam place restrictions on the use of foreign words in displays, trade names and advertising. In the longer term, best practice in these areas may require the negotiation of international agreements for the recognition of rights and reduction of non-tariff barriers caused by the ways in which regulations and policies are used to confer rights.

### (b)    Transparent legal and regulatory systems

Business cannot grow and develop in the absence of a legal and regulatory framework.  All countries have legal systems, laws and regulations.  Inevitably, there are wide variations in the nature of these systems, depending on a host of historical, political and social considerations, as well as economic and business ones.  The issue here is not so much whether one system is better than another, but rather the transparency and interpretation of regulatory frameworks.  Transparent regulations are those that are clearly codified and interpreted consistently.

By contrast, opaque regulations leave much administrative discretion in interpretation to individual officials, who are under no obligation to interpret them consistently. Opaque regulations or regulations that are interpreted in opaque ways are a real impediment to business development, especially for SMEs.  Small businesses are particularly disadvantaged by the transaction costs of finding out what regulations apply, and how they are applied.  Obtaining this information is usually a fixed and sunk cost, and a small business has to pay the same as a large one; this puts the former automatically at a competitive disadvantage.  Also, opaque laws and regulations tend to encourage corruption (see box VI.1).

---

**Box VI.1.  Opaque regulations and corruption**

Transparency in legal systems and regulations means that it is easy for investors to see what the regulations and laws are, and what the consequences are of breaching them.  The opposite n  opaque regulations n are often quoted by SME investors as a major source of difficulty because they encourage corruption.  For example:

- An SME developer of property in a developing Asian economy was required to make a payment for each approval for construction.  In all, there were over fifty separate approvals needed for one relatively straightforward construction.  Anyone involved in the approvals could hold up the process by saying that the documentation was inadequate or that particular regulation had not been complied with.  There was no recourse if a delay occurred.  A foreign investor in another development in a different city was in a similar situation and eventually gave up.  The local partner then walked away with the title to the partially developed land, without paying any compensation.

- Another SME foreign investor was using a range of subcontractors and employing local staff as well as managers from its home country.  The management found that police visits were a regular feature to check documentation, contracts, workers' visas and work permits.  It appeared that no matter what papers were provided, the police could almost always fault them.  This was in part because of ambiguities in the regulations themselves relating to eligibility.

- An SME manufacturer using imported parts in assembly was required to place them in a bonded warehouse.  The parts were released only at the discretion of the warehouse staff, who always demanded fees in addition to the prescribed warehousing fees; the contract covering this already contained payments to cover their wages.  If fees were not paid, the warehouse was not opened, and production stopped.  The warehousing staff quoted "standard practice" and overriding regulations, which were sufficiently imprecise to make it not worth challenging the payments.

*Source:*  based on the case studies conducted by UNCTAD.

---

The challenge is therefore to ensure that whatever legal framework is adopted is transparent and interpreted consistently. The lesson from leading economies in Asia is a little mixed on this issue. Singapore is commonly cited as being one of the least corrupt countries in the region, and one with the most transparent legal and regulatory system. It has also been the most successful in attracting FDI for its SMEs. It thus seems that best practice consists in making efforts to simplify and avoid unnecessary complexity in regulations, and ensuring that regulations are as transparent as possible.

## B. Releasing the potential of SMEs

What can governments do to use their limited resources most effectively to release the potential of SMEs? Providing a business environment conducive for SMEs (and for large firms) is a good and necessary condition, but the lesson from the countries in which SMEs play an important role is that this is not sufficient by itself. It is also necessary for governments to invest actively in specific programmes designed to assist SMEs. SMEs face many impediments that inhibit their growth and their potential to contribute fully to economic development. As discussed, two main groups of SMEsn those indigenous SMEs and entrepreneurs that have the potential to internationalize and grow, and those SMEs from abroad engaged in foreign trade and FDI, in particular n are major components of the entrepreneurial engine (see chapter II).

By examining the lessons learned from successful countries, it is possible to pinpoint some characteristics of best-practice policies. There are five main challenges faced by policy makers in this regard:

- Which SMEs and entrepreneurs should receive most attention? This means providing specific programmes to help the target SMEs (those that are growth-oriented and internationally oriented) to overcome short-term impediments that inhibit their longer-term potential to grow.

- What should be the role of government in assisting SMEs? The main lesson is to focus on those areas in which additionality can be achieved -- that is, where gains can be made that would not otherwise be achieved. In general, this is in the areas of finance, human resource development, information, access to markets, regulatory reform and technology.

- How to accommodate to changing SME needs as the economy develops? Appropriate administrative mechanisms depend on knowing what the needs and problems of SMEs are. To this end, monitoring mechanisms, particularly diagnostic services, provide an important source of information. The second main lesson is that an emphasis on internationalization is now a crucial aspect of all SME policy.

- How to meet the wide range of SME needs in a coordinated manner? The best-practice approach seems to be to have some sort of planning and coordination for SME programmes and priorities serviced by a single administrative unit (e.g., a government department or agency) with responsibility for monitoring SME priorities and needs, but which may not necessarily be responsible for delivering actual programmes to SME clients.

- How can SME programmes be delivered cost-effectively? This usually requires some form of cost sharing or cost recovery, plus cooperation with the private sector in the delivery of programmes, plus internal benchmarking and comparison of programme effectiveness.

These challenges and the approaches to addressing them are discussed in greater detail below.

## 1. Which SMEs and entrepreneurs should receive most attention?

As specific government programmes cannot address all SMEs, the question arises as to which should receive most attention. The challenge is to identify those SMEs that should receive priority for policy makers' attention. Approaches to this differ, and governments adopt different programmes to address the needs of different types of SMEs. Best practice seems to be that government programmes give priority to SMEs that have the potential to grow and develop. The target firms for encouraging SME FDI are a subset of this subset of SMEs; only some SMEs are oriented towards growth and only some growth-oriented SMEs will have the ability to internationalize.

This approach should not be confused with "picking winners" n a policy approach that is very difficult to implement. The approach is more to provide the necessary tools to those firms seeking to start up, grow and internationalize. Thus, if a firm seeking to grow faces problems it can, if it wishes, seek assistance from programmes to provide it with credit-guarantee facilities, programmes to help it develop a credible business plan, or programmes that provide it with the necessary management skills. With these tools, an SME is in a better position to overcome the obstacles it faces, and expand. Without such programmes, its expansion may be stalled and its development potential will be lost.

In the case of FDI by SMEs, the investing firm tends to find a suitable local partner in the target economy; about half or more of all cases of SME FDI (more important for smaller firms) are such cases (see chapter III). A partner may be an existing local SME or an individual entrepreneur. From the point of view of developing countries (which seek to encourage SME FDI), this means that it is very important to adopt policies that encourage entrepreneurs and local firms with the capacity to be suitable partners and to grow. Failure to do so means not only less SME FDI, but also fewer benefits from the FDI that does occur. The leading economies in Asia have all adopted policies that focus on growth-oriented SMEs. Within that focus, there is increasing emphasis on SMEs that have the capability to compete internationally. For example:

- In Singapore, the SME Master Plan introduced in 1988 identified as its target group those local enterprises which have the critical mass, capacity, capability and commitment to innovate and grow. It helps those SMEs that are likely to develop and grow themselves.

- In Taiwan Province of China, the basic policy thrust since 1991, has been to promote the healthy development of SMEs and to help them grow through their own efforts.

- In the Republic of Korea, the plan adopted in 1982 for the promotion of SMEs was aimed at their long-term development, and focused on the promotion of promising SMEs in industries identified as priority ones. Previously (in 1965), the Basic Law on Small Business was adopted as the legal foundation for SME policies.

- In Japan, the concept underlying the Small and Medium Enterprise Law is to promote the growth and development of SMEs and to enhance the economic and social well-being of entrepreneurs and employees of SMEs. The main emphasis of programmes to achieve this is on modernization and structural upgrading.

A focus on those firms most likely to develop and grow does not necessarily mean that the social aspects of SMEs are ignored. Roughly speaking, only about 10 per cent or so of SMEs are growth-oriented. The remaining 90 per cent, though important in the economy, do not seem to contribute much to growth. These SMEs are typically small retailers, restaurants and manufacturers. They do not normally seek to grow beyond a given size, usually defined by the owner's management capability. Many die; and many are born each year. This volatility has extensive social consequences, and most countries also have programmes to address these issues, but these programmes are not necessarily intended to contribute to economic development.

## 2. What should be the role of government in assisting SMEs?

SMEs are not homogeneous, and they face many problems. Governments cannot solve all the problems of all SMEs. What, then, should be the role of government in assisting SMEs to realize their development potential? The policy challenge is to identify those areas to which governments can make a useful contribution.

There is broad agreement on the areas where governments *can* have most impact in addressing the problems facing SMEs. The areas identified by, for example, APEC and OECD include human resource development, advisory services and management training; technology, technology transfer and technology sharing; finance; market access; information access; and regulatory burden and regulatory infrastructure. Two additional areas are also sometimes cited: cooperation between the private sector and government; and cooperation between large and small firms (APEC, 1994; OECD, 1997).

The best-practice lesson is that government action in these areas has the greatest likelihood of providing additionality -- benefits to the community that would not accrue otherwise. Thus the lesson from leading economies, both in Asia and elsewhere, is that government *does* have a legitimate role to play in establishing specific programmes to help SMEs to overcome the problems they face.

SMEs range from TNCs with hundreds of employees abroad to micro ventures with a single person working part-time. They range from manufacturers using sophisticated technology to farmers using primitive technology. They range from SMEs that have no interest in growing beyond their present size to those that pursue an aggressive path to achieve international growth. They range from established firms to those that are really only ideas in entrepreneurs' minds. The only really common thread is that they are not large, and that they all face problems arising from three main sources:

- Problems that are intrinsic to SMEs themselves -- for example, when SMEs lack the necessary management skills to develop, or the inherent risks associated with being a single-product firm or relying on a single major client. To the extent that governments can address these issues, they usually require programmes that are directed specifically at SMEs. All the leading economies in Asia have developed healthy and vibrant SME sectors, and all offer a portfolio of services and programmes to SMEs that is designed to address problems intrinsic to SMEs. The policy emphasis placed on these areas differs over time, and across economies. For any given country at a given time it is thus necessary to monitor the relative importance of differing needs over time. This is dealt with further in the section immediately below. The annex table (to Part Two) shows how policy emphasis differs between economies. The programmes are usually provided to transnational SMEs as well as to local SMEs, although there may be some qualifying conditions in some circumstances.

• Problems that are intrinsic to governments -- for example, when unnecessary regulations or corruption impede SME development. Similarly, macroeconomic management policies (such as exchange rate, monetary, taxation and fiscal policies) can sometimes unintentionally discriminate against SME development. These issues have to be addressed at the government level, and thus have a much wider scope than just SMEs.

• Problems that are intrinsic to market systems -- for example, when markets fail. Financial markets may fail to provide finance to SMEs at a price that accurately reflects the real risk and transaction costs, or unfair competitive practices may be used to disadvantage SMEs. Similarly, the failure of the markets to provide information on technology or about business opportunities can impede development. These issues have to be addressed at the market level, for example by taking steps to correct the functioning of market. As with the second point, the scope of these actions is usually wider than just issues pertaining to SMEs, although sometimes second-best solutions can be directed specifically at SMEs. For example, if financial markets fail to provide SMEs with finance at rates reflecting their real risk, it may be easier to give financial subsidies to SMEs rather than trying to rectify the market.

## 3. How to accommodate to changing SME needs as the economy develops?

For policies and programmes to be effective, they need to reflect the needs of SMEs in the economy. As economies develop, so do their SMEs, and the needs of those SMEs change. Changes also take place in the administrative capability of the economy to provide services to SMEs. For example, SMEs in a predominantly agricultural economy in transition to a light industrial economy are more likely to gain from assistance in forming cooperatives, basic technology programmes and the development of basic infrastructure in areas such as communications, education, law and property rights. By contrast, SMEs in a more sophisticated, advanced technology- and services-based economy need a more comprehensive and integrated package of services, and need access to international technology and skills if they are to survive in an internationally competitive market. Policy makers in developing countries now face two main challenges: first, developing appropriate administrative mechanisms to meet SME needs; and, second, how to compress the development of SME administrative processes to meet the increased pressure for international competitiveness.

The first main lesson which seems to emerge from the experience of leading economies in Asia is that appropriate administrative mechanisms depend on knowing what the needs and problems of SMEs are. To this end, monitoring mechanisms, particularly diagnostic services, provide an important source of information. The second main lesson is that an emphasis on internationalization is now a crucial aspect of all SME policy. In the leading Asian economies, administrative mechanisms were able to evolve over a period of decades, and were progressively adapted to the changing needs of SMEs (see table VI.4). However, increased globalization, international competition and international economic integration mean that almost all economies now have to adopt policies that make their advanced SMEs internationally competitive. Even in the leading economies, there have been differences in approach (table VI.4).

**Table VI.4. Evolution of SME policies in leading Asian economies**

| Japan | Republic of Korea | Singapore | Taiwan Province of China |
|---|---|---|---|
| In the immediate post-war period, SME policy tended to be predicated on the assumption that SMEs were weak and needed protection. A number of government institutions (such as the Small Business Finance Corporation) were set up to provide SMEs with access to finance, and a credit-guarantee programme was established. The Small and Medium Enterprise Cooperative Association Law was enacted to encourage SMEs to form into larger groups. | There has been a marked shift in the attitudes and polices towards SMEs in the post-war period. Initially, SMEs were seen as peripheral to economic development; then, in the 1970s, it was realized that this view had led to a decline in SMEs and a weakening of the whole economic structure. A policy reversal took place, and now considerable emphasis is placed on the international competitiveness of SMEs. | Administrative support for SMEs has pursued an evolutionary path. Initially, the focus was on needs for technological upgrading of domestic SMEs, and this was met by a relatively simple set of programmes. This has remained an important aspect of SME policy, but emphasis has shifted progressively to a more comprehensive system of programmes aimed at promising local enterprises (including SMEs) which are, or have the potential to be, leaders in internationally competitive markets. | There have been about four distinct periods since the 1950s, in each of which the main policy emphasis has changed to reflect the changing needs of the SME population. Taiwan Province of China is somewhat unique in that, since the 1960s, its SMEs have led the economy's export drive. Throughout the past 30 years, there has been a strong emphasis on policies to enhance the international competitiveness of SMEs. |
| The focus of policy shifted in the 1960s more to technological upgrading and modernization. Plans were drawn up on an industry-by-industry basis and financial and tax incentives were provided to encourage SMEs to invest and grow. It was at this time that the SME Basic Law was enacted, and SME policy became more systematic and coherent. | In the 1960s, the Republic of Korea embarked on a development strategy based on export-oriented industrial expansion. The first five-year development plan was initiated in 1962, and emphasized heavy industry. The accompanying structural changes meant that during the 1960s SMEs declined in relative importance; for example, their contribution to value added in mining and manufacturing declined from about 50 per cent of all value added in 1963 to 27 per cent in 1973. Although SME policies were adopted and a basic law was introduced, SME needs were not addressed in any systematic way. | The foundations for Singapore's SMEs were established in the 1950s with an emphasis on education and a stable pattern of economic development. The first specific programmes for SMEs were initiated in 1962 by the Economic Development Board (EDB). Assistance was provided for equipment upgrading, working capital and site relocation. In addition, advice was provided on technology, management and marketing. | During 1945-1960 n the period of post-war reconstruction n SMEs were mostly small, and faced shortages of capital, skilled labour, foreign exchange and technology. Policy focused on providing loans to assist the development of SMEs, and on encouraging a suitable infrastructure for entrepreneurial small firms to thrive. There was no specific SME administration; rather, assistance was provided by the United States Aid Committee of the Executive Yuan. |
| In the 1970s, a more comprehensive approach to SME programmes was adopted; this covered human resource development, financing, technology, access to information, assistance with exports, and so on. Major structural problems affected the economy in this period (as a result of the oil shocks), and SMEs required assistance in obtaining the resources and skills needed to adjust. At the same time, some policies (now mostly reversed) were adopted to limit competition from larger firms, especially in retailing. | In the latter half of the 1970s, the decline in the SME sector emerged as a problem in the development of heavy industry, as subcontractors were less able to adapt to the changing and more competitive needs of the main suppliers. Pragmatic efforts were made to promote SME specialization and subcontracting, for example, by designating certain products to be supplied by SME subcontractors, and by encouraging government and public organizations to buy from SMEs. | From the mid-1970s onwards, increased emphasis was given to forming joint ventures with foreign TNCs and larger local firms. This approach emphasized the role of the market in developing SMEs, but a specific set of programmes were developed to encourage market cooperation between large and small firms. As before, the EDB was primarily responsible for SME development (through its Investment Services Division). | From 1960 to the mid-1970s, a period of rapid export growth, SMEs were encouraged to develop low-cost light industry with a strong export orientation. Specific programmes to assist SMEs were developed, and implemented by the Medium and Small Business Administration.

During the period from the mid-1970s to the mid-1980s, SMEs were affected by the volatility associated with the "oil shock", and with changes in the international economic order. |

/...

(Table VI.4, cont'd.)

| Japan | Republic of Korea | Singapore | Taiwan Province of China |
|---|---|---|---|
| The strongly rising yen and the rapid internationalization of the Japanese economy (at least in manufacturing) gave rise to a new set of needs and priorities in the 1980s. In particular, this generated a need for a strong emphasis on the internationalization of SMEs. In the 1990s, these issues continued, but policy needed to address also the shift into a prolonged period of slow growth, and the continued structural changes in the economy. Japanese SME policy remains a mix of policies aimed at encouraging growth and development, combined with programmes aimed more at social and structural adjustment. | It was not until 1982 that the long-term plan for the development of SMEs recognized a wide range of needs of SMEs and sought to address them in a systematic way via a number of programmes and initiatives. For example, the plan provided specific measures for assistance (e.g., assisting start-ups, requiring contractors to pay accounts on delivery); established the Small Business Training Institute, established several financial support and taxation measures; introduced a general programme for modernization and technology upgrading of specific sectors; and expanded the number of sectors designated as exclusively for SMEs.<br><br>In the 1993 New Economy Plan, the focus shifted more towards encouraging competition in domestic and international markets through deregulation and the removal of protection measures. SMEs are no longer considered to need protection, but programmes are aimed at giving them the capability to compete in international markets. | A period of economic instability and recession in 1985 led to an increase in SME business failures, and to the formation of a one-stop agency for SMEs, the Small Enterprise Bureau (SEB), still within the EDB. The SEB focused on the needs of SMEs that had the potential to export or were already doing so, SMEs in the supporting industries sectors, and those SMEs which could be upgraded and modernized.<br><br>The SME Master Plan was developed in 1987 and 1988. This emphasized the role of a multi-agency approach to provide a comprehensive range of services to SMEs. This range of services takes a promising enterprise, and assists it through the stages from start-up, to growth, to expansion and to internationalization.<br><br>In 1996, the emphasis shifted slightly again. The EDB now focuses mostly on larger enterprises, while the Productivity and Standards Board (PSB) emphasizes the delivery of programmes to smaller enterprises. EDB programmes are geared more to regional development opportunities, while those of the PSB are more domestically oriented. However, there is still a strong underlying emphasis on the development of promising local enterprises to achieve international competitive standards. | SMEs were encouraged to adopt better technology and to move to more value-added products, and many were encouraged to become satellites of larger companies. Policy delivery emphasized cooperation with banks (especially the Small and Medium Business Bank) and foundations.<br><br>From mid-1980 to the present, many traditional SMEs started to lose their international competitiveness as a result of rising labour costs, protectionism, increasingly stringent environmental controls, and labour disputes. At the same time, globalization pressures meant that, to survive, many SMEs needed to shift part of their production chain abroad. Ten guidance systems were established to provide a comprehensive and internationally competitive SME policy and a portfolio of services to SMEs. |

*Source:* UNCTAD.

## 4. How to meet the wide range of SME needs in a coordinated manner?

SMEs face many impediments, and governments can provide many forms of assistance to overcome these impediments. There is some commonality as to the areas in which governments can most likely have an impact (see section 1 above). However, these areas are very wide ranging. SME policy requires a holistic approach, and is difficult to implement in a segmented fashion. For example, there will be little benefit from addressing human-resource-development impediments if finance remains a limiting factor. This means that it is not sensible to deal with questions of human-resource-development policy (or technology policy, or access to markets) in isolation. This poses two difficulties. The first is that it is administratively difficult to bring such a wide range of capabilities and programmes within the purview of one department or administrative unit. The second is that SME clients have difficulties if there are many different functional departments to deal with n it is easier for them to go to one point. The challenge is how best to coordinate government assistance to SMEs in such a way as to provide a holistic approach to SME needs, to be accessible and seamless to SME clients, and to be administratively workable.

The approaches adopted differ, but the best-practice approach seems to be to have some sort of planning and coordination for SME programmes and priorities serviced by a single administrative unit (e.g., a government department or agency) with responsibility for monitoring SME priorities and needs, but which may not necessarily be responsible for delivering actual programmes to SME clients. This unit, sometimes in the guise of a one-stop or first-stop shop, also acts as the main contact point for SME clients. The implementation of a programme is then shared between the SME administrative unit and a variety of other agencies. This can cause some problems with budget allocations and a degree of administrative tension, but it is usually administratively workable, and in some cases actually seems to increase accountability, transparency and responsiveness. (See table VI.5 for different approaches to the coordination of assistance to SMEs in leading economies.)

## 5. How can SME programmes be delivered cost-effectively?

All governments face the question of financing. Furthermore, there is the usual moral hazard problem: if services to SMEs are free, they will be overutilized. SME programmes can be a good investment. For example, a study on the counselling activity by the United States Small Business Development Centre (SBDC) suggests, on the basis of comparison of sales and employment figures for clients for two years before and after counselling, and estimation of a weighted contribution to increased tax payments as a result of growth, that the benefit-cost ratio for counselling services was 4.3 and the ratio for all SBDC operation 2.6 [1] (Chrisman and Katrishen, 1994). Their growth was then discounted by state growth to arrive at the likely "additionality" contribution due to counselling. As a crude indication, for every $1 spent on SBDC counselling activities, at least an additional $2.6 was generated in tax revenues. These returns are large by normal investment standards, but some care must be taken in interpreting them. The reason that the SBDC benefit-cost ratios are so large is that human-resource-development consultancy and advisory services often have the effect of getting an SME over an immediate hump, so that it can take advantage of a specific opportunity. Nonetheless, it is evident that many programmes do provide additionality.

There are two related challenges: how to pay for SME programmes and how to ensure that they are delivered cost-effectively. Approaches to these challenges vary widely. Best practice seems to involve some form of cost recovery or cost sharing with clients, and this is a fairly common form of solution to the first challenge. Most governments only provide partial subsidies (usually up to 50

**Table VI.5. Different approaches to coordination of assistance to SMEs in leading Asian economies**

| Japan | Republic of Korea | Singapore | Taiwan Province of China |
|---|---|---|---|
| The Ministry of International Trade and Industry (MITI) coordinates SME programmes via the Small and Medium Enterprise Agency. The agency is responsible for planning, review and providing guidance in respect of a range of specific programmes and policies. However, for the most part it does not actually implement these programmes; that is left to implementing agencies and corporations, such as the Japan Small Business Corporation and the Japan External Trade Organization. | In 1996, the Small and Medium Business Administration (SMBA) was established to act as a central coordinating point for SME policy and programmes. It is made up of bureaus to deal with assistance (e.g., start-up, human resource development), technology and specific industries, and has 11 regional offices. The National Institute of Technology and Quality is affiliated with the SMBA. To a greater extent than in other countries, it appears that the SMBA actually implements and delivers its own programmes, but it still works in cooperation with other agencies -- for example, the Korean Trade-Investment Promotion Agency and the Industrial Bank of Korea -- for delivery. | A multi-agency and holistic approach is pursued, under which multiple agents work broadly within the framework of the SME Master Plan. Different agents, from both the public and private sectors, deliver services to SMEs, in accordance with programmes and schemes designed and engineered by the Economic Development Board (EDB), in close cooperation with the relevant agent. For example, the Singaporean National Computer Board, the National Science and Technology Board and the Trade Development Board all provide some services specifically to SMEs, but they also provide other services and functions to other clients. This approach has a particular advantage; because Singapore's SME development strategy has emphasized linkages between TNCs and local SMEs, it is thus important to have government agents with specialist capability in dealing with TNCs, but which can also link to local SMEs.<br><br>Administratively, the achievements of the SME Master Plan have been continually reviewed by the EDB (and now also the Productivity and Standards Board, previously the National Productivity Board), which has in turn reviewed and upgraded the various programmes and schemes to meet the needs of SMEs in Singapore. The Enterprise Development Council, composed of 16 people from politics, government, large and small businesses, and academia acts as a source of ideas and advice. The EDB and the Productivity and Standards Board act as overseers of the SME services, but do not necessarily deliver them. Where funding is required to operate a programme, the relevant agents are allocated line budgets under the annual budget process. | Since the mid-1980s, the economy has adopted a programme of 10 guidance systems for SMEs, in the areas of pollution control; production technology; industrial safety; research and development; marketing; quality enhancement; mutual cooperation and support; information management; finance and credit; and management.<br><br>This approach requires cooperation between a variety of agencies, and the Ministry of Economic Affairs plays a coordinating role through the Small and Medium Enterprise Agency. Most programmes are implemented by specific agencies and associations such as the China Productivity Centre and the Small and Medium Business Credit Guarantee Fund. |

per cent of the cost), and cap the total amount of subsidy available to a given SME (box VI.2). This helps to pay for services and to overcome some of the moral hazard problem. Best practice in achieving cost-effectiveness in delivery can be enhanced by cooperating with the private sector to deliver services and internal benchmarking and monitoring of the effectiveness of programmes. A wide range of programmes, such as advisory, diagnostic, consultancy, technology and information-provision services, can be readily provided with the assistance of the private sector -- consultants, chambers of commerce, non-governmental organizations etc. By having the private sector actually responsible for the delivery of services, it is possible to avoid crowding out the private sector by government intervention. Also, private sector provision introduces some market pressures and thus encourages more cost-effective and efficient programme delivery.

---

**Box VI.2.   Examples of advisory and consultancy services**

**Australia**

AusIndustry's *National Industry Extension Service (NIE)* is a joint State-Federal Government initiative that provides a range of programmes, covering provision of information on regulations and assistance programmes, general business diagnostics and advice, and specialized advisory and training programmes related to skill acquisition in the areas of benchmarking, exporting, total quality management, integrating manufacturing etc. Services are funded up to 50 per cent of cost, subject to approval, and with some limits on the size of subsidy available. Targeting is mostly to firms likely to be able to achieve international competitiveness. Delivery is through accredited and trained private sector consultants. About 2,000 to 4,000 SMEs use the NIES services, and total costs are about $20 million per annum.

**Canada**

The *Canadian Business Service Centres (CBSC)* provide one-stop or first-stop access to government information services and assistance programmes. *The Federal Business Development Bank* provides management courses and, through a programme of *Community Business Initiatives,* provides counselling and advice. The *Counselling Assistance for Small Enterprises* (CASE) programme uses retired business people to provide counselling and advice. AMTAP (Advanced Manufacturing Technology Application Programme) offers subsidized consultancy to upgrade manufacturing. As regards funding, programmes are typically funded to a maximum of 75 per cent subsidy. Targeting depends on the programme, but generally is on SMEs with growth potential. Delivery is through regional offices, and use is made of private consultancy services, colleges and universities.

**Taiwan Province of China**

The *Medium and Small Business Administration of the Ministry of Economic Affairs (MOEA)* provides a number of guidance programmes aimed at improving management, production technology, research and development, safety etc. These rely on experts from within relevant government agencies, or private consultants. Funding is up to 50 per cent of the cost of services. Delivery is via Small and Medium Sized Business Centres in regional locations. Consultancy services were budgeted at about $NT 190 million in 1994, although some of this was for general consultancies to improve the conditions of SMEs.

**Finland**

The *Ministry of Trade and Industry (MTI),* through the *Regional Business Service Offices,* delivers programmes such as the Kunto (or condition) programme, which diagnoses SMEs' needs, provides training for setting up a business, general management training etc. subsidizes up to about 60 per cent of the cost of the programmes; the rest is borne by the client. The programme targets SMEs, and about 60 per cent of participants are start-up or young companies. Delivery is by MTI-trained consultants. There have been about 9,000 participants in 850 courses and about 1,540 consultancy days.

*/...*

**(Box VI.2, cont'd.)**

### Japan

*Small and Medium Enterprise Agency of the Ministry of International Trade and Industry (MITI)* is responsible for programmes and the *Japan Small Business Corporation (JSBC)* provides personnel training and consultancy services to government officials responsible for SMEs and to SME managers. Subsidies are available which usually cover two thirds of the cost. No specific targets are set, although the basic law aims to help SMEs in need of technical upgrading. Delivery is through a chain of nine Small and Medium Enterprise Institutes located in provincial centres. Chambers of commerce assist in the delivery of advice on tax and management. Specialized JSBC advisers provide consultancy services to particular industry segments, such as SMEs in retailing. About 12,000-15,000 people attend training courses each year.

### New Zealand

*Business Development Boards* provide a number of programmes, such as the *Expert Assistance Grant Scheme* to support consultancy advice to increase international competitiveness, and the *Business Development Investigation Scheme* to carry out feasibility studies. Funding is usually subsidized up to 50 per cent of the cost of approved projects, subject to upper limits. Targeting varies by programme, but most are aimed at growth-oriented companies. Delivery is via private sector consultants selected by the client.

### Singapore

*Enterprise Promotion Centres*, now coordinated by the *National Productivity Board* (and previously by the Economic Development Board), assist SMEs with a range of programmes aimed at business development, facilitating expansion and growth via training, special technical assistance etc. Funding is generally subsidized up to 50 per cent of costs, subject to limits. Targeting is at SMEs' needs at different stages of growth, from start-up, to growth, expansion and internationalization. Delivery is via a multi-agency approach. The Skills Development Scheme had, between 1978 and 1988, approximately 3,000 cases per annum.

*Source*: Hall, 1996.

# Note

[1]    Only clients who indicated that the SBDC counselling was useful were included in the benefit calculation.

# CHAPTER VII

## SPECIFIC POLICIES AND PROGRAMMES
## TO ENCOURAGE INWARD FDI IN AND BY SMEs IN ASIA

What can host country governments do to attract more SME FDI? With the exception of Singapore, Asian countries have not used FDI in and/or by SMEs as an explicit development strategy. Singapore actively encouraged large TNCs (not SMEs) to invest in its SMEs (box VII.1). Taiwan Province of China has encouraged technological partnerships between its SMEs and SMEs abroad. None of the other economies in Asia has really used inward FDI by SMEs in SMEs as a component of their development strategies. It is thus difficult to distil lessons and best practice from Asian experiences. What lessons one *can* distil come from the experiences of Singapore and Taiwan Province of China, and the more general experiences of efforts to encourage increased FDI flows in the region.

FDI in and by SMEs makes up only a small proportion of FDI in host Asian economies (chapter II). The potential is there, however, to increase it quite significantly. For developing countries facing the need to expand their SME sectors rapidly, and to internationalize them, increasing inward SME FDI could be an attractive policy option. Best practice in increasing inward SME FDI is mostly a matter of actively encouraging foreign SMEs, and large firms, to invest in SMEs in a host country, by means of a mix of policies and programmes designed to:

- encourage the development of growth-oriented, internationally oriented SMEs in the domestic economy;

- provide accurate information to foreign investors;

- encourage linkages between SMEs across borders;

- provide appropriate incentives;

- provide access to support services and infrastructure; and

- address specific impediments and barriers to SME FDI.

---

**Box VII.1  The Singaporean model**

The Singaporean model of development has been one of the success stories of encouraging FDI as a means to develop local SMEs. It has not focused so much on SMEs abroad as a source of FDI, as on encouraging large firms to set up smaller affiliates in Singapore, and using this FDI to develop local SMEs.  This has been done by encouraging foreign TNCs to form partnerships with local SMEs, and by encouraging foreign affiliates to establish linkages with local SMEs. The key features of the Singaporean model are as follows:

- *An emphasis on internationalizing local industry.*  In the early stages of development, in the 1950s and early 1960s, Singapore adopted a fairly protectionist approach and encouraged import substitution. However, from 1967 onwards, Singapore moved to an export-oriented strategy. Tariffs and quotas had largely been abolished by 1970.

- *Encouragement of FDI in local industry and industrialization.*  The Economic Development Board (EDB) actively sought foreign firms that would invest in manufacturing, especially for exporting, through its centres established in New York, San Francisco and Hong Kong, and through targeted approaches to firms seeking to expand into Asia. Special incentives were provided, in particular for firms granted pioneer status, mostly in heavy industries such as shipbuilding, chemicals and oil. Provision of local infrastructure (transport, housing) and skills (education and language capabilities, especially English) was given a high priority.  Subcontractors were reliable. This provided an environment in which TNCs felt comfortable investing, because they knew that supporting infrastructure and skills existed.  FDI into Singapore increased sharply in the 1970s, typically making up about 80 per cent of total investment and growing at a rate of around 16 per cent per annum.  The result was a steady increase in levels of employment and exports. There are no statistics that give the breakdown of FDI by size of firm, but available data show that since the early 1980s, about 20 per cent of Singapore's manufacturing establishments have been foreign-owned (in the sense of having a capital structure that is less than half locally owned). Since only 15 per cent of Singapore's manufacturers employ more than 100 people, and only 3 per cent employ more than 500 people, a significant amount of FDI appears to have gone to SMEs.  Anecdotal evidence suggests that investment by TNCs in local SMEs, or in setting up small local affiliates, has been an  important aspect of Singapore's longer-term success. It has helped to provide the physical capital and developed the human capital (especially in enterprise management) necessary for the longer-term growth of new ventures.

- *Shifting the emphasis on FDI and development to more advanced technology and services.*  Through the 1970s and 1980s, the EDB encouraged the development of more technologically oriented industries and service industries by means of technology transfer and FDI. Foreign investors were given various incentives, including five-year tax holidays. This was done in conjunction with programmes aimed at increasing the skill and technology levels of local enterprises. Foreign TNCs were encouraged to establish joint vocational training centres to help train local employees.  Similarly, a Local Industry Upgrading Programme was established in 1986 to encourage TNCs to provide assistance to local SMEs and to subcontractors in upgrading technology and quality.

- *An SME Master Plan and support system.*  SMEs were recognized explicitly as a key part of Singapore's development strategy, with the release of the SME Master Plan in 1988. This brought together a framework of programmes supplied in a multi-agency approach. These programmes seek to support SMEs as they go through stages of start-up, growth, expansion and internationalization.

*Sources*:  Singapore, Economic Development Board, *Yearbook*, various years;  Singapore, Economic Development Board (1993); and Van Elkan (1995).

---

The challenges and the best-practice solutions to them are summarized in table VII.1. An overriding challenge is to establish priorities so that the emphasis and mix of programmes and initiatives provides the greatest possible impact per unit of expenditure (or expenditure equivalent). Establishing such priorities requires effective monitoring mechanisms for identifying the gaps and deficiencies in existing programmes and the likely gains from increasing activity. For example, simply increasing incentives to foreign SMEs to engage in FDI may not be as effective as alternatives (such as encouraging partnerships) and may not be effective at all unless foreign SMEs can access accurate information. This issue is dealt with in more detail in Part Three.

**Table VII.1. Best-practice policies for host countries seeking SME FDI**

| Challenges | Best-practice solutions |
|---|---|
| How best to encourage growth-oriented SMEs with an international orientation. | Encourage internationalization and growth, both generally, and specifically with respect to SMEs that have the potential to grow and do business internationally. |
| How best to provide accurate information. | Provide accurate information to potential foreign investors on such things as market conditions; opportunities; and government regulations and requirements, by means of a portfolio of different channels. |
| How best to encourage linkages between SMEs across borders. | Encourage the development of linkages (e.g., partnerships and alliances) between SMEs across borders by means of a mix of available channels. |
| How best to provide appropriate incentives. | Best practice requires that incentives be part of a broader strategy for encouraging FDI tailored to the development of target industries (or to aspects of industrial development such as export promotion); are designed so that they actually have an additionality effect; discourage rent seeking by clients; and are consistent with broader multilateral agreements or practices, so that bidding competition between countries or regions is avoided. |
| How best to provide access to support services and infrastructure. | Adopt a mechanism that anticipates the needs of those investors a country is seeking to attract, and allows those support and infrastructure needs to be met in priority order. |
| How best to address the specific impediments and barriers to SME FDI. | Establish mechanisms that monitor and respond to the problems or impediments faced by foreign investors; and integrate the findings into action plans to reduce more systemic problems. |

*Source:* UNCTAD.

## A. Encouraging growth-oriented internationalized SMEs

Best practices seem to be to encourage internationalization and growth, both generally, and specifically with respect to SMEs that have the potential to grow and do business internationally. Few SMEs, except high-technology SMEs, move immediately to FDI. FDI by SMEs is usually preceded by more exploratory international activity n arm's-length trading, exporting using an agent or a representative office, establishing an inter-firm agreement to develop a business opportunity, and so on. As in the case of other firms, it is only when sufficient knowledge, trust and experience have been built up that SMEs are willing to take the risks and make the commitment associated with capital investment abroad. Thus, if the business environment is not attractive to SMEs, FDI is less likely to occur. However, the converse does not automatically and immediately follow: making an environment attractive to SMEs will not immediately lead to SME FDI, because, first, it may take several years before a sufficient number of SMEs have built up and, second, other more specific factors may discourage SME FDI. Encouraging growth-oriented international SMEs is a matter of a mix of general policies and more specific ones.

The key lessons from the discussion in chapter VI, section A, are that it is important to have a commitment to stable and predictable economic growth and an environment conducive to investment, an explicit political commitment to the development of SMEs, usually in the form of a law or strategy, and a stable and predictable framework of legal and regulatory processes. Similarly, chapter VI, section B, provided some basic policy lessons specific to SMEs if governments in developed countries are to encourage SME FDI successfully and sustainably. Key points are as follows:

- Policy efforts should focus on those SMEs that have the potential to grow, and to build business internationally. This means both domestic SMEs and foreign SMEs that have established a domestic foothold.

- It is necessary to identify the requirements of these SMEs and to adapt policies so that they are appropriate to the needs of the target SMEs and to the stage of development of the economy.

- It should then be possible to design and implement a portfolio of suitable programmes aimed at assisting SMEs in the target categories to overcome short-term problems that inhibit the realization of their longer-term potential.

- Administrative mechanisms to coordinate the delivery of these programmes should be put in place, and some mechanisms for cost recovery or cost sharing should be instituted.

## B. Providing accurate information

Leading economies in Asia have information services that are aimed at providing information to their own firms (including SMEs) about opportunities and conditions abroad, and to firms abroad seeking to invest or trade about opportunities in their own economies.

The costs of obtaining accurate information are a sunk cost. For SMEs, this cost is large in relation to an investment, and it tends to be a barrier to entry. Information also has public-good characteristics. The best practice is to provide accurate information to potential foreign investors on market conditions, opportunities, and government regulations and requirements. It should be emphasized that information is of little use if it is out of date or not accurate.

The main problem in doing this for SMEs is the cost of disseminating information to target audiences. Again the best practice seems to be to use various different channels and media such as commercial attachés at embassies, trade missions, trade shows, networking systems, chambers of commerce and their publications, international agencies and programmes, technology-exchange programmes, international forums and conferences, web sites, specific market research consultants, and other national trade-promotion bodies.

Japan, the Republic of Korea, Singapore and Taiwan Province of China have all used these avenues at different times, and with differing emphasis. All have specific programmes for providing information to domestic firms. Singapore's approach to providing information abroad and to its domestic firms is probably more targeted than that in other countries, although Taiwan Province of China is also now adopting a targeted approach in an effort to attract and develop certain "hub" industries (finance, media etc.).

Most developed countries and countries with successful programmes for SMEs also offer financial assistance to SMEs (and large firms) to access some channels. For example, general information is only of limited use to some SMEs simply because they generally operate in niche markets. Consequently, countries also offer consultant programmes, usually subsidized, so that a client firm can use the services of a market research consultant to gather specific information about a market, government regulations etc. Typical is the Singaporean model, which offers grants of up to 50 per cent of the eligible costs of participating in trade shows, and of obtaining reports, data and intelligence on markets abroad, or on new technologies or joint-venture partners.

## C. Encouraging linkages between SMEs across borders

By forming a partnership or alliance, an SME can significantly reduce the risks and costs associated with doing business across borders, be it for trade or investment purposes. Both sides can gain. The local partner (either an SME or a manager) can assist by providing local knowledge and contacts, and, in turn, gains from the capital, technology and training provided by the foreign SME. As observed in Part One, the existence of local partners is a significant factor in encouraging FDI by SMEs. A local partner can provide a low-risk, low-commitment entry point to a market for a foreign SME, especially for smaller SMEs for which a fully fledged move into FDI may stretch managerial and staff resources.

The best practice is to encourage the development of linkages (e.g., partnerships and alliances) between SMEs across borders by means of a mix of channels. Forging and maintaining successful partnerships and alliances between SMEs involves several steps, and governments can have an important role in a number of these. They include:

- *Creation of a pool of suitable partners.* As stressed in section A, the existence of a pool of SMEs and managers with the ability to become partners or allies with foreign SMEs is an important aspect of encouraging inward SME FDI. Governments (both in host and in home countries) have an important role to play in this regard.

- *Introduction.* Matchmaking requires an introduction between two suitable partners with some common interest. Given the number of SMEs in the world, and the huge variations in markets and interests, this is not an easy task. Intergovernmental cooperation is usually an important aspect of successful introduction and matchmaking, even where the private sector plays an important role.

- *Formalization.* Only some introductions will lead to a decision to proceed further to an alliance or to a partnership, or even a take-over. Before such formalization occurs, however, the potential partners may need to obtain finance, arrange legal agreements to cover licences or trade processes, establish banking facilities, etc. In almost all cases, they will need access to professional advisers or to larger institutions with the capability to assist them. This area is important to SMEs, but governments typically play a less direct role.

- *Management and conflict resolution.* Managing a small, fast-growing organization stretched across borders has its own strains and stresses. Not all matchmakings, even those carefully matched, are problem-free, and the conflicts that result often need some assistance in order to be resolved. Governments can play a role in this area, for example by providing access to suitable management training and conflict-resolution mechanisms.

In the past, most activity in this regard has been bilateral, and been based on fairly traditional mechanisms of trade encouragement (e.g., trade missions). In recent years, international activity is emerging to encourage SME partnerships, especially amongst the Asia-Pacific Economic Cooperation (APEC) economies in the Asian region. To date, most of this activity has focused on the introduction stage -- how to get two potentially interested SMEs to meet. There has also been an increase in the number of private providers, and this is likely to continue with the development of global electronic commerce.

When it comes to encouraging linkages between SMEs, a variety of methods are used to introduce SMEs to potential partners, but they do not guarantee that the SMEs involved will actually link up. One emerging problem is the proliferation of means. There are so many different options for an SME seeking to explore a linkage that the SME manager may not have the necessary skills to determine which ones are more suitable or even reliable. Examples of these are:

- *Investment and trade missions.* In these, an investment-promotion agency invites a group of foreign SME managers to visit and meet with local SME managers. The activity is targeted at specific industries and countries. Thus, a mission of machine-tool producers from Japan or fruit canners based in Taiwan Province of China may be invited to visit and meet with suitable SMEs in a developing Asian country.

- *Conferences and investment/trade shows designed to encourage business matching.* These often have a theme or themes (e.g., focusing on particular industries or markets). They draw participants from many different countries together at a single location, where business-matching discussion can take place. Some Asian trade shows are already successful, for example the Global Business Opportunity Convention (GBOC) held in Osaka, and APB Net (APEC Business Opportunity Network) conferences. Both are held every year and have successfully offered introduction and trading opportunities to thousands of SMEs.

- *Electronic business-matching services.* These typically provide a service in which a list of potential partners can be viewed, and partners of interest are selected according to a set of criteria. This usually initially requires an access point (e.g., direct to the Internet or Web site, or via an accredited agent) which then allows potential partners to view-anonymously-limited details (also anonymous) on other potential partners with common interests. Before more details are released, it is necessary to declare identity and, in some cases, to have this verified by an accredited agent. Examples of such arrangements vary. For instance, UNISPHERE is one of the oldest and best-established electronic services designed to encourage linkages between high-technology firms seeking partners. Similar systems are operated by IBEX (International Business Exchange) and the Global Business Exchange, the latter being designed by chambers of commerce and designed specifically to accommodate the needs of SMEs in developing countries. Similarly, UNCTAD's Tradepoint system is primarily designed to facilitate trade opportunities, not FDI, but it is likely that firms using it will use it to seek investment opportunities as well. Also, ACTETSME (the APEC Centre for Technology Exchange and Training for SMEs) is exploring the use of electronic forums and meeting points. Finally, there are many bulletin boards and forums that encourage electronic introductions.

- *Chambers of commerce and other facilitators.* Some chambers of commerce provide introduction services, as well as facilitating trade missions; some bilateral chambers are set up primarily with this in mind. Similar services are being offered by export-import banks, accounting firms and a range of other facilitators.

- *Clustering programmes.* Clustering programmes have been used successfully in Europe for some time, especially as a means of encouraging the internationalization of SMEs. The usual model is for a manager to be appointed to help a cluster of SMEs to do business. Thus, a cluster may be formed of disparate SMEs which, together, can invest and produce products abroad, but which individually would not have the skills, contacts or time to do so. Although clustering is normally designed as a means of bringing together domestic firms, the same techniques can be used to encourage linkages across borders as well.

## D. Providing appropriate incentives

Incentives have often been used to attract FDI, but there are usually no specific incentives for SME FDI. Whether it is best practice to use incentives is questionable (UNCTAD, 1996; Lecraw, 1996). It can be argued that, in imperfect markets, the use of incentives can be justified as best practice, but the level and type of incentives depend very much on what other competing destinations are offering as incentives. The danger is that offering incentives can become a lose-lose situation where competing destinations simply bid to increase their share in FDI flows. The investors benefit, but it may not lead to a significant increase in investment or much net gain to the community.

Best practice thus requires that incentives:

- Be part of a broader strategy to encourage FDI and tailored to the development of target industries. More generally, this means that FDI should be directed at increasing the longer-term viability and growth of the economy. In a globalized world, this usually means encouraging greater international competitiveness. Since there are many routes and options for achieving this in a particular economy at a particular time, it requires some strategic focus to establish priorities.

- Be designed so that they actually have an additionality effect, i.e., they lead to investment that would not have otherwise taken place, and which generates greater benefits to the community than the costs of providing the incentives. This requires mechanisms to be in place which monitor the needs of client groups, and the impact of the incentives.

- Discourage rent seeking by clients. Rent seeking arises when the client SME engages in an activity primarily in order to obtain an incentive payment. Discouraging rent seeking requires policing, cost sharing and, performance-related payments, and sometimes requires that incentives be reversible, or have a sunset clause, so that they do not become permanent corporate social welfare.

- Be consistent with broader regional or multilateral agreements or practices, so that bidding wars between countries or regions are avoided. The increasing role of APEC in the Asian region means that incentive payments are more likely to be scrutinized carefully for their role in acting as non-tariff barriers.

All the leading countries in Asia have selectively used incentives to assist specific industries or firms. In most cases (Japan has been an exception until recently) incentives have also been used to encourage inward FDI. In many cases, they are contingent upon certain conditions (for example, they depend on the proportion of the output being exported, or on a certain volume of FDI) and are negotiable; this tends to discriminate against SME investors, who then receive relatively less by way of incentives.

Incentives typically provided to encourage FDI are typically divided into:

- *Fiscal incentives*, which usually involve governments' forgoing taxable revenue, including tax reductions (i.e., reductions in the rate of tax levied on foreign investors); tax holidays (taxes on investors are waived for several years after setting up); accelerated write-offs (depreciation is permitted at a higher rate than normal); and investment allowances (instead of an investment being depreciated, a proportion of it can be written off in the first year or so, and then the losses held over or sold to another firm).

- *Financial incentives*, which usually involve governments in subsidizing investor activity or forgoing income that would otherwise be earned by government agencies, including specific grants or subsidies (for installation of infrastructure or worker training); preferential loans (subsidized loans, or loans made more accessible to certain types of investor or investment); "peppercorn" leases (state property is leased at a nominal rate of rent); rent holidays (facilities in foreign trade zones, foreign access zones or industrial parks are offered rent-free for a period); and profit-repatriation rights (some foreign investors may be exempt from some profit-repatriation restrictions for a period).

- *Other incentives*, which include resource access and guarantees as regards the supply of inputs (power, water, labour, raw materials etc. provided to foreign investors on a priority basis); protective tariffs or quotas (import competition is restricted by tariffs and quotas and the market reserved for foreign investors); foreign exchange rights (restrictions on foreign exchange are waived or modified for foreign investors); and import rights (foreign investors are permitted to import machinery or raw materials which would otherwise be prohibited).

These incentives are sometimes targeted at specific segments of the economy, for example taking the form of special industry/region concessions (special incentives may be attached to particular industries or regions); incentives for subcontracting (incentives may be paid or given to large firms if local firms are given subcontract work), or for small and medium-scale industries (some industries are reserved only for SMEs); and export- or import-substitution programmes (incentives are offered to investors who generate exports or produce import substitutes). In some cases, incentives are a short-term solution to overcoming more difficult structural impediments. For example, if complex regulatory frameworks exist that restrict business generally (such as restrictions on the import of machinery, or licensing systems which limit competition), incentives may be a useful means of getting around this problem, by exempting foreign firms from the regulations or licensing requirements). Such incentives should really only be seen as a stopgap measure, which allow time for a gradual transition to an internationalized economy.

## E. Providing access to support services and infrastructure

Both SMEs and large firms require tangible and intangible infrastructure to provide a foundation for business development. Tangible infrastructure takes the form of ports, roads, bridges, railways, telecommunications systems etc. Intangible infrastructure includes education, management training, technical training, research and technology, banking systems, legal and regulatory systems etc. Without access to suitable infrastructure, firms are less likely to invest in the first place, and less likely to transfer benefits to the rest of the community. The infrastructure needs of foreign investors are not particularly different from those of domestic investors, but it is sometimes more economic to provide them with specific support services and infrastructure than to try to do so for the whole economy.

Most development planning tends to focus on tangible infrastructure associated with larger (and usually more profitable) engineering projects. There is usually enough inbuilt spare capacity in such projects to look after the needs of SMEs without any special planning for them (although sometimes they are unnecessarily discriminated against in terms of access itself, access charges and tariff rates). Intangible infrastructure is a rather different matter, and SMEs have needs that are important for development -- for example, technical and management training is a key aspect of the development of SMEs. Investment in intangible infrastructure does not offer the same profit as construction activity, and is often less appealing to aid agencies, even though it can provide good rates of social return.

Best practice seems to be that there is a mechanism in place that anticipates the needs of those investors a country is seeking to attract, and allows those support and infrastructure needs to be met in priority order. Examples of the sort of approaches to this are:

- One-stop or first-stop shops that handle foreign investment approvals, and also provide advice and assistance to foreign investors. This is now common practice in the Republic of Korea, Taiwan Province of China and Singapore.

- Programmes designed to develop appropriate skills or intangible infrastructure in conjunction with foreign companies and their needs. Singapore established joint industrial training centres with foreign investors and provided TNCs with incentives to train and upgrade the skills of workers, so that they had a reliable supply of skilled staff (Tan, 1996).

- Cooperation with trading companies (for example, the Japanese *sogo shosha*) to establish industrial zones or to assist in the development of subcontracting links and supply lines.

- Establishment of foreign trade zones, industrial zones, technology parks, incubators etc. which provide access to reliable infrastructure and allow guaranteed rights to power, water etc. This is an effective way of providing some certainty to investors and reducing their risk premiums. In many cases in Asia, industrial parks are increasingly being provided by large private companies working in conjunction with governments. These industrial parks are often designed to provide SMEs with ready access to suitable physical infrastructure.

## F. Addressing specific impediments and barriers to SME FDI

Foreign investors often face problems that inhibit their investment and impede the spin-off or transfer of benefits to the broader indigenous business community. For example, foreign investors might face problems finding suitable partners, obtaining access to reliable power and resource supplies, and finding skilled labour. Some problems are as much symptoms of a deeper problem as they are problems in their own right. For example, "difficulties finding a suitable partner" is sometimes just a symptom of "difficulties with access to property rights and tenure of land". If it is not possible for a foreign firm to own land, it must find a local partner, but it is more difficult to find a suitable partner when there is a considerable unsecured investment in property than it is if a partner is simply required to help overcome cultural differences in management approaches or distribution systems. In such circumstances it is useful to know what the more fundamental problem is, and the extent to which it impedes investment and growth. Only then can policy makers make informed decisions about the benefits and costs of addressing more fundamental issues and systemic problems.

SME FDI is not very different from that of large firms in the problems it faces, but there are more SMEs, and so it is harder to monitor them and their needs. In the case of large projects, the consequences are fairly apparent. For example, investors in a petrochemical plant, or a major build-operate-transfer infrastructure investment may make it clear that they will not proceed unless certain problems are addressed, and so the economy may stand to lose, say, $100 million in investment. With SMEs, the problems and issues may be much more diffuse; it is harder to keep track of 100 individual $1 million investors. Although the direct consequences may still be $100 million, the loss of spin-off benefits to the economy may be even greater if SMEs are discouraged by unnecessary problems and a failure to deal with them. For this reason, more systematic methods of monitoring the extent and size of problems become important for establishing government priorities.

Best practice seems to be to establish mechanisms that monitor and respond to the problems or impediments faced by foreign investors, and to integrate the findings into action plans to reduce more systemic problems. To some extent this is just part of a more fundamental issue of how to provide a good business environment (see chapter VI, section A), and how to provide administrative support and release the potential of SMEs (see chapter VI, section B). Monitoring mechanisms can be put in place through the following, for example:

- Chambers of commerce, international business associations (e.g., the ASEAN Chamber of Commerce and Industry) and bilateral business associations. Business associations and chambers of commerce are a common conduit for complaints by members to governments; most have regular meetings with relevant ministers or departments, at which key issues can be raised.

- Problem hotlines, and one-stop shops attached to boards of investment or relevant government agencies. These allow investors to raise issues directly with a government agency, usually the one responsible for foreign investment or trade. The problem is that the power of such an agency actually to do something to address fundamental issues may be quite limited, but it can at least alert other agencies to problems.

- Periodic surveys and reviews, usually by industry, and usually as part of a broader industrial development strategic planning exercise.

It needs to be stressed that such mechanisms are useless unless there is a political commitment to address the issues, and that they do not provide the information necessary to identify priorities for addressing impediments. In Part One, an attempt was made to compare the relative importance of a number of impediments and barriers faced by SMEs. This was supplemented by case studies of individual SMEs in order to provide an extensive list of impediments. The main conclusion was that these impediments vary widely between countries, and that often what is a major impediment to one SME may only be a minor nuisance (or even of assistance) to another. It is thus not sufficient just to know that something is an impediment. It is necessary to know to whom it is an impediment, and the extent to which it impedes investment. Without this knowledge it is impossible for governments in developing countries to allocate their limited resources to addressing those impediments that most limit their potential to attract SME FDI.

# CHAPTER VIII

## SPECIFIC POLICIES AND PROGRAMMES TO ENCOURAGE OUTWARD FDI BY SMEs IN ASIA

What can Asian home country governments do to encourage their SMEs to invest abroad, particularly in developing countries in Asia?  Responsibility for this lies with:

- *Governments.*  Most governments in the developed and more advanced developing Asian economies have policies to encourage exports and the internationalization of their firms (UNCTAD, 1995a).  These are usually a mix of fiscal, financial and other incentives, combined with a portfolio of services.  However, few if any of these policies are designed specifically for SMEs; even fewer policies are specifically designed to encourage SME FDI; and fewer again are targeted at increasing SME FDI in developing countries.

- *Regional/international organizations.*  Organizations such as UNCTAD, OECD, APEC, WTO and ASEAN all have an increasingly important role to play in building up a cooperative environment between governments.  It is the process of international cooperation that offers the greatest potential gains for developing countries, because it will open up possibilities for SMEs that would otherwise be difficult for them to size. Increasingly, there are limits on what governments can do unilaterally to encourage FDI without breaching more general best-practice policy.

Encouraging outward SME FDI involves much the same issues and challenges as those dealt with in relation to inward FDI by and/or in SMEs.  It too requires:

- General initiatives, which are part of a broader policy approach to internationalization, for example programmes to encourage the development of more internationally competitive SMEs.

- Specific initiatives aimed at those SMEs engaged in FDI, or with the potential to invest abroad, for example, to address impediments or systemic problems, or to provide specific incentives and financial support for such firms.

The main challenges, and the best-practice solutions to them, are summarized in table VIII.1, and then examined in more detail in the sections that follow. As with inward FDI, there is an overriding issue of how best to establish priorities so that the emphasis and mix of programmes and initiatives provide the greatest possible impact per unit of expenditure.

## A. Home country options

There are two broad avenues available for home countries to stimulate SME FDI, especially from and into developing countries:

- Focusing on their own SMEs -- for example, by helping to provide them with the necessary skills, financial services, incentives, information etc. to invest successfully and trade abroad.

- Focusing on host countries and their SMEs -- for example, by helping host countries to develop and implement policies to encourage their SMEs to be suitable partners for FDI, or to help host countries to identify and address impediments to SME FDI.

Why should countries encourage their SMEs to engage in FDI in developing countries? The main reasons are much the same as for any process of internationalization:

*Push factors.* Rising input costs (land, labour etc.) in some countries have meant that if SMEs are to remain internationally competitive, they must seek lower production costs. In Asia, this has been particularly apparent in Singapore and Taiwan Province of China. For Japan, the rising yen in the past decade has reduced the competitiveness of SMEs engaged in export and led to their seeking lower-cost bases for production. The increasing globalization of many SMEs has meant that competitive pressures are often greater. From a government perspective, encouraging such SMEs to invest abroad makes sense if it helps them survive and prosper as small and medium-sized TNCs. Even though this is sometimes perceived as encouraging a hollowing out of industries, it is often not so much a matter of exporting jobs as preventing bankruptcies and remaining competitive internationally.[1]

*Pull factors.* Growing market opportunities in developing countries (especially the larger economies such as China, Indonesia, India and Viet Nam) are often seen as a major incentive for SMEs to invest abroad. Similarly, large firms (especially in Japan and the Republic of Korea) have pulled along their subcontractor SMEs. From a government perspective, helping SMEs to pursue new market opportunities abroad, by FDI or by trade, is a means of encouraging growth that may not otherwise take place. In the longer term, it helps set the foundations for the TNCs of tomorrow.

*Management factors.* Management with an international view and the commitment and ability to internationalize is more likely to be successful when investing abroad. Encouraging enterprises to develop such management ability makes sense from a government point of view, because it opens up new growth opportunities. For example, Singapore and Taiwan Province of China have both taken advantage of their management resources (particularly ethnic Chinese managers) to encourage investment abroad.

**Table VIII.1. Best-practice policies for home countries
and international organizations to encourage SME FDI**

| Challenges | Best-practice solutions |
|---|---|
| How to encourage SMEs to invest abroad. | National: adapt support programmes (human resource development, finance, technology transfer etc.) to encourage SME FDI.<br>International: greater international cooperation on a range of policies and programmes designed to encourage exports, investment, technology transfer, recognition of quality standards, credit guarantees etc. |
| How to provide accurate information. | National: make information services more accessible and useful to SMEs seeking to invest abroad.<br>International: cooperation and sharing of information between providers. |
| How to encourage linkages between SMEs. | National: use a mix of channels to introduce potential partners.<br>International: joint initiatives on networking and business partnering. |
| How to provide appropriate incentives. | National: subject incentives to specific guidelines to make them as effective as possible.<br>International: cooperation possibilities to deal with excessive incentives competition. |
| How to encourage the development of appropriate infrastructure in host countries. | National: encourage large firms and invest directly in physical infrastructure. Assist developing countries with technical and other advice on intangible infrastructure for SMEs.<br>International: develop best-practice models for infrastructure development. |
| How to identify and reduce impediments to SMEs seeking to invest or internationalize and generally facilitate SME FDI. | National: identify and act on impediments in home country, bilateral liaison with host countries in cooperation with chambers of commerce, etc.<br>International: cooperation in setting up mechanisms to address impediments. Cooperation on means of monitoring the competitiveness of countries seeking to attract SME FDI. |

*Source:* UNCTAD.

The main reasons for *encouraging* SME FDI are thus that it opens up growth opportunities that may not otherwise be available, and that it could help make the home country's SME sector (or parts of it) more internationally competitive. Governments may also have reasons to *discourage* outward FDI by SMEs. For example, most of the advanced economies in the Asian region now face the political problems of SME FDI being seen to lead to "hollowing out". Similarly, the Republic of Korea has had approval processes that control FDI activity through foreign-exchange controls in the face of a serious current account deficit. Prior to 1986, it was difficult for individuals or smaller family-based SMEs to engage in outward FDI from the Republic of Korea, as all investors were required to obtain permission from the Bank of Korea. In 1986, a notification system was introduced to apply to investments of less than $0.2 million, for which approval was no longer needed. This level was later raised to $10 million. It is, however, still a requirement that an investing firm has to have at least 20 per cent of the overseas affiliate's equity, or meet other conditions (specifically, to have at least one person on the board of directors of the foreign affiliate, or sign a trading or technology-transfer contract).[2] This requirement may tend to discourage some forms of alliance-making by SMEs across borders.

On balance, in the longer term, the net benefits of encouraging SME FDI probably outweigh the benefits associated with discouraging it. Moreover, it should be recognized that SME FDI is different in some respects from FDI by large firms. Compared with large firms, SMEs investing abroad tend to be:

- affected disproportionately by the sunk or fixed costs associated with obtaining information (which then poses a barrier to entry);

- less likely to have in-house capability to deal with specific problems that occur and that may impede their development; and

- more likely to work with a local partner and to transfer technology.

There is thus a case for some special treatment of SME FDI. However, this may be better done by modifying SME policy to encourage those SMEs engaged in FDI, and not just by reviewing FDI policy. Most of the developed and more advanced developing economies in Asia already have programmes to assist SMEs, and the previous chapter showed how other countries can adopt polices to attract more SME FDI. For some areas (particularly providing information, and encouraging linkages between SMEs across borders), the policy lessons are basically the same for encouraging home-country SMEs to invest abroad. In other areas, it may be useful to adapt the policies more specifically to encourage outward SME FDI, including encouraging growth-oriented international SMEs, providing appropriate incentives, providing access to support services and infrastructure, and addressing specific impediments and barriers to SME FDI. Most of the more developed economies in Asia have adopted programmes to encourage their own companies to internationalize and to be more internationally competitive. The following thus focuses more on how initiatives in these four areas can be adapted specifically to encouraging SME FDI, and particularly to encouraging SMEs to invest in other countries, especially developing countries. In this respect, there are not many lessons that can be drawn on, simply because there has not been much by way of efforts to encourage SME FDI (as distinct from FDI generally), and even less by way of efforts to encourage SME FDI to other countries.

## 1. Adapting support programmes to encourage internationalization

Almost all the developed and more advanced developing economies in Asia now have fairly comprehensive support programmes to assist their SMEs. As outlined, the emphasis differs between economies, but all now have a strong internationalization aspect. Adapting these programmes to help SMEs to invest abroad, and to invest in developing countries, is a logical step. This is particularly relevant in the areas of human resource development, advisory services and management training, technology, technology transfer and technology sharing, and finance.

*(a)   Human resource development*

Human resource development programmes can help SMEs to engage in FDI successfully by being directed at:

- providing home country SMEs with the necessary information and skills to operate in a different country and culture; and

- providing opportunities for managers and staff of foreign SMEs to acquire skills and experience, either in the home country or in the host country.

For example, Japan, Singapore, the Republic of Korea and Taiwan Province of China all offer their SMEs access to consultancy services at subsidized rates to assist firms in evaluating and finding out about markets and labour conditions. Japan, in particular, provides country-by-country training courses to management personnel assigned to posts abroad, and a significant part of these courses is devoted to labour management and business practices in the host economy. These courses are offered by the Japan Small Business Corporation via its various SME training institutes. Similarly, Japan has offered training programmes for foreign trainees to promote technical cooperation. These are usually offered in cooperation with Japanese SME cooperatives, and chambers of commerce.

*(b)   Technology and technology transfer*

Technology transfer by home country firms can be facilitated by a range of initiatives, such as:

- bilateral agreements between countries on licensing and technology. These can help to provide increased security for the intellectual capital related to technology, and so tend to be relatively more important to smaller firms. The greater the number of agreements, the wider the protection offered;

- encouraging the use of franchise agreements and licensing agreements (e.g., by providing firms with the knowledge and legal basis to implement these in foreign countries), and encouraging systems to allow home firms to find suitable partners in foreign countries; and

- establishing databases or technology-exchange partnering systems. These systems allow home country firms to indicate technologies that they are willing to license to other firms, and allow firms in host countries to find suitable technology and partners to help them to finance and implement its introduction. Such systems are increasingly becoming more multilateral, but they still rely on support from home and host governments to provide access and encourage firms to participate.

*(c)   Finance, credit guarantees and insurance*

Investing abroad poses proportionally greater financial risks for SMEs than for larger firms because it is usually harder for SMEs to manage the risks. These risks tend to increase if the investment is in developing countries. The provision of forms of credit guarantees suited to SMEs and adaptable to developing countries is a major factor in encouraging SME FDI. For example, in the Republic of Korea, SMEs investing abroad are given slightly more favourable treatment in that they can obtain insurance against political risks for up to 95 per cent (as against 90 per cent for larger firms) of an investment from the Korea Export Insurance Corporation. Commercial banks can lend up to 80 per cent of the value of a project to SMEs (70 per cent in the case of larger firms). The Export-Import Bank of Taiwan Province of China gives SMEs up to 85 per cent coverage for insurance against political risks for approved investors investing abroad.

## 2. Providing appropriate incentives

All economies offer incentives for export and to a lesser extent to encourage outward FDI by their firms. Although these are not usually specific to SMEs, they can be used by them. These incentives are normally offered as part of a package of services. For example, partial subsidies may be given for market research and consultancy services associated with exploring a foreign market and establishing a market foothold. As noted, incentives have the potential to be distorting; their use needs to be justified on a case-by-case basis. In general, therefore, best practice for home countries (encouraging their SMEs to engage in outward FDI) regarding incentives is that they:

- be part of a broader strategy for increasing the international competitiveness of SMEs and of industry generally;

- have an additionality effect;

- discourage rent seeking; and

- be consistent with the spirit of broader multilateral (e.g., WTO, APEC, OECD) agreements.

Given the problems that they face in engaging in FDI, there may be a case sometimes for special incentives for SMEs. For example, the sunk costs associated with obtaining information (and the public goods aspects of information) may justify providing SMEs with subsidized information, or with subsidies to obtain information.

## 3. Supporting the development of infrastructure

Home countries can assist in the internationalization of SMEs by helping host developing countries to develop suitable infrastructure. This can be:

- in physical infrastructure n e.g., in the form of investment in business/industrial parks, telephone systems, road and transport infrastructure. By its very nature, this sort of infrastructure is of benefit to large firms as well as SMEs, regardless of whether they are foreign or domestic, and usually involves direct foreign aid or support for private sector infrastructure investment; and

- in intangible infrastructure n e.g., through directly assisting training and education programmes for SMEs, or less directly in the form of assistance to developing SME policies and programmes.

For example, Singapore has actively pursued a policy of regionalization since the late 1980s. It has established industrial parks in Suzhou (China), Bintan (Indonesia) and Bangalore (India), and has an agreement with Viet Nam to develop an industrial park. These parks are not designed specifically for SMEs, and they have not been markedly effective in attracting SMEs, but they do provide some SMEs (usually larger SMEs) with a secure environment in which to establish a physical presence in another country. These SMEs then, in turn, tend to subcontract out to local SMEs. Singapore has also initiated a S$ 1 billion programme in a Cluster Development Fund, targeted at cooperative ventures with TNCs in the region (e.g., with Daimler Benz in Viet Nam) and in Singapore. Singapore's Economic Development Board specifically seeks to develop Singaporean local enterprises through such investments, but there are spin-offs to other SMEs in the region as well.

Similarly, Japan and Singapore (since 1994) have offered a joint technical cooperation programme aimed at human resource development in developing countries. Although not specific to SMEs, it aims at providing technical support to the private sector in areas such as productivity improvement, quality management, worker participation, management training and supervisory training. The main purpose is to help managers and professionals in developing countries (mostly Asia and Africa) to better understand market systems and ways of managing resources more effectively.

## 4. Liaising to reduce impediments to SME FDI

Impediments to SME FDI can exist both in home countries (e.g. approval procedures, lack of understanding of financial risks in markets abroad) and in host countries (e.g., approval procedures, local regulatory requirements, corruption, lack of infrastructure).

### (a) Home countries

The most immediate role that governments can play in reducing impediments is to reduce regulatory impediments and complicated reporting and approval procedures. For example, since the mid-1980s the Republic of Korea has removed and simplified some of the regulatory impediments and approval procedures for outward FDI. This has made it easier for SMEs to invest abroad because, for investments of less than $10 million, a firm is required only to notify its choice of foreign exchange to the authorities, and no further approvals are required. The regulations were originally introduced as a means of foreign exchange control, and so their removal is mostly a matter of improved trading conditions, and the country's commitment to the OECD and APEC. Similarly, Taiwan Province of China has simplified and removed some of the reporting requirements for firms investing abroad (UNCTAD, 1995a). These were originally introduced as a means of monitoring and controlling the pattern of strategic investment by its firms so as to prevent excessive dependence on particular areas.

### (b) Host countries

Host countries may need liaison in order to address impediments in their own countries. At present, most efforts at liaison to reduce the impediments faced by SMEs are initiated by complaints made by SMEs themselves, either directly to government or via a bilateral or other channel such as joint chambers of commerce. For example, a Singaporean SME having problems with bureaucracy in Viet Nam, or with a partner absconding in China, may approach the Government of Singapore or the Singapore Confederation of Industry for assistance. The problem can sometimes be resolved by their approaching a counterpart organization for help and advice.

Alternatively, a problem may be raised via diplomatic channels, for example in communications between trade attachés or, more formally, via ministry communications. However, anecdotal evidence suggests that SMEs are often unwilling to raise complaints via official channels, because they tend to believe that such complaints are unlikely to carry much weight in official negotiations and thus are unlikely to be solved. Rather, it is more likely that their complaints will be simply passed down to the authorities about which they are complaining, thus making their situation possibly even more difficult.

## B. International policy options

International bodies and international cooperation organizations in the Asian region, such as APEC and ASEAN, have endeavoured to move towards more liberalized investment regimes, but they have not focused specifically on SME investment. General moves towards investment liberalization benefit both SMEs and large firms. In addition, many international agencies -- such as UNCTAD, UNIDO, ESCAP, ADB and the World Bank -- have initiated technical and aid programmes directed at developing SMEs. For example, UNIDO provides an extensive package of services aimed at developing an infrastructure of programmes for assisting entrepreneurs and SMEs. These programmes are important to the longer-term development of a good business environment (see chapter VI, section A), and thus in providing a foundation for internationally oriented SMEs. However, SMEs investing abroad face some special barriers and impediments, and these are not necessarily overcome by broadly based liberalization moves. The focus of this section is thus on what multilateral initiatives can possibly do, beyond broad liberalization moves and the provision of technical support to developing local SMEs, to facilitate SME FDI.

### 1. Cooperation on joint-support programmes and other initiatives

The more developed economies in Asia already have comprehensive support programmes for SMEs. Some other economies are in the process of developing such systems. International cooperation between SME policy makers is still in its infancy, but there is considerable potential for it to expand. Such cooperation can have three main advantages:

- It can lead to the adoption of better programmes, by allowing governments to benchmark and learn from each other's experiences. For example, since 1995 APEC has hosted a policy-level group devoted to SME issues. This has facilitated the exchange of information about policy initiatives and allowed officials to learn from the experiences of others. Staff-exchange programmes can also assist in this regard.

- It can lower programme costs by sharing information and infrastructure. For example, once training programmes are developed, they can be offered to developing countries, thus saving them the development costs. Internet access to web pages is making it easier for SMEs in developing countries to access the advice and training packages available in developed countries.

- It can help to harmonize regulations and to simplify regulatory burdens. Some regulations act as impediments to FDI. For example, efforts are being made by international finance providers (e.g., the Export-Import Banks of the United States and Canada) to work with finance providers in other countries to facilitate lending for investment and the international development of SMEs. The United States Export-Import Bank may extend a line of credit to finance providers in a host country, to be used to assist local SMEs. However, in some countries loans by an export-import bank to a local SME (or to a partnership of a local and foreign SME) are subject to withholding taxes on interest. This can be quite high (in the order of 25 per cent or more) and makes a significant difference to the cost of the loan. Cooperation in the form of bilateral tax treaties, and multilateral initiatives to develop models for bilateral agreements can assist in providing credit-guarantee facilities to SMEs (Kaiser, 1996). A similar potential exists for regulatory harmonization in areas such as standards (for things such as labelling, packaging, and electronic data interchange protocols), customs-clearance procedures, business registration and reporting, copyright and patent registration.

## 2. Cooperation in networking, information systems and global commerce

It is important for SMEs engaged in international investment to have access to information and, for some, to have access to partners. Governments can unilaterally provide services in this regard; but in an increasingly globalized world it makes more sense for these services to be offered cooperatively. International cooperation can assist in making it easier for SMEs to access information about markets, investment opportunities, partners and networking opportunities. This opens up a wider range of opportunities for SMEs wishing to invest abroad. Also, it can help to reduce the costs to governments of providing services in such areas as business matching, technology transfer and market information.

Global electronic commerce has the potential to allow SMEs to reduce transaction costs associated with shifting money, obtaining finance from abroad and accessing a much wider range of services (such as trade documentation, electronic data interchange, risk management, information, specialized advice and consulting). It has the potential to make it much easier for smaller companies to expand and manage businesses across borders, including through FDI. Cooperation by governments to adopt common protocols (e.g., for data transfer, forms, registration procedures) will be important if global commerce is to be of much use to smaller companies. The UNCTAD's Global Trade Point Network (GTPNet) is a worldwide Internet-based network of Trade Points that provides trade information and facilitates the exchange of electronic trade opportunities. The UNTPDC web page (//www.unicc.org/untpdc) contains information of the developments of the GTPNet.

The World Bank's Multilateral Investment Guarantee Agency (MIGA) has recently launched a global investment marketplace, IPAnet (//www.ipanet.net) on the world wide web. This is intended to provide a "shopping mall" for one-stop global investment. It is designed to provide ready access to investment intermediaries, private investors and technology providers.

## 3. International cooperation on regimes for investment and market access

International cooperation, such as that in process within the APEC with respect to rules, regulations and practices related to investment, will generally improve the environment for FDI, and thus for SME FDI as well. SMEs are likely to benefit more from international cooperation.

However, there are some specific issues of liberalization that perhaps warrant more attention, precisely because they create unnecessary barriers to the contestability of markets by SMEs. Access to markets across borders is obviously important to SMEs, and especially important to growth-oriented, innovative SMEs in smaller economies. A survey by the Pacific Economic Cooperation Council suggests that about 78 per cent of services industries in the APEC region are effectively closed to international transactions (1995, p.11) . SMEs are heavily represented in the services sector, and the functions they need to move across borders are often services functions. Since many successful internationalized SMEs work in partnership with other SMEs, these impediments may be significant. The APEC Non-Binding Investment Principles (UNCTAD, 1996a) provide a foundation for more specific work that addresses the issue of SME FDI, and also provide a "best-practice guide" for economies to follow.

## 4. International cooperation to identify and reduce barriers to SME FDI

A major issue facing SMEs are impediments to their international activity. In addition to tariff barriers and customs regulations, a host of factors may limit market access, intentionally or unintentionally: approval procedures, the costs of establishing a legal entity, the difficulties in using flexible organizational arrangements (such as alliances or franchises), immigration restrictions on the use of skilled staff, protection of brand names or techniques or innovative processes or products, cultural impediments to distribution channels or resources, corrupt local officials, and so on. Although it is not always possible for governments to do something about such impediments, it is useful to know of their existence. At present, there is no way of knowing how significant they are, what problems they cause, or what opportunities are lost because of them.

If a smaller firm faces impediments to FDI activity, it can:

- Give up, or find another way to get round the problem. This is probably the most common approach, but it is not known how much potential investment is lost as a result, or how much is lost in unnecessary transaction and search costs.

- Make representations via existing channels in its home economy, such as approaching a government office direct or through an industry organization (e.g., a chamber of commerce). The complaint or suggestion is then forwarded via normal diplomatic channels on a bilateral basis. The problem with this is that as SMEs are small, individual complaints at the bilateral level are easy to ignore or get lost amongst bigger issues. SMEs are thus often wary about initiating anything where they feel that their formal complaint may lead to retaliation; they usually have little to gain and much to lose from making their complaint known via formal diplomatic channels. Bilateral approaches also make it hard to monitor whether the issues are more widespread, and thus there is less incentive to look for more effective broader initiatives. For example, none of the chambers contacted for this study could provide any broad overview of the nature and extent of the complaints, or potential complaints.

- Initiate legal or formal procedures in the economy concerned. Only a very small minority of SMEs adopt this approach, and it is usually less than satisfactory. In some countries, recourse to such methods is regarded as a major failure in itself.

If there was some channel by which SMEs could report difficulties without causing a dispute with a host government, it would be much easier for international organizations to identify key issues as they emerge, and to address them. This could be done, for example, via APEC's APB Net, supplemented by other industry associations (chambers of commerce, APEC's PBEC, bilateral friendship associations etc.), which could channel submissions to a central register, which could in turn be reviewed regularly by an international panel of experts and officials. Feasibility studies are, indeed, under way on an APEC notification system.

## 5. Assisting countries in monitoring their competitiveness in attracting SME FDI

Governments increasingly compete to attract FDI. For large firms and large projects, the investors and their financiers make it clear to governments if particular locations are not competitive. International financial and risk-rating agencies also assist in this regard. It is much harder for governments to monitor how competitive they are when it comes to attracting SME FDI. SMEs are more diverse, and there are more of them. If governments want to attract SME FDI, it is important for them to know how their locations perform relative to their competitors' locations. How can governments monitor their competitiveness and how might international agencies help them to do so? There seem to be two main ways:

- *Systematic comparison of government regulations, incentives and services.* The attractiveness of a destination for SME FDI, relative to other destinations, can be affected by government regulations, incentives and services. A systematic means of comparing these would make it easier for governments to see where they stand. For example, the withholding tax on profits may be lower in other destinations, or regulations relating to approvals may be less complex, or foreign SMEs may have automatic access to financial and advisory services in some destinations. This information can be collected by any government; however, there is an advantage in having an international agency regularly collect and put together a comparison of participating countries, based on a common format. APEC currently reviews the investment regimes of its member economies each year, and publishes the results. However, that survey is primarily concerned with regulations; a broader ambit which would allow a comparison of incentives and services accessible to SMEs is necessary for comparing locational attractiveness.

- *Monitoring of SME perceptions of impediments and assistance.* For governments seeking to attract more SME FDI, and to compete with other destinations, it is also useful to know:

    - How attractive do SME investors and potential investors rate a particular economy or market as a destination for investment? For example, does a sample of potential SME investors see a country as being more attractive than another, or vice versa?

    - What impediments do foreign SME investors face or perceive? For example, what proportion of existing investors have major problems with corruption, or what proportion of potential investors have a poor view of the investment prospects in a given country on the basis of their knowledge about volatile conditions and lack of a systematic legal framework?

    - What forms of assistance do foreign SMEs see as being helpful? For example, if business partnering and matching services are seen as helpful by many firms, this may justify devoting more resources to expanding those services in order to attract more SME FDI.

Some of these issues were reviewed in Part One. Much of this information can be collected directly by governments -- for example, by using sources such as boards of investment, one-stop shops and chambers of commerce. However, comparisons would be facilitated by a more independent approach which would permit systematic surveying of SMEs in a range of participating countries. This could be done in collaboration with chambers of commerce, and based on a common format.

# Notes

[1]  According to one SME manager, "setting up overseas has cost jobs here; we now only employ 50 per cent of the people we used to; but the fact is that if we had not set up overseas, we would not be employing anyone here. As it is, we have doubled our total workforce (i.e., at home and abroad) and more than doubled our revenue".

[2]  This, however, is not required in the following cases: the executive director is appointed by the Republic of Korea investor to serve on the board of the corporation invested in; a sales contract (longer than a year) is signed for raw materials or products from the home country; and either a contract to provide or introduce essential manufacturing technology, or a contract for joint research development, is signed.

# Annex to Part Two

## The portfolio of SME services and programmes in selected Asian economies

How governments have sought to help SMEs overcome problems is illustrated in this annex, which examines the portfolio of services offered by leading Asian economies. The key points emerging out from the experience of these economies are that:

- all of them have quite comprehensive programmes of assistance for their SMEs;
- although the programmes are organized in different ways, and the emphasis and method of delivery vary, they all share a common emphasis on certain key aspects such as finance and technology; and
- all of them have a strong emphasis on increasing the international competitiveness of their SMEs, although how this is done varies.

### Japan

Japan's portfolio of services is the most comprehensive in Asia and reflects the importance attached by this country to SMEs. It also reflects the need to internationalize the SME sector. In recent years, special attention has been paid to SMEs in the retail and wholesale trade, to adjust to structural reforms in the economy precipitated by recent changes in government regulations and competitive pressures. Programmes and services for SMEs are listed and described below.

*Programmes* aimed at strengthening the management base of SMEs, and designed to rectify the social and economic disadvantages that SMEs face, and to provide an environment that makes SMEs become more competitive.

- Organization (Law on Small and Medium Enterprise Organization, Law on Cooperative Association)
- Management guidance:
  - Diagnosis and guidance (by consultants, prefectural governments etc.)
  - Technical guidance (by public research and testing institutions etc.)
  - Human resource education and training (Japan Small Business Corporation (JSBC) etc.)
  - Information provided to SMEs (Japan Small Business Corporation, JETRO etc.)
- Subcontracting:
  - Law promoting subcontracting by SMEs (Law on Promotion of Subcontracting Small and Medium Enterprises)
  - Law preventing delays in the payment to subcontractors (Law on the Prevention of Delay in the Payment of Subcontracting Charges and Related Matters)
- Credit guarantee

*Programmes* aimed at supporting structural reform, designed to facilitate the adaptation of SMEs to changes in the social and economic environment and to assist in structural reform of SMEs.

- Measures by industry:
  - Modernization (e.g., the Small and Medium Enterprises Modernization Promotion Law)
  - Rationalization of distribution:
    - Measures for SME wholesalers
    - Measures for SME retailers
    - Measures for efficient distribution
- Measures by issue:
  - Integrated development of SMEs (Extraordinary Law Concerning Promotion of the Development of New Business Areas through Fusion of Knowledge of SMEs in Different Industries)

- Promotion of the development of new business areas and the fusion of knowledge

- Shortening of work time and assistance in securing human resources:
  - Measures for shorter working time
  - Law relating to improved management and securing of labour force (Law Concerning the Improvement of Employment Management Aimed at Securing a Labour Force for Small and Medium Enterprises)
- Technological development:
  - Technology development and promotion for SMEs
  - Assistance measures
  - Development of suitable technology by public institutes
- Environmental issues
- Internationalization:
  - Encouragement of FDI:

Provision of information on overseas investment opportunities
  Consulting guidance (Japan Chamber of Commerce and Industry, JSBC)
  Employment information on overseas employment and recruitment (JSBC)
  Exchange of information on overseas investment (JETRO)
  Information on overseas investment opportunities (JSBC)
  Overseas investment promotion missions (JETRO, Japan Chamber of Commerce and Industry)
Human resources
  Reception and training of foreign employees/trainees
Financing
  Financing for overseas investment (government-affiliated financial organizations)
  Funds for overseas investment (Japan Overseas Development Council)
Projects to facilitate import and export
  Provision of information, e.g., research on overseas markets, trade fairs, displays etc. (JETRO)
  Import promotion (JETRO, JSBC)
  Financing, e.g., provision of finance for promotion of imported goods (Small Business Finance Corporation, the People's Finance Corporation)
  Commercial arbitration, e.g., processing of claims related to international trade by SMEs (International Commercial Arbitration Association)
Projects for foreign trainees
  Joint training programmes for foreign trainees
  Programmes to support foreign trainees
Projects for overseas public relations
  International exchange programmes
  Overseas public relations for SMEs
Projects for international design exchange

- Promotion of local SMEs:
  Measures for local industry readjustment
  Law to organize and activate SMEs (e.g., cooperatives; Law to Organize and Activate Specified Small and Medium Enterprises)

*Programmes* aimed at promoting small-scale enterprises: these are specific programmes designed to supplement other programmes in addressing the needs of micro enterprises with only a few employees.

- Guidance
- Small-enterprise mutual relief projects

### Republic of Korea

The Small and Medium Business Administration (SMBA) of the Republic of Korea was established only in 1996. It comprises headquarters, 11 regional offices and the National Institute of Technology and Quality, as well as the following four major bureaus:

*The Assistance Coordination Bureau* provides general services, including provision of financial and human resources, start-up services, and business and international cooperation. Furthermore, it operates a number of programmes to foster internationalization through for example:
- the Korean Trade-Investment Promotion Agency (KOTRA), which provides information on opportunities abroad, including for investment;
- training programmes and consultants to assist SMEs in dealing with foreign buyers;
- providing opportunities for participation in trade shows and international exhibitions;
- general programmes to improve quality and lower the defect rate in production; and
- credit guarantees and loans.

*The Technology Bureau* is in charge of technology development, technology cooperation, technology assistance and technology evaluation.

*The Industry Bureau* looks after the interests of SMEs in various specific industries, such as machinery, metals, electrics and electronics, textiles and clothing, chemicals and consumer goods.

*The Distribution and Logistic Bureau* encourages joint use of warehouses and distribution centres, and looks after wholesale marketing, general business retailing and speciality business.

Information services for Republic of Korea outward investors are provided as follows:

- *KOTRA* has 82 overseas Korea Trade Centers in 64 countries that are linked via Global Network, a computer-based system to disseminate information quickly and efficiently. It can assist SMEs through a range of services, including information on general economic trends, regulations and policies in foreign markets, coordinating trade fairs and exhibitions, and providing the Strategic Marketing Initiative programme which facilitates export to and entry into foreign markets.

- *The Korean Brand Export Support Centre* offers information on registration and development of trade marks, and on improving the quality and recognition of Republic of Korea products.

- *The Export-Import Bank of Korea* provides a free service (Overseas Investment Information Service) on-line, which covers such things as FDI procedure in each country, general information on specific countries, conditions for FDI in each country, the Republic of Korea's FDI policy and rules, the situation of Republic of Korea companies investing in each country, standard documentation and forms required, and a list of companies that hope to joint-venture with Republic of Korea companies.

- *The Korean Foreign Trade Association* is a non-profit private organization to promote international trade for Republic of Korea firms. Most Republic of Korea firms engaged in international trade are members. Its services to members include business inquiry services using a database that can be searched for Republic of Korea suppliers for specific product or technology inquiries, seminars on investment opportunities abroad, and trade shows and exhibitions.

## Taiwan Province of China

Taiwan Province of China uses guidance systems that are coordinated by the Small and Medium Enterprises Agency. Each of these guidance systems is implemented by public and private organizations. A services network delivers the programmes under the different to regional centres in Taiwan Province of China. There is no specific guidance system for the internationalization of SMEs; rather, this is integrated through the 10 guidance programmes, with specific aspects being dealt with by different guidance cells. For example, an internationalizing SME may seek advice on international management which may be delivered by the China Productivity Centre; international credit guarantee facilities may be provided by the Small and Medium Business Credit Guarantee Fund, and so on. The 10 Guidance Centres are:

- finance n providing finance and assistance and advice to SMEs in financial management;
- management n setting up management systems, improving management efficiency and improving human resources development;
- production technology n improving technology and productivity and adopting new technologies;
- research and development n supporting research-and-development efforts;
- information management n assisting in computerization and the use of databases and sophisticated information management systems;
- marketing n helping SMEs to gather the necessary market intelligence;
- industrial safety n establishing and improving industrial and worker safety systems;
- pollution prevention n assistance in resolving pollution control problems and in improving pollution control facilities;
- mutual support and cooperation guidance n encouraging SMEs to work cooperatively and to engage in joint activities to boost their competitiveness;
- quality enhancement n improving product and service quality and quality management systems.

## Singapore

Singapore offers SMEs a range of programmes that are designed to help firms to go through various stages, from start-up to internationalization. These have been coordinated by the Economic Development Board (EDB), although some of the responsibility for smaller enterprises is now the domain of the Productivity and Standards Board (PSB — previously the National Productivity Board). A multi-agency approach is used to deliver programmes, including the following:

- export development and internationalization, delivered through the Trade Development Board, the EDB and PSB;
- technology programmes, delivered via the Singapore Institute of Standards and Industrial Research in conjunction with polytechnics and universities;
- computerization programmes, delivered by the National Computer Board and the Enterprise Promotion Centres (usually joint arrangements with foreign TNCs);
- automation programmes, delivered by the Automation Applications Centre;
- training and human resource development programmes, delivered by the PSB, the National Computer Board and the EDB.

Examples of programmes that have been or continue to be offered under these broad groups of programmes are:

*Start-up:*

    Local enterprise computerization programme
    Local enterprise finance programme
    Product development assistance scheme
    Research-and-development incubator
    Skills development fund
    Venture capital

*Growth:*

    ISO 9000 certification
    Local enterprise technical assistance scheme
    Local enterprise finance scheme
    Local industry upgrading programme
    Market and investment development assistance
    Product development assistance
    Software development

*Expansion:*

    Automation leasing scheme
    Brand development assistance
    Business development
    Franchise development
    Pioneer status (giving tax relief to firms setting up and introducing new technology)
    Investment allowances
    Promising local enterprise scheme
    Total business planning

*Going overseas:*

    Enterprise financing scheme in overseas investment
    Overseas enterprise incentive
    Overseas investment incentive
    Double deductions for overseas investment development expenditure
    Overseas business development scheme
    Market development assistance scheme

*Source:* UNCTAD.

# PART THREE

# TECHNICAL COOPERATION MANUAL: PRACTICAL MEASURES TO ASSIST SME INVESTORS

# INTRODUCTION

## HOW TO USE THIS MANUAL

This part of the *Handbook* contains a number of practical measures designed to enhance the skills of national policy makers from developing countries in Asia in formulating policies and programmes to attract foreign direct investment (FDI) by small and medium-sized enterprises (SMEs) and to maximize the contribution of SME FDI to development. The manual is divided into three main sections. Chapter IX provides guidelines to help policy makers to appraise the benefits and costs of alternative programmes for encouraging increased SME FDI. Chapter X suggests policy options available to increase SME FDI, based on what appear to be "best practice" characteristics of policy, focusing mainly on initiatives that can be pursued in developing host countries. Chapter XI suggests initiatives that may be pursued in cooperation with the principal Asian home countries of SME outward investors, or in cooperation with international agencies. In chapters IX and X, first the rationale for each main group of initiatives is briefly explained. Specific practical measures or steps are then described which could assist in increasing SME FDI, and increasing its contribution to development. Issues are discussed that need to be taken account of in order to assess the appropriateness of initiatives to particular situations, and to increase the success and effectiveness of measures.

Host country governments seeking to use SME FDI as a means for development have a wide array of options from which to choose. Table 1 gives a summary overview of the main actions available to host country governments in developing countries to encourage more SME FDI. The broad options available for increasing inward SME FDI, and the likely impact can be seen as a simple scale, as set out below:

| Policy options | | |
|---|---|---|
| Do nothing. | Target specific initiatives at impediments to SME FDI, and provide incentives etc. | Comprehensive strategy aimed at international integration and developing the SME sector. |

| Likely impact on SME FDI | | |
|---|---|---|
| SME FDI likely to grow at 10-30% per annum. | Impact fairly immediate (one to two years; 25-50% per annum growth), but may not be sustained. | Potential for large increases in SME FDI (e.g., 100%), but takes several years to implement and requires longer-term strategic commitment. |

It can be reasonably assumed that, in the absence of policy initiatives for increasing it, SME FDI is likely to grow in line with FDI trends generally. Although this obviously depends on the economy in question, expected growth rates of 10 to 30 per cent per annum may not be unreasonable, judging from recent FDI growth. However, SME FDI may not increase as a proportion of total FDI.

In the short term, it should be possible to achieve relatively higher increases in SME FDI of, say, 25 to 50 per cent per annum by more directed initiatives targeted specifically at SME investors, such as addressing impeding regulations, providing specific incentives for SME FDI, and providing targeted information to investors. The danger is that these initiatives may be addressing symptoms, but not underlying factors, in which case the SME FDI growth is not sustainable. The initiatives may lead only to a spurt of increased investment, which then drops off again as reality reveals a less attractive fundamental investment picture.

To have a sustained impact on development, especially in countries in which the absence of a large group of SMEs is a significant structural problem, increases in SME FDI of 100 per cent per annum or more may be needed. To achieve such rates requires a fairly comprehensive programme of activities that serves to integrate the country with the rest of the world, thus making it easier for SMEs to invest and do business across borders. This sort of programme requires time to implement and to show results, and so it requires a longer-term view and a strategic commitment to the development of the SME sector as a whole.

There is no standard recipe to follow for increasing SME FDI. The situation facing each government is different. The best way to use this manual is therefore to review the summary of options available (table 1; see also Part Two); to review the existing planning mechanisms in comparison with the framework set out in this Part, in particular the practical steps for assessing policy options; to review the monitoring, performance and planning measures in chapter IX; and to use the practical suggestions and considerations in chapters X and XI as a guide to what initiatives are most likely to be appropriate to the particular circumstances and objectives.

### Table 1. What can governments do to attract more SME FDI?

| Actions | Reasons |
|---|---|
| **Establish monitoring and performance systems** | |
| • Set development objectives and targets.<br>• Assess contribution of SMEs to development.<br>• Develop SME FDI strategic plan.<br>• Make best-practice policy comparisons.<br>• Make international comparisons regarding attractiveness of locations | Attracting SME FDI is a means to development, not an end in itself. To ensure that SME FDI contributes as much as possible to development requires coordination and planning of initiatives. |
| **Develop the local SME entrepreneurial engine** | |
| • Establish SME basic law/SME strategic plan.<br>• Identify target SMEs to benefit from FDI.<br>• Establish an able coordinating SME agency.<br>• Work with developed countries on programmes.<br>• Promote stable growth<br>• Build transparent legal, regulatory system. | For SME FDI to contribute to development it is necessary to "prepare the garden" so that local SMEs can take advantage of opportunities offered by the entry of SME FDI. Some local SMEs make better targets for assistance than others. |
| **Provide SME investors with access to information** | |
| Design and target a suitable mix of trade shows, trade and investment missions, first-stop or one-stop shops, business associations, facilitators and trading companies, trade publications, web sites, key-entry sites, and other national investment and trade promotion organizations. | Information is essential for SME investors to make decisions. Lack of accurate and timely information is a barrier to SME FDI. |
| **Encourage linkages/networks with SMEs abroad** | |
| Develop a programme of matchmaking conferences and electronic matchmaking services by chambers of commerce and/or bilateral associations. Encourage clustering and networking, work with major contractors and trading companies, encourage franchising and licensing, and assist in appropriate regulation of networks. | Much of SME FDI depends on the investor finding a suitable local partner, in or jointly with whom to invest. Encouraging opportunities to make linkages with SMEs abroad reduces the chance element in this search process. |
| **Use appropriate incentives** | |
| Design a mix of fiscal, financial and other incentives, ensuring that benefits exceed costs. | Incentives offer a fast way of attracting more FDI, including SME FDI. However the costs, especially the hidden costs, can easily outweigh the benefits of their use. |
| **Provide investors with access to support services** | |
| • Advice from one-stop shops, first-stop shops.<br>• Skill-development programmes.<br>• Infrastructure in industrial zones, foreign trade zones etc.<br>• Credit guarantee arrangements. | It can be very cost-effective to have support services designed specifically to help SMEs from foreign countries to cope with temporary problems. |

/...

**(Table 1, cont'd)**

| Actions | Reasons |
|---|---|
| **Address impediments to SME FDI** | |
| Set up mechanisms to identify impediments and review options for dealing with common impediments in the short and the longer term. Help SMEs to cope with impediments. | Impediments (such as corruption, or difficult approval procedures etc.) to FDI are often systemic, but if they are not dealt with they are a significant barrier to SME FDI. |
| **Make use of international cooperation at bilateral and multilateral levels** | |
| • Technical assistance programmes.<br>• Accessing information and other networks.<br>• Adopting international standards.<br>• International monitoring. | Cooperation with other governments and with international agencies offers developing countries access to a range of measures to facilitate SME FDI. |

*Source:*   UNCTAD.

# CHAPTER IX

## MECHANISMS TO APPRAISE THE POTENTIAL BENEFITS AND COSTS OF INCREASED SME FDI

Encouraging SME FDI involves both costs and benefits. The challenge facing policy makers is to design policy initiatives to derive the greatest net benefit from SME FDI. There is no simple recipe for this; it is a matter of each government tailoring its policies to the circumstances and to its strategic needs. This chapter sets out a basic framework to assist host country governments in appraising the options available to them, as well as a series of steps or mechanisms for assessing the costs and benefits of programme alternatives.

### A. A basic framework for assessing benefits and costs of SME FDI

FDI in general has now gained widespread acceptance as a useful means for facilitating development -- which suggests that the benefits of attracting more FDI are quite high in comparison with the costs involved. Similarly, SME FDI is expected to emerge as an attractive and effective means of developing a more competitive and flexible economic base. For some developing countries in Asia this makes SME FDI especially important. It is clear from Part One that the potential is there to increase SME FDI quite significantly. From Part Two, it is clear that governments have a wide range of policy options for encouraging more SME FDI, but there is no point in encouraging SME FDI for its own sake -- the benefits of attracting more SME FDI must exceed the costs involved.

Governments can pursue policies that maximize the net benefits of SME FDI only if they are able to assess the benefits associated with SME FDI and can compare these with the costs of various policy options. This requires some understanding of the benefits associated with SME FDI, and the policy options for increasing SME FDI as well as their likely impact and cost.

## 1. The benefits from SME FDI

The benefits which arise from SME FDI are both direct and indirect, public and private. These are illustrated in the matrix below. SME FDI is associated with transfer of technology, management and other skills, and training. Although the variations are large in a typical SME FDI, the flow of equity funds usually amounts to less than $1 million, the value of technology flows to about half of that, and that of training, to around $100,000 (see Part One). The technology and training flows may be in kind, not in the form of a flow of funds. In crude terms, every 100 additional SME investors attracted are likely to inject the equivalent of about $160 million of direct and indirect gross private benefits into a host economy.

The immediate benefits from SME FDI are private, and they take the form of returns from investment opportunities that would otherwise not be available. In the longer term there also are indirect private benefits associated with having a foreign equity position, because it gives access to intangible assets, including training and technology, thus increasing productivity and the chances of success. The private benefits of SME FDI in host economies presumably outweigh the private costs (e.g., costs of the dividends payable on foreign equity, and loss of some degree of control), because otherwise FDI would not occur. The immediate benefits are likely to be relatively modest. SME FDI is quite small relative to total FDI flows, and even if it can be increased by 100 per cent will still be relatively modest. As shown in Parts One and Two, the potential exists to increase SME FDI quite significantly if appropriate policy measures are adopted.

| | Direct (immediate) benefits | Indirect (long-term) benefits |
|---|---|---|
| Private benefits | Additional returns (to investors in the SME ventures, employees and input providers) due to new investment and production opportunities and better utilization of existing investment/ production opportunities because of immediate additional access to funds, technology and training. | Access to technology and training increases, eventually, chances of success and productivity of new and future ventures.<br><br>Multiplier effects from investment. |
| Public benefits | No significant benefits (except some tax revenues). | Technology and productivity spillovers through forward and backward linkages, turnover of employees and competition.<br><br>Increased base of entrepreneurial activity -- enhanced entrepreneurial engine. |

The public or social benefits tend to be more indirect and intangible, and take time to materialize. The potential social benefits from SME FDI are large. As argued in Part One, as much as 70 per cent of growth can come from SMEs, and most of this from the entrepreneurial engine that SMEs provide. Without this entrepreneurial base (the "missing middle") developing countries have lower sustainable growth, based on low-cost industries. FDI creates opportunities for other firms; for example, an investment in a new factory or hotel leads to opportunities in construction for other indigenous firms that supply to (or buy from) the new enterprise, as well as spillovers of, for example, technology or knowledge yielding benefits beyond those reflected in the flows of payments between the FDI enterprise and the related firms. Similarly, in the longer term, SME FDI provides local entrepreneurs with management skills and experience that would not otherwise be available, and leads to a stronger entrepreneurial base. SME FDI is more likely to lead to multiplier effects through linkages to local industry, whereas large-firm FDI is more likely to "leak" back out of the economy in imports. SME FDI can also lead to the growth of medium-sized firms which fill the missing middle, and it can help provide a flexible, internationally competitive supply industry.

## 2. Policy options, impact and cost

For governments to intervene to increase SME FDI requires that the potential public benefits outweigh the costs of intervention. The role of host country governments in increasing the benefits from SME FDI is twofold:

- First, governments can actively encourage a greater volume of SME FDI. For example, by reducing impediments to SME FDI (e.g., by making regulatory processes more simple and flexible) or by actively providing a more conducive business environment in which to invest, they may be able to increase the number of SME investments, thus increasing the resource flows of capital, technology and skills.

- Second, governments can take steps to encourage more public benefits to flow from SME FDI. For example, they may encourage SME investors to provide more management training to local staff by means of fiscal incentives, and cooperation in developing training programmes and management training institutions. Similarly, if a government sees a need to develop a technologically advanced supply-industry capability, it may seek to attract SME FDI from suitable foreign SMEs as a means of building up that capability.

There are several options as regards policy measures for increasing the benefits from SME FDI (chapter X). In isolation, none will necessarily have much impact. For example, just increasing the information available to potential SME investors, or just providing fiscal incentives to invest, will not necessarily have much effect if other impediments remain significant problems. Similarly, developing a conducive business environment may make a location more attractive to SME investors, but only if they have access to information will they be likely to be attracted. A programme, or a combination of initiatives, is required. Thus, a programme of initiatives providing easier access to information could be coupled with a programme aimed at reducing impediments and combined with programmes to give fiscal incentives and support for those SMEs which invest in training. To establish a coherent programme of initiatives requires that priorities be established, and this requires a framework for assessing the policy options for increasing the contribution of SME FDI to development.

## 3. A basic framework

A basic framework for appraising options for increasing the SME FDI contribution to development is set out in table IX.1. In brief, ultimately, governments are interested in SME FDI as a means of encouraging development. SME FDI is well suited to contributing to development in particular ways -- for example in developing an entrepreneurial base. If this is important to the strategic development needs of a government, encouraging SME FDI offers an attractive policy option. However, encouraging SME FDI is only an attractive policy option to the extent that the benefits flowing from it exceed the costs of attracting it. As SME FDI involves working with many different investors, the administrative costs could be higher than those associated with FDI by large firms.

**Table IX.1.  A framework for assessing options for increasing the contribution
of SME FDI to host country development**

**Strategic development objectives:**

*How can SME FDI contribute to overall development and public benefits?*

Public benefits of SME FDI -- for example, creation of supply-industry capability, filling of the "missing middle", creation of a flexible and competitive export base, acceleration of economic restructuring, growth of indigenous SMEs -- tend to be indirect and take time to materialize.  Achieving development objectives depends on the potential to achieve net public benefits.

**Net public benefit:**

*How to ensure that there are net public benefits from SME FDI?*

Net public benefits depend on the public benefits exceeding the costs of policies designed to increase the flow of SME FDI and encouraging SME FDI which provides more public benefits.

**Potential for increased SME FDI:**

*How will SME investors respond to policy initiatives?*

The ability to increase SME FDI, as well as technology and training flows associated with it, depends on the response of investors to policy initiatives.  This requires the maintenance of close links with SME investors and potential SME investors.

**Policy options and initiatives:**

*What programme of policy options is best suited to increasing benefits from SME FDI
and meeting development needs?*

Which policy initiatives are likely to have the most effect will depend on establishing priorities by comparing:
* existing policy initiatives with best practice to identify gaps relative to best practice;
* proposed and existing policy initiatives with those in competing destinations; and
* proposed policy initiatives with the needs and requirements of target SME investors.

The package of policy initiatives will then be composed of appropriate domestic options and international options.

*Source:*  UNCTAD.

The extent to which policy initiatives are successful in attracting more SME FDI, or in attracting desired types of SME FDI, depends on the response of SME investors to those initiatives.  SME investors are not homogeneous; their needs, and the problems they face, vary widely.  Governments seeking to attract more SME FDI need to be able to monitor and anticipate the needs of the SME client group they are seeking to attract.  The design of an appropriate programme of policy initiatives to encourage SME FDI depends on establishing priorities amongst the wide range of options available.  The priorities depend on the strategic development objectives of the government concerned, the response of the SME investors to the programme, the initiatives in competing destinations, comparison with best practice, and the costs and strategic benefits associated with implementing the programme.

## B.  Practical steps for assessing policy options

There are five main practical steps that draw together the remainder of the manual and that are important in making best use of available policy options to encourage SME FDI.

*Establishing mechanisms for monitoring SME FDI and providing accurate information on SME FDI.*  In order to monitor the benefits flowing from SME FDI, it is necessary to have some knowledge of the levels of SME FDI flows and the benefits associated with those flows.  Existence of a reliable statistical information system is an absolute precondition.  The first step is to establish some baseline or benchmark from which to compare.  Ideally, this means having information on *actual* FDI flows by size of investor.  Most developing countries have information on *approved FDI projects* by the amount of FDI approved, but information on *actual* flows (including transfer of intangible assets such as technology and training) by size of investor is more difficult to obtain.  Few countries collect the information on FDI broken down by size of recipient or investor.  However, it would not require much more than a refocusing of the role of investment boards to make it easier to collect useful information.  It is important to provide such information without alteration to SME investors.

*Identifying strategic priority areas for SME investment and development.*  The identification of strategic priorities is an important practical part of attracting and making best use of SME FDI. However, strategic development planning with respect to SMEs is something of a contradiction.  It is a government's prerogative to decide on priority areas for development.  It is a market's prerogative to agree or disagree with the government's assessments and priorities.  Governments can create a conducive business environment, they can provide information to potential SME investors, they can offer incentives to SME investors -- but they cannot force them to invest.  Much of the benefit of SMEs and SME FDI comes from flexibility and ability to adapt.  SMEs are not suited to being pushed into bureaucratic five-year plans.  Even so, government planning and targeting can still be useful by:

- Identifying priority areas and recognizing the role of SMEs in development.  A government can signal to SME investors those areas most suitable for investment.  For example, if a government sees an opportunity for the development of supply-industry capability in moulded parts, it may work with larger firms to establish a network of smaller suppliers, and invite overseas SME suppliers to establish a presence by means of FDI.

- Putting the infrastructure needed by SMEs in place.  For example, a government may establish that the development of a dynamic SME sector may need a significant increase in the number of people with some level of formal management training.  To achieve this might require a programme of cooperation with foreign agencies, large foreign investors, local training institutes and universities, chambers of commerce, as well as with SMEs and SME investors.

A critical element in making effective use of the potential offered by SME FDI is for governments to make a strategic assessment of the role of SMEs and SME FDI in the development process.  Though the issues differ from country to country, this requires making an assessment on the extent of the "missing middle" -- that is, the need to develop a dynamic group of entrepreneurial growth-oriented SMEs; the availability of technical and managerial skills in indigenous entrepreneurs, relative to the future needs of the economy; the need for local entrepreneurs to gain managerial and business experience, especially in international business; the accessibility of equity finance available to local entrepreneurs; and the importance of being able to develop an internationally competitive supply or subcontracting sector, both generally and in specific industries. By comparing the present economy and its SME entrepreneurial engine with where the government would realistically like to see the economy in a few years' time, it is possible to develop plans and policy initiatives which make more effective use of the potential offered by SME FDI. These aspects are pursued in more detail in chapter X, section A.

***Establishing priorities for policy options to increase SME FDI.*** A wide range of policy options exists for increasing SME FDI. These are set out in chapters X and XI. They range from general initiatives to provide a more conducive business environment to quite specific incentives. They cover initiatives in the host economy and international initiatives, both bilaterally with home countries and multilaterally. No single initiative on its own will have much impact. What is required is a programme of initiatives -- a programme made up of many elements. For example, it may be made up of regulatory reform, establishment of first-stop or one-stop shops for SME investors, changes in the operation and reporting requirements of boards of investment, and cooperation with TNCs on establishing training centres. Because there are many elements, it is necessary to identify which elements should take priority. The practical steps in developing priorities for the elements of a programme start with identifying those areas where the current policies are most evidently deficient relative to best-practice policy and relative to policy initiatives in competing destinations. These aspects are examined further in chapter X, section A.

***Assessing how SMEs will be likely to respond to these options.*** Only by knowing how SME investors are likely to respond to different initiatives is it possible to refine priorities in the elements of programmes to derive the greatest effect, or the greatest potential net benefit. This can only really be done by maintaining close links with SME investors and potential investors. The practical methods of doing this are examined in chapter X, section A.

***Assessing the likely direct and indirect benefits and costs of the options.*** Assessing the benefits and costs of SME FDI is made difficult by the sheer number and various kinds of investments, and by the difficulties in defining what costs are necessary to secure the benefits. For large-scale investments involving foreign funds (e.g., infrastructure projects such as highways or electricity-generating plants) the benefits and costs are fairly clearly defined by the project. SME FDI depends on a wide range of programmes and initiatives, and is much more diverse. For some specific initiatives to encourage SME FDI (e.g., a trade show, a targeted marketing campaign or the introduction of a specific fiscal initiative), it is sometimes possible to make an assessment of the likely benefit in terms of attracting a given amount of investors and investment relative to the costs of the initiative. However, even here, there is a problem with the preconditions needed to ensure SME FDI. The problem is analogous to attributing the benefits of building a bridge to the costs of adding the last span. The bridge is largely useless without the last span, and so a high benefit-to-cost ratio can often be demonstrated: the last span may not cost very much and without it there may not be any benefits, but this is obviously misleading. Similarly, a specific initiative to encourage SME FDI (such as a trade show or a targeted marketing campaign) may lead to more FDI, but only if other initiatives are also in place. For example, it may be that without efforts to simplify investment approval procedures (or to reduce investment impediments generally), or to make local SMEs "investment ready", the efforts on a specific initiative will come to nothing. Therefore, an assessment of the programme as a whole is essential. This means that care must be taken in any benefit-cost assessment to ensure that both project and programme approaches are used, and that any project assessment is carried out in the broader context offered by the strategic planning process.

# CHAPTER X

## PRACTICAL MEASURES AVAILABLE TO HOST COUNTRY GOVERNMENTS TO MAXIMIZE BENEFITS FROM SME FDI

### A. Establishing measures for monitoring performance and planning

#### 1. Rationale

Without effective measures and mechanisms for monitoring and planning it is almost impossible to make good use of the development potential offered by foreign direct investment (FDI) by small and medium-sized enterprises (SMEs). In order to develop suitable initiatives to attract more SME FDI and encourage its flow to desired activities, it is necessary to have information on how a country is performing with respect to SME FDI. This requires the establishment of systematic means of gathering appropriate information so as to be able to:

- Measure the role and contribution of SMEs in the economy, including the levels of SME FDI.

- Identify and monitor the relative importance of different factors that are attractive to SME investors, and those that impede those investors. For example, if investment approval procedures or customs procedures are seen as a distinct impediment to a large proportion of SME investors, that information is useful in deciding how important it is to remodel those procedures. SMEs are not homogeneous. Their needs, and the problems they face, vary widely. In order to establish policy and programme priorities it is necessary to know what needs they have, what problems they face, and how important these are for different types of SMEs.

- Monitor or compare government policy relative to best practice.

- Measure the relative attractiveness of one destination against other competing destinations. Competition between destinations for FDI is increasing. Investors are increasingly able to access and compare information about competing destinations, and resources are increasingly mobile. This means that it is imperative for policy makers to know where they stand relative to competing destinations and relative to the needs of the investors that they may be seeking to attract. For example, if other countries have adopted initiatives that streamline their investment-approval procedures, they may become relatively more attractive in the eyes of potential investors.

Information by itself is of little practical use. It is necessary to put the information into a form which allows it to be acted on in a practical way. Strategic planning is the most common way to do this, and is widely used in the more developed economies in Asia.

## 2. Practical measures and examples

### (a) *SME strategic plan: identifying areas of greatest potential for SME FDI*

Most of the more developed economies in Asia have adopted either an SME strategic plan or an SME basic law or Magna Carta. Japan's Basic Law provides an illustration (box X.1). These laws or policy statements serve to provide a set of objectives and responsibilities for governments. They also serve to help coordinate administrative activity by a variety of agencies or programmes relevant to SMEs. Examples were given in Part Two, and their application was described in chapter VII.

Many developing countries have development plans, usually based on a rolling five-year time span. However, few such plans address the issue of SME development, and rarely do they seek to use SME FDI as an means of development. The steps that governments need to take to make best use of SME FDI in economic development are as follows:

*The first step*. Identifying broad strategic development objectives at the economy, sectoral and/or industrial level.

*The second step*. Identifying the potential role of SMEs in economic development. As noted in Part One, SMEs play an important role in sustainable economic growth, and can contribute to upwards of 70 per cent of long-term growth.

*The third step*. Identifying how SME FDI can contribute to development of indigenous SMEs and the broader development process. The greatest potential for SME FDI to contribute to development is where, for example:

- Access to technology geared to smaller firms and local market conditions is important to the development of indigenous SMEs (e.g., in agricultural industries, and in town and village industry development);
- There is a lack of the managerial skills necessary to expand the number of SMEs in line with economic development targets;
- Access to finance (especially equity finance) is limited for the development of SMEs;
- Entrepreneurs in the informal sector are unable to develop indigenous SMEs further; and

- Access to foreign markets and experience offers an important channel for the development of SMEs and for the economy in general.

---

**Box X.1.  Japan's Small and Medium Enterprise Basic Law**

**Introduction**  (Objectives)

**Generality (Chapter 1)**

| | |
|---|---|
| **Targets of policies (Article 1)** disadvantages improvement of their | Growth and development of SMEs; enhancement of economic and social well-being of entrepreneurs and employees of SMEs.  Measures include rectification of faced by SMEs and support of their self-help efforts, leading to productivity and business conditions. |
| **Definition of SME (Article 2)** | • Manufacturing and other industries: enterprises with capital of less than ¥100 million or with 300 or less employees.<br>• Retail and service business: enterprises with capital of less than ¥10 million or with 50 or less employees.<br>• Wholesale: enterprises with capital of less than ¥30 million or with 100 or less employees. |
| **Government policies (Article 3)** | • Modernization of equipment.<br>• Improvement of technology.<br>• Rationalization of management.<br>• Structural upgrading.<br>• Prevention of excessive competition and making proper subcontracting.<br>• Stimulating demand.<br>• Ensuring fair opportunities for business activities.<br>• Promoting appropriate labour-management relations. |
| **Policies of local public organizations (Article 4)** | Local public organizations must implement policies based on governmental policies. |
| **Legislative measures (Articles 5-7)** | Specification and establishment of legislative and financial measures required to implement SME policies. |
| **Annual report (Article 8)** | Publication of the *White Paper on Small and Medium Enterprises.* |
| **Structural upgrading of SMEs (Chapter 2; Articles 9 to 16)** | Policies concerning commerce, service business, changes of business and labour with respect to modernization of equipment, improvement of technology, rationalization of management, proper scale of enterprise and adjustment for cooperative business. |
| **Rectification of disadvantages in business conditions (Chapter 3; Articles 17 to 22))** | Prevention of excessive competition, ensuring proper subcontracting, ensuring fair opportunities for business activities, securing appropriate guidelines from public authorities, promotion of exports. |
| **Small-scale enterprise (Chapter 4; Article 23)** | Improvement and development of management of small-scale enterprises; living standards of employees balanced with those of employees of other enterprises. |
| **Financing and taxation (Chapter 5; Articles 24 to 25))** | Smoothing of financing; consolidation of corporate capital. |
| **Administrative authorities and SME organizations (Chapter 6; Articles 26 to 27)** | Maintenance of organizations related to SME administration.<br>Maintenance of small and medium enterprise organizations. |
| **Small and Medium Enterprise Policy Making Council (Chapter 7;Articles 28 to 32)** | Request for establishment, authorities, organization, submission of materials and monitoring of entrusted organizations. |

*Source:*   UNCTAD, based on information provided by Japan's Small and Medium Enterprise Agency.

---

*The fourth step*. Appraising (using, for example, cost-benefit analysis) the options for initiatives to increase SME FDI, and the potential for doing so. The basic framework for this was set out in chapter IX.

*The fifth step*. Engaging in consultative processes with stakeholders, government agencies, industry groups, chambers of commerce, potential SME investors etc. to refine the plan, explain it and gain acceptance for it.

*The sixth step*. Formalizing the plan as a document and disseminating it.

*The seventh step*. Coordinating the implementation of the plan via the relevant agencies.

### (b)   *Monitoring policy performance against best-practice guidelines*

#### i.   *Selecting performance indicators*

Government policy plays a critical role in making the best use of SMEs and SME FDI in development. Part Two set out this role in detail, and developed a set of guidelines as to best-practice approaches in three key areas: how to develop a generally conducive business environment; how to design and implement administrative policies aimed at encouraging SMEs; and how to implement policies aimed specifically at encouraging SME FDI. In an increasingly international environment, it is becoming more important for governments to be able to compare their policies and policy performance with those of other economies, and against best-practice benchmarks. This requires that governments identify areas where there are potential gaps -- areas where government policy seems to lag significantly behind other economies in its effectiveness, or where it falls below best-practice standards. This can be of assistance in establishing both short-term and longer-term policy priorities. All policy comparisons inevitably contain a subjective element, and this is no exception. Therefore, in order to tell how an economy is performing relative to best practice, there is a need for an indicator, or a set of indicators, for each of the characteristics. The use of indicators can take three forms:

- Results of a survey analysis (such as that described in Part One), or of regular monitoring. For example, by using the techniques set out in section G it is possible to assess the extent to which corruption or the prevailing legal systems are seen as a problem by SME investors, or the extent to which SMEs find government-sponsored networking and matchmaking programmes to be of assistance.

- Qualitative assessment of policy based on consultant reports, discussions with officials and business people. Using these informal channels to tap key opinion leaders, it is possible to assess the extent to which SMEs are included in and taken account of in the development of national strategic plans, or whether the investment environment is as conducive as it might be.
- Independent or objective indicators. For example, it is possible to compare economic growth rates, or country risk indices.

Table X.1 summarizes best-practice guidelines and identifies the broad indicators by which an evaluation can be made of the policies of a specific country.

**Table X.1. Indicators with which to compare and assess policy effectiveness against best practices**

| Best-practice characteristics | Indicators |
|---|---|
| **Creating a conducive business environment** | |

*Develop a business environment which is conducive to investment by SMEs and large firms, both from abroad and domestically. The main characteristics of this include:*

| | |
|---|---|
| • A clear and transparent commitment to SMEs. The best-practice solution appears to be the adoption of a clear statement of political commitment to SMEs. This takes either the form of a basic law, which sets out the obligations of the government to SMEs and SME policy, or the form of a strategy document, which sets out the broad directions and aspirations of the government policy in relation to SMEs. | Existence of such a statement, or of planning commitment to SME development in broader strategic economic and industry development planning. |
| • Economic growth with a degree of certainty about the future. Best practice requires sustained and sustainable economic growth. It also requires policies which address investor uncertainty concerns. There is no single effective way to achieve this. What is important from a best-practice point of view is that economic growth be seen by investors as sustainable and sustained, and that economic indicators point to this. | Rate of growth measures; variability-in-growth measures; inflation measures; country-risk indicators. |
| • Definable and transferable property rights. Best practice requires that property rights be defined and transferable, especially for physical assets (land and buildings). | General property rights for land, land transferability; specific rights of foreign investors to hold and transfer property; extent of property rights for intangibles (copyright, patents etc.); and adoption of international conventions on patents, copyright. |
| • Transparent legal and regulatory systems. Best practice requires that efforts be made to eliminate unnecessary regulatory complexity, that laws and regulations be transparent and codified, and that they be interpreted consistently. | Legal codes; survey evidence on corruption in legal systems etc. |

**General administrative mechanisms to assist in the development of SMEs**

*Providing a conducive business environment is not sufficient in itself to release the full potential of SMEs, and best practice is that all governments in the leading economies have administrative mechanisms for assisting the development of SMEs.*

| | |
|---|---|
| • Focus on growth-oriented SMEs. Best practice is that government programmes should give priority to SMEs which have the potential to grow and develop. The target firms for encouraging SME FDI are a subset of this subset of SMEs; only some SMEs are oriented to growth and only some growth-oriented SMEs will have the ability to internationalize. | Existence, availability of programmes for growth-oriented and internationally oriented SMEs; existence of targets or objectives of programmes. |

**(Table X.1, cont'd.)**

| Best-practice characteristics | Indicators |
|---|---|
| • Focus on those areas where governments can provide additionality. Best practice is that governments establish programmes and mechanisms to facilitate the development of SMEs generally, and that these be directed at areas where additionality is most likely to occur (i.e., where net benefits will accrue that would not otherwise accrue). The areas most commonly identified are: human resource development, advisory services and management training; technology, technology transfer and technology sharing; finance; market access; information access; and regulatory burden and regulatory infrastructure. Two additional areas are also sometimes cited: cooperation between the private sector and government; and cooperation between large firms and small firms. A second main aspect is that policies increasingly reflect the need to encourage international competitiveness in SMEs. | Existence of a portfolio of programmes and type of programmes offered; availability of a range of programmes geared to encouraging internationalization of SMEs. |
| • Monitoring of needs, providing diagnostic services, revising priorities as necessary. Best practice requires that programmes be adapted to the changing needs of SMEs as circumstances change and as the economy evolves and develops. This is usually achieved by means of diagnostic services (which help SMEs to identify what their real problems and needs are). | Availability of diagnostic services; existence of strategic planning process for monitoring needs now and in the future. |
| • Central agency, one-stop or first-stop shops. Best practice is that SME programmes be coordinated, and that SME clients have fairly seamless and ready access to programmes. This is typically achieved by a central or coordinating agency which acts as a one-stop or first-stop shop. | Existence of organizational structure for programme delivery; method of coordinating programmes for SMEs. |
| • Cost recovery, cooperation with private sector. Best practice generally requires some cost sharing and cost recovery of SME programmes. It also involves the private sector (consultants, chambers of commerce, finance providers, accountants etc.) to deliver programmes and services. | Delivery methods for programmes; cost-recovery practices. |

### Specific policies to encourage SME FDI

*SME FDI could be an effective and attractive policy option for accelerating the development of an indigenous SME sector.*

| | |
|---|---|
| • Encouraging internationalization (and growth) generally. Best practice seems to be to encourage internationalization and growth of SMEs that show potential in these respects. | Existence of effective programmes to encourage internationalization of domestic SMEs; absence of impediments to internationalization of SMEs; proportion of SMEs that are engaged in export, directly or indirectly; proportion of SMEs with links to foreign firms. |

/...

**(Table X.1, cont'd.)**

| Best-practice characteristics | Indicators |
|---|---|
| • Providing accurate information. Best practice is t o provide accurate information to potential foreign investors on market conditions, opportunities, and government regulations and requirements. It is emphasized that information is of little use if it is out of date or not accurate. | Availability and accessibility of reliable information on investment conditions and opportunities etc.; use of one-stop access for potential investors seeking information; range of media used for conveying information to targets. |
| • Encouraging linkages. Best practice is to encourage the development of linkages (e.g., partnerships and alliances) between SMEs across borders. By forming a partnership or alliance an SME can significantly reduce the risks and costs associated with doing business across borders, whether this be for trade or investment purposes. Both sides can potentially gain. | Existence of partnering programmes; access of SMEs to international partnering programmes and exchanges. |
| • Providing appropriate incentives. Best practice requires that incentives be part of a broader strategy for encouraging FDI and tailored to the development of target industries (or to aspects of industrial development such as export promotion); designed so that they actually have an additionality effect (they lead to investment that would not have otherwise taken place); and generate greater benefits to the community than the costs of providing the incentives. This requires mechanisms to be in place that monitor the needs of the client groups, and the impact of the incentives. It also sometimes requires that they are reversible, or with sunset clauses, so that recipients do not become permanent candidates for "corporate social welfare"; and designed to discourage rent seeking by clients wherever possible, consistent with broader multilateral agreements or practices, so that the risk of bidding competition between countries or regions is minimized. | Range and type of incentives offered for attracting FDI; existence of overall strategy for encouraging desired SME FDI; evidence of mechanisms to encourage additionality; mechanisms to discourage rent seeking; conformity with spirit of multilateral agreements. |
| • Providing access to support services and infra-structure. Best practice seems to be that there is a mechanism in place which anticipates and puts in place the support and infrastructure needs for those investors a country is seeking to attract. Institutionally, this takes the form of an agency that has broader responsibility for SMEs and development (such as, for example, the Economic Development Board in Singapore). It can then work with chambers of commerce, boards of investment etc. to maintain links with SME investors and potential investors. | Existence of mechanism to establish priorities for tangible infrastructure required by SME investors; private-public sector cooperation in developing tangible/intangible infrastructure; existence of support services and mechanisms for developing intangible infrastructure and accessibility to foreign investors. |
| • Addressing the specific impediments and barriers to SME FDI. Best practice seems to be to establish mechanisms which monitor and respond to the problems or impediments faced by foreign investors, and to integrate the findings into action plans to reduce more systemic problems. | Existence of mechanisms to monitor problems faced by foreign investors; overall strategy and action plans to reduce impediments. |

*Source:* UNCTAD.

*ii.    Systematic assessment and priorities*

Mechanisms for selecting and measuring suitable indicators having been established, the next question is whether a government is able to use these to identify priorities. This requires a systematic (but simplified) assessment of all the main areas. Table X.2 compares two hypothetical countries to show that such an assessment can be undertaken and can help in comparing policy, both with best practice and with policy in competing destinations. The evaluation is necessarily subjective and is for illustration purposes. In each major best-practice area an assessment is made, on the basis of the overall evidence available, as to whether the policy adopted is poor, moderate, good or best practice. The key points emerging from this illustrative analysis are that it is possible to undertake a useful and systematic analysis at relatively low cost. This analysis can be supplemented by more detailed assessment in more specific areas.

If either hypothetical country shown in table X.2 were to be successful in attracting SME FDI, it would need to develop fairly comprehensive strategies to do so. Attempts just to adopt specific policies to encourage SME FDI are unlikely to be effective in attracting SME FDI or enhancing its contribution to development, if policy in other, more general areas diverges much from best practice. This is particularly the case as regards providing general administrative support systems to facilitate the development of growth-oriented, internationally oriented domestic SMEs and SME managers. This area is particularly deficient in both hypothetical countries. There are specific areas in each hypothetical country which diverge considerably from best practice. The analysis serves to highlight these divergences. This does not necessarily mean that governments should seek to achieve best practice in all areas. Some areas may be less important than others, and in some areas it may simply be too expensive to warrant achieving best practice in the immediate future. However, there is a *prima facie* expectation that the greater the divergence between actual and best practice, the greater will be the potential benefits of making improvements.

*(c)    Establishing mechanisms for monitoring international competitiveness in attracting SME FDI*

In an international world, destinations (whether they are countries or regions within countries) compete with one another for FDI. Investors are increasingly able to access information and make comparisons between destinations. Reliable and accurate information is necessary. If such information does not exist, meaningful monitoring is not possible. Investors are usually interested in comparison of such things as economic fundamentals (economic growth, inflation, interest rates, government deficit, exchange rates, reserves etc.), risk (e.g., risk of personal injury and kidnapping, risk of appropriation of assets, risk of unpredictable delays in projects), and policy initiatives, incentives, regulations etc. (as they relate to foreign investment, at both the general level and at specific industry or provincial level).

In most circumstances, whether a destination is attractive or not depends on a balance of factors. For example, an investor may be willing to take more risks in investing in a fast-growing market. It is not usually a matter of one destination clearly standing out as better than another; it is a matter of some aspects of some destinations being more attractive than others and some, less. However, governments can play an important role in changing that balance. If larger TNCs find some aspects of a destination unattractive, they are generally in a position to make their views known to the government. The government can then decide whether it is worth offering a specific package of incentives to overcome the unattractive aspects, whether it should address more fundamental problems, or whether it should simply ignore the advice proffered. The situation is different for SME investors. They are less likely to have direct access to government, and thus less likely to be able to make their views known. Also, they are likely to have a much wider range of views.

**Table X.2.  Examples of two-country comparisons of policy assessment**

| Indicator | Country A | Country B |
|---|---|---|
| **Providing a conducive business environment** | | |
| Transparent commitment to SME development | Moderate. No specific SME law or strategy. Plans do not address SME issues. | Moderate. No specific SME law or strategy. Plans do not address SME issues. |
| Economic growth with certainty | Economic growth: good - moderate | Economic growth: good |
| Property rights | Good. Land transferable on leasehold. | Moderate. Some problems with transferability and specification of title. |
| Transparent legal system | Moderate - good. Legal system fairly transparent. Corruption regarded as a moderate problem for SMEs. | Moderate - poor. Legal system not regarded as transparent. Corruption regarded as a major problem. |
| **General administrative systems to assist in development of SMEs** | | |
| Focus on growth-oriented SMEs | Poor. No programme. | Poor. No programme. |
| Focus on areas of additionality | Poor - moderate. No specific SME programmes. | Poor - moderate. No SME programmes, except some private sector ones. |
| Monitoring of SME needs | Moderate. Some monitoring of needs by industry. | Moderate. Some monitoring of needs by industry. |
| Central agency for SMEs | Poor. No plan. | Poor. No plan. |
| Cost recovery | Poor. No programme. | Poor. No programme. |
| **Specific policies to encourage SME FDI** | | |
| Encourage internationalization | Poor. Internationalization impeded by exchange-rate system. | Moderate. Inhibited at SME level. |
| Accurate information | Moderate. Limited information, difficult to get. No effective targeting at SMEs. | Moderate. Limited information, improving but still difficult to get. No effective targeting at SMEs. |
| Appropriate incentives | Moderate. No general SME strategy. Incentives geared more to larger firms. Limited additionality. | Moderate. No general SME strategy. Incentives geared more to larger firms. Limited additionality. |
| Access to support | Moderate - good. Limited mechanism via board of investment, chambers of commerce. | Moderate. Limited mechanism via chambers of commerce. |
| Efforts/mechanism to address impediments | Moderate. Limited mechanisms via board of investment, but not really suited to SMEs. | Poor. No real effort to address impediments. |

*Source:*   UNCTAD.
*Note:*   The comparison is based on existing countries.

This points to two closely related requirements for governments seeking to take advantage of the opportunities for development offered by SME FDI.  The first is that of monitoring what SME investors' needs and problems are.  This is dealt with in section G below.  The second is the need to compare systematically and regularly the relative attractiveness of a destination *vis-à-vis* other competing destinations.  Although this is possible for a single government to do, it is easier to do at a multilateral or international level. (This is examined further in the next chapter.)  APEC member economies have, for example, already undertaken a systematic yearly comparison of investment regimes (box X.2).  This allows fairly ready comparison of most of the major competing destinations in Asia, at least in respect of government policy and regulations.  From a government point of view it is relatively easy to see whether government regulations are likely to make a given destination significantly more or less attractive to a foreign investor.  Because changes in the APEC countries are taking place relatively quickly, non-APEC countries need to be aware of their relative position, and to respond to those changes appropriately if they are not to become relatively less attractive places in which to invest.  Comparison with non-APEC developing countries is more difficult, but no less important.  An SME investor may consider investing in Myanmar, Pakistan or Central and Eastern Europe.  Changes in the attitude to foreign investment are taking place quickly in all these areas, and to remain competitive it is necessary to move with the changes.  In practical terms, there are four steps to take:

- *The first step*.  Identifying those regulatory and other aspects which are most important to determining the relative competitiveness of a host country's competitiveness in attracting FDI, and particularly in attracting the type of SME FDI that it seeks.

- *The second step*.  Developing a clear, concise and accurate record of the country's own performance or position on those aspects.  For example, if repatriation of profits or foreign exchange control is a major determinant of attractiveness, the country's position on those issues should be clearly stated.  More generally, this information should be disseminated effectively to target investors.  This issue is pursued further in section C.

---

**Box X.2.  Guide to investment regimes of APEC member economies**

Information on this guide is widely available in electronic and published format.  Information is updated each year on a common comparable format which covers the following:

- The background of principles underlying policy on foreign investment.

- The regulatory framework used to manage FDI, including transparency, most-favoured-nation treatment, national treatment, repatriation and convertibility, entry and stay of personnel, taxation, performance requirements, capital exports, investor behaviour and other measures.

- Investment protection offered to foreign investors in relation to expropriation, nationalization, compensation and settlement of disputes.

- Summary details of promotion and incentives, including contact details for the agencies responsible for implementing these initiatives.

- International investment agreements and codes to which the economy is a signatory.

*Source:*  UNCTAD.

---

- *The third step.* Collecting the necessary information from other competing destinations and comparing it in a systematic way. As outlined in the next chapter, there is a role for international organizations such as UNCTAD to arrange for the systematic collection of relevant information.

- *The fourth step.* Using the information gleaned in this way to revise regularly and improve the effectiveness of the SME strategic plan, outlined above in this section.

## B. Creating an indigenous entrepreneurial engine: maximizing the contribution of SME FDI to development

### 1. Rationale

SME FDI is a means to an end, not an end in itself. It could be an effective means to encourage development, but it is not itself always sufficient to engender development. In other words, governments cannot simply hope to attract FDI (whether it is by large firms or by SMEs) and expect indigenous SME development to flourish. For seeds to flourish in a garden requires that some preparation be undertaken by the gardener. The experience of the more developed economies in the Asian region (examined in Part Two) is that SMEs are an important element in their economic growth, and that the government plays an important role in the development of SMEs. In Part One, it was shown that many of the developing countries in the region face the problem of a "missing middle". The development of dynamic, growth-oriented SMEs is an important aspect of economic development for these economies. The effective use of SME FDI as a means of development requires that governments "prepare the garden" and ensure that it is maintained. Failure to develop a foundation for SME growth will simply mean that the risks facing SMEs are higher. SME investors are not interested in investing in longer-term aspects of business which bring significant externalities to the economy as a whole, such as management training and product development. There are a number of key practical issues that governments need to consider if they are to "prepare the garden" so that their indigenous SMEs can benefit from SME FDI.

### 2. Practical measures and examples

#### (a) SME basic law, Magna Carta or SME strategic plan

As shown in Part Two and illustrated in section A.2 of this chapter, many of the more developed economies in Asia have adopted an explicit political statement of support for developing their SMEs. This has taken the form of an SME basic law or SME Magna Carta (setting out government objectives, obligations and commitments to the development of SMEs), and/or an SME strategic plan (periodically revised and giving guidance to the various government agencies responsible for SMEs). The impact and success of these explicit political commitments to the development of the SME sector depends on how government policy is implemented. The commitments and documents mentioning them have little impact unless they are supported by a substantive framework of policy and administrative mechanisms supporting that policy. In practical terms, governments that seek to develop a suitable foundation for SME growth need to consider several issues:

- First, what is the appropriate form of explicit political commitment to SMEs and their development, if any? This is a matter of balance between the rigidity of a basic law and the flexibility of a strategic plan. For example, in economies where political power may shift from one party to another, a basic law may be seen as less appropriate, because it is difficult to change and thus limits flexibility and the right of parties to change policy direction. On the other hand, if a non-partisan set of common commitments can be agreed on amongst all parties, this might provide the basic foundation needed to guarantee some stability needed by SMEs. A political commitment is essentially useless to business if it cannot be fulfilled.

- Second, the extent of this basic political commitment. For example, in Japan the Basic Law is quite specific about areas where the Government should enforce measures (box X.1). In Singapore the 1988 Master Plan document simply sought to achieve four broad aims, one of which was the internationalization of SMEs. In Taiwan Province of China, the guidance principles relating to SME development are more flexible, but the Statute for the Development of Small and Medium Enterprises provides for a process (in the form of a council) for revising the details of the strategic plan.

- Third, the mechanics of how the responsibility for implementing the commitment should be designated. As discussed in Part Two, most of the more developed Asian economies give a ministerial portfolio the responsibility for SMEs; at an administrative level, responsibility is coordinated by a single agency. The nature of this coordinating agency is discussed further below.

- Fourth, how to move to more specific planning, especially as it relates to SME FDI. The broad process for this was set out in section A.

### (b)   Identifying target SMEs and entrepreneurs suitable for development

As discussed in Part One, all SMEs do not contribute equally to development. Those SMEs which are more growth-oriented and have the capability to grow are more important than others to the development process. The point of targeting is to encourage the former SMEs as they are most likely to benefit from an injection of FDI. There is usually no point in using resources for encouraging SMEs geared to a small scale to absorb FDI or to grow beyond a certain size. This does not mean that these lower-growth SMEs are unimportant to an economy; but by concentrating on suitable target SMEs, it is possible to have a more effective policy impact and thus derive the most benefit from FDI. The issue of targeting is a difficult one -- it is often associated with "picking winners", a practice which is largely discredited. In fact, the issue is a little different, as illustrated in the following figure:

**Existing high-growth firms.**
Small proportion -- usually less than 5 per cent of all firms.
Target at reducing impediments to growth so as to increase growth rate and more effective use of FDI.

**Growth-oriented medium-sized firms**.
Perhaps 10-20 per cent of all firms.
Target at getting these to increase growth rate, encourage more use of FDI.

**Firms (mostly small but some medium) most of which are not growth-oriented.**
About 80-90 per cent of firms.
Not a major target. Encourage self selection of firms that might be able to benefit from FDI.

**Nascent entrepreneurs and informal-sector SMEs.**
Not a major target. Encourage self selection of entrepreneurs who might be able to benefit from FDI.

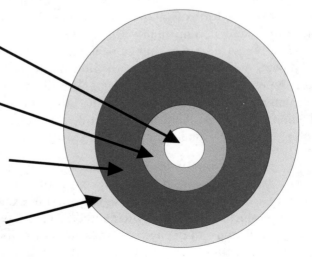

As one moves from the central circle of growth-oriented firms, the targets are more difficult to identify, and SME FDI policy initiatives more difficult to implement. Different policies are suited to different target groups. There are then two main issues: how to identify the target group and how to design policies to make best use of FDI in each target group.

**The first group** of existing fast-growth SMEs are the ones most likely to be or have already been engaged in some form of international linkages. The main issue is to work with them to identify the factors that prevent them from growing faster, and the things that might help them to grow faster. FDI is only one of a number of policy initiatives which may be relevant to these SMEs. The lead time required for these firms to take advantage of any potential offered by SME FDI is relatively short, because in most cases the firms in this target group are usually "investment ready" or close to it. In Singapore, for example, there are specific "promising local enterprise" schemes that seek to identify fast-growth firms and provide them with access to a range of support programmes designed to facilitate their growth. These SMEs can usually be identified fairly easily. They are typically firms that have been in existence for more than five years, have more than 20 employees, and have turnover growth in excess of 20 per cent per annum. They can usually be identified by chambers of commerce, boards of investment and government officials working with firms. Although this target group is quite small, their "investment readiness" and their experience with managing growth mean that benefits from targeting them are likely to be immediate, and can be quite significant relative to the cost.

**The second group** is probably the main group that will benefit most from SME FDI. It is made up of growth-oriented firms, and so the main distinguishing feature is that the manager is keen to make the firm grow and has some sort of realistic plan for doing so. Identifying these firms is not always easy, and in most cases it is better to allow self-selection for programmes designed specifically for growth-seeking SMEs. However, sometimes banks, accounting firms, regional authorities etc. can all be used to help identify such firms. SME FDI may be of assistance to these firms, but to take advantage of it they may need access to other forms of advice and assistance. For example, they may need access to advisory services to help them improve their accounting systems, or to restructure their firms to allow an equity injection, or to negotiate a technology-licence agreement. Moreover, by providing access to basic management training, or by encouraging networks and trade shows, it may be possible to introduce some indigenous entrepreneurs to foreign investors, and to allow them to benefit from FDI. This target group is less likely to be "investment ready", and so it takes longer to derive benefits from increasing SME FDI. Similarly, the group is larger, and so it usually costs more to provide access to the advisory and other services needed to help them prepare better for taking advantage of SME FDI. However, as the group is larger, in the longer term it also offers significant benefits.

**The third and fourth groups** are much larger, and less likely to be able to directly benefit from SME FDI. Although, within these groups, there will be some SMEs with more potential than others to benefit from FDI, the nature and the sheer size of the groups make it difficult to target policies effectively. This suggests that these groups are not really suitable policy targets for encouraging SME FDI. However, in the longer term, the growth of firms from this sector by means of general programmes of development will provide the seedbed of entrepreneurs and SMEs that are more able to take advantage of growth potential and SME FDI. In some circumstances, clustering or networking programmes may help SMEs in these groups to benefit directly from FDI.

### (c)    *Preparing local SMEs to take advantage of FDI*

The main benefits of FDI (including that by SMEs) for indigenous SMEs lie with increasing access to capital, technology, training, technical and managerial advice, experience and foreign markets. However, for indigenous SMEs to benefit from FDI requires them to be prepared. For example, to take an injection of equity through FDI requires that the management of the domestic SME be prepared to relinquish some of its control, and to share responsibility and decision-making with the investor from abroad. As noted in Part One, the aims of SME investors from abroad are often very sympathetic to economic development objectives and to the needs of domestic SMEs; SME investors are much more likely than larger foreign investors to see as very important the training of unskilled staff, the training of local managers, the provision of new products, and better-quality products suited to the needs of a local market, and adaptation of technology to local needs. Decision-making on critical issues (such as strategy or marketing) is also more likely to be split between the domestic SME and the foreign investor.

"Preparing the garden" in this area means providing assistance to domestic SMEs and entrepreneurs so that they are better able to take advantage of the potential benefits of SME FDI. At a practical level this is to provide SMEs in the target group with access to advice and assistance in areas such as negotiation skills, corporate legal structures, equity dilution and control, currency exchange, dividend planning, intercultural management training, technology and licensing agreements, business planning and accounting systems.

### (d)    *Establishing a coordinating agency for SME policy*

SME planning and policy implementation cut across most parts of the economy and of government. SME policy typically involves providing a wide portfolio of services (see Part Two). If a government sees SMEs as being important to economic development, and if there is a genuine political commitment to the development of the SME sector, there is a need to find a way to deliver effectively and to coordinate programmes and services to SMEs. As noted, the best-practice approach is to have planning and coordination for SME programmes and priorities serviced by a single administrative unit (e.g., a government department or agency) with responsibility for monitoring SME priorities and needs. The actual programmes and services may be delivered to SME clients by other functional departments within government. For example, agricultural cooperative programmes may be delivered by the ministry of agriculture, while management training in agribusiness is delivered in programmes funded and implemented by the ministry of industry or ministry of education. However, the existence of an SME agency of some form can act as a coordinating point, and serve to develop and monitor the implementation of broader SME development strategy. This is important with respect to taking advantage of SME FDI, as well as encouraging broader SME development.

Although there is a clear need for a coordinating point for SME policy, there are two main practical issues that need to be considered in the actual design and empowering of such an agency. There is no simple solution to these issues; the nature of SMEs is such that there will always be some tension between the different government departments dealing with them, and it is more a matter of how that tension is managed in the area of funding and responsibility.

- *Funding*. Should the coordinating agency have its own budget, and what should it be allowed to fund? For example, it may have a budget for programme development in its own right, but once developed, it may be required to offer the programmes through other ministries.

- *Location and ministerial responsibility.* Most coordinating agencies are located in industry ministries, and report to a minister responsible for small business or SMEs. This can involve tension if part of the role of the coordinating agency, and thus of the minister, is to audit the role of other ministries and departments in fulfilling the SME strategic plan.

The established coordinating agency should not be just an additional government body; it should have power and an impact on the SME sector.

### (e) Working with more developed economies and with the private sector to establish suitable, cost-effective support programmes

One of the biggest problems facing most developing countries seeking to provide support programmes to SMEs is the cost of designing and implementing these programmes. To "prepare the garden" so that domestic SMEs can effectively take advantage of SME FDI requires that they have access to programmes of advice and assistance on financial management, business planning, quality control, negotiation techniques, technology licensing etc. By cooperating with governments in more developed economies, and with the private sector, it may be possible to:

- receive technical assistance in developing or adapting new programmes. For example, technical assistance may be available to take an existing programme on quality control and adapt it to local needs;

- draw upon the more developed economies for suitable programmes to assist domestic SMEs. For example, a training course on export financing may be provided in cooperation with one of the credit-guarantee agencies in the Republic of Korea or Taiwan Province of China;

- have SME managers and staff attend training programmes in foreign countries. For example, technical staff in manufacturing in a developing host country may be invited to attend a training programme offered by the Japan Small Business Corporation; and

- access existing programmes offered abroad n for example, by accessing information services via the Internet, or by using distance learning.

This reduces the cost of programmes and increases quality and accessibility. Some further examples of the ways in which this can be done were given in Part Two. Practical steps for governments seeking to pursue this path are:

*First*, assessing the needs of indigenous SMEs and entrepreneurs, especially in respect of making more effective use of FDI. This is part of the overall SME strategic planning process set out in section A.

*Second*, reviewing the existing programmes available domestically and revising them to better meet the needs of target group SMEs.

*Third*, reviewing what opportunities there are to invite technical assistance and cooperation from more advanced economies, business associations or international agencies. This may involve making ministerial approaches to seek information on programmes available and relevant to the identified needs of target group SMEs.

*Fourth*, engaging in bilateral discussions with other governments and with international agencies to establish cooperative or technical assistance programmes.

## (f)   *Policies to promote stable economic growth*

All investors benefit from stable growth, but SMEs tend to be affected more by instability because they lack the hedges available to larger investors.  To the extent that governments wish to attract SME FDI, there is a case for adopting a "stability premium" in considering growth strategies.  In other words, it may make sense to emphasize stability over growth if there is any serious conflict between the two.  At a practical level this requires governments to:

- identify major sources of instability  (e.g., exchange-rate movements, sudden changes in tax rates or interest rates);

- seek ways whereby governments can reduce instability or volatility (e.g., by developing more mature and efficient markets, limiting speculative flows etc.);

- examine ways of assisting investors to hedge or avoid the instability (e.g., setting up free trade zones or special zones).

## (g)   *Development of secure and transferable property rights*

Property rights are not an issue for SMEs alone, but they can pose real barriers to SME investors.  The defining of secure and transferable property rights is usually associated initially with agricultural land reform.  This usually requires the codification of processes for surveying and registering ownership rights to land.  Without this, it is difficult to establish a base for SMEs to develop.  For example, in Taiwan Province of China land reform took place in the 1950s, and provided a foundation for later economic development (Zheng, 1992).  Furthermore, property rights now go beyond simple rights to agricultural land.  Urban property titles are also important for SMEs to access office space and manufacturing space.  Similarly, governments seeking to attract SME FDI need to be able to give investors some assurance as to the rights associated with patents, trademarks and copyright as well as rights of repatriation of capital and profits.  The broad practical steps that governments need to consider are:

*First*, auditing existing property rights entitlements in a broad range of areas relevant to SMEs and especially investors from abroad.

*Second*, examining ways in which general reforms can be introduced, and the time-frame and resources required to implement desired reforms.

*Third*, if the time-frame for general reform is long relative to the time-frame targeted for attracting increased levels of FDI, it may be worth considering temporary measures that provide differential property rights for some investors or classes of SMEs.

## (h)   *Development of transparent legal and regulatory systems*

The absence of transparent legal and regulatory systems poses a major impediment to SME FDI.  In Part One, it was shown that corruption is seen as a significant problem by about 75 per cent of survey respondents.  The problem is typically not so much corruption itself, which is usually just seen as something of a tax. Often, SME managers make the comment that although they would prefer not to pay either a tax or the corrupt official, they are sympathetic when the official has no other real source of income. The problem is the unpredictability and lack of transparency in the process, which make it difficult for an investor to plan. As with instability and property rights, the issue of regulatory and legal systems goes well beyond considerations related to SME FDI. Nevertheless, there are three broad practical issues that governments need to consider if they wish to attract more SME FDI:

- Review regulatory processes and simplify them wherever possible. Approval processes which require many different steps (or "shops") simply cause delays and invite corruption and bribes.

- Consider the setting up of special administrative arrangements and channels for foreign investors. This can be linked to one-stop or first-stop shop procedures for FDI (outlined further in section G). For example, officials in the one-stop investment shop can be placed on a different career path and payment system and subject to much more stringent checks for bribery or corruption. They can then act on behalf of an investor in dealing with other agencies and departments to ensure that only the correct and scheduled fees are paid. Many investors would not object to higher charges if there was more certainty in the approval processes.

- Consider options for reducing corruption, and for making the legal process more transparent and accountable. This is difficult, because many cases of corruption cited arise from the existence of ambiguous or even conflicting regulations and laws.

*(i)    Improving the relationship between SMEs and the banking sector*

Established domestic banks as well as foreign banks seem to be interested only in large firms and often even refuse to work with SMEs. It is therefore very difficult for SMEs to find appropriate funds for their development. Significant results could be achieved by improving the relationship between SMEs and banks. Specific programmes could include pilot schemes on financial arrangements between banks and SMEs. In some leading countries, there are special banks exclusively for SMEs (Small Business Finance Corporation, People's Finance Corporation and Shoko Chukin Bank in Japan; the Industrial Bank of Korea and the Citizens National Bank in the Republic of Korea). In other countries, such as the Philippines, banks are encouraged to have a certain percentage of loans earmarked for SMEs.

## C.   Providing accurate information to foreign investors

### 1.   Rationale

Information is an important element in any strategy to attract SME FDI. To arrive at decisions, SME investors as well as potential investors (most of which are SMEs) need information on both the approved and actual size of SME FDI, government regulations and requirements, market and economic conditions, opportunities and potential partners. Expenditure on information is a sunk cost, and the cost of obtaining information is the same for an SME as for a large firm (or higher). SME investors are thus relatively disadvantaged when it comes to obtaining information. A lack of information, or uncertainty about the accuracy and timeliness of the information, creates a barrier to entry and discourages SME FDI. Having access to accurate information for investors and potential investors is an important aspect of encouraging more FDI, especially from SMEs.

Governments seeking to use SME FDI as a means of development can play an important role in providing information. However, the challenge is to find cost-effective and targeted channels for delivering the information to the firms most likely to invest. Relatively few SMEs engage in FDI, and there are many SMEs. Providing information to many SMEs abroad can be very expensive, and some information channels may not be very effective for the purpose of attracting more FDI. As shown in Part One, "chance" is an important factor for many SME investors, and there is considerable room for improvements in the area of information and intelligence. It also has to be noted that as few firms move immediately to investment and many first engage in other means of international transactions such as trade, agency agreements and licensing, information has to be geared to this evolutionary process.

## 2. Practical measures and examples

### (a) Design and targeting of information

The overriding practical issue in making use of information to attract more SME FDI is in the design and targeting of an information strategy and implementation of an information programme. The key issues to consider in doing this are:

- What are the information requirements of various target audiences? For example, the information needs of an SME manager abroad who is considering international operations but who is not yet even trading internationally are likely to be much more general than the information requirements of an SME that is trading (but not investing) internationally, and that in turn will be more general than the information needs of an SME that is already actively investing abroad. Identification of target SME investors and potential investors and understanding their needs are part of overall SME strategic planning.

- What information should be provided by governments, and what by the private sector? What should be charged for and what should be free of charge? The more specific the needs of an information user, the more sensible it is to levy some sort of charge and to encourage the private sector to provide the information. For example, if a potential investor wants very specific market research done, it makes more sense to provide access to reliable consultants who can research the questions. The role of the government may be limited simply to providing a register of suitable consultants. On the other hand, if an investor just needs general information on the state of the economy, or on the nature of regulations, information is more likely to already be available in some form and be able to be provided free by governments.

- What emphasis should be placed on the active dissemination of information to target users, relative to information provided passively for users to access? Active dissemination means identifying the audience and then sending the information to it, including direct mail advertising campaigns aimed at potential investors and/or having trade attachés contact potential investors. Passive dissemination means having information available (for example, in the form of brochures or on a web site) but leaving it to potential investors to seek it out. Actively targeting audiences is usually more expensive, though in some cases, if the targeting is done well, it may be more cost-effective.

- What are the advantages and disadvantages, costs and benefits of using different information channels and media?  There are many different channels and media for conveying information, and the relative merits of these need to be assessed.

- What portfolio or mix of channels and media is best for a given country's needs?  In practice, the strategy and programme that are most effective will be aimed at a mix of targets, will have a mix of government and private-sector participation, will comprise a mix of active and passive dissemination, and will use a mix of different channels and media.  There is no simple recipe to say which is best for a given country.

### (b)  Trade shows

Trade (or industry) shows bring together exhibitors in a single place to display their products and technologies.  A country seeking to attract SME FDI might run its own trade shows, encourage its firms to go as exhibitors to trade shows abroad, send government-sponsored exhibitions to display opportunities for FDI, or send delegates to attend trade shows to talk to exhibitors and encourage them to invest or trade or build alliances with suitable domestic firms.  "Virtual" trade shows may also emerge -- groupings of web pages brought together so that someone attending can "walk" through a virtual exhibition of products, technologies and services that are of interest to them, and make initial contact with the firms.  This may make it much easier and cheaper for developing countries to participate in trade shows, but will require a level of technology and skill beyond that available to many SMEs in developing countries.

The main **advantage** of trade shows is that they bring together firms with specific common interests which are seeking opportunities for business.  As such, they reduce the "chance" element of making contacts.  Trade shows are usually more effective if they have a clear focus or theme, such as a specific industry or technology (e.g., electronic components, agribusiness or forestry technologies).  It is typically harder to attract a good audience or good exhibitors to an event that is not fairly specific to their interests, simply because they are less assured of there being a suitable pool of potential firms to buy from, sell to or invest in.

The main potential **disadvantage** of trade shows is the cost-effectiveness.  This depends on the cost of exhibition space, which is often expensive, and the hit rate and conversion rate.  The hit rate defines the number of positive contacts that are made.  It can be quite low.  Trade shows are sometimes difficult for SME investors or potential investors to attend, and so they are likely to attract larger firms, not SMEs.  If the intention is to attract SME FDI, trade shows may offer only a limited hit rate.  The conversion rate is the number of potential investors that are actually induced to invest.  In most cases, trade shows provide only an initial contact and expression of interest.  If the people at a trade show are not properly trained and briefed, or do not have proper supporting materials, the hit rate and conversion rate are lower, and the cost-effectiveness is reduced.

### (c)  Trade and investment missions

Trade and investment missions involve either inviting selected groups of "trade" people from abroad to visit and review opportunities for trade and investment,[1] or sending delegations abroad to hold meetings with potential investors.  The success of such missions lies very much in the preparation and planning undertaken.  Rarely can trade missions be focused on SME FDI.  In most cases, such missions tend to focus more on trade than investment (simply because most firms start off by trading before they invest), and in most cases SMEs are only part of a mission.

The main **advantages** of trade missions are that if they are well planned, they can be a cost-effective way of introducing potential investors to opportunities; to a large extent, they can be self-financed by the participants (and in some cases SME participants can piggyback or free-ride, participating in the mission at a reduced cost, where the overheads of the mission are covered by the larger firms participating); and, finally, trade missions often gain access to government officials and opportunities that would not otherwise be accessible to any of the individual participants, especially SMEs. The main **disadvantage** is that they require bilateral cooperation, usually with governments or industry associations, to undertake the planning aspects abroad, and thus planning is more complex and requires more time.

### (d)  *Commercial attachés*

Commercial attachés are usually quasi-diplomatic staff located in embassies abroad. Usually, it is the role of commercial attachés to seek trade and investment opportunities, and to do this, they need to be fairly knowledgeable about opportunities and firms, both in the domestic market and in the foreign market where they are located. This offers **advantages** in that it allows a much more specific targeting of efforts to increase trade and SME FDI.

The **disadvantage** is that commercial attachés are expensive to maintain. Because it is more difficult and perhaps more costly to deal with SMEs relative to larger firms (since there are more SMEs and they are smaller and more diverse but require much the same level of attention), most commercial attachés tend to focus primarily on larger firms. Similarly, most developing countries cannot afford to maintain extensive networks of diplomatic and commercial representation abroad. "Privatizing" some of the functions of commercial attachés may be worth some consideration: it could reduce costs by cooperating with specific industry associations in other countries, or by commissioning consultants.

### (e)  *First-stop shops: access to information on regulations and requirements*

Potential investors seeking information, particularly information about regulations and approval procedures, can benefit from access to a first-stop shop or one-stop shop. *First-stop shops* are single points (usually an office or agency) that are intended to listen to the investors' broad ideas and questions; identify or distil relevant regulations to assist the investors; help the investors refine their questions and ideas; and direct them to where they can obtain answers to their questions. They are essentially advisory and referral centres. *One-stop shops*, in principle, go one step further -- they are able to implement the actions necessary to meet an investor's requirements. For example, at a one-stop shop, a potential investor should be able to obtain all the information necessary to know how to comply with government requirements, and should also be able to obtain the necessary approvals.

It is usually more difficult to establish one-stop shops because it is necessary to wrest control over administrative procedures from other agencies. This is particularly difficult in countries with multiple levels of government where a foreign investor needs approvals at national, provincial and local levels. For practical reasons, most one-stop shops are really first-stop shops, that is, they are really referral centres rather than genuine one-stop shops. However, first-stop shops can extend their role to assist investors in dealing with other agencies, for example in an advocacy or agency role. Such a role means that they actively help an investor to approach other agencies or to deal with problems that the investor may face, without actually subsuming the role of the other agencies. In this respect, they can sometimes be used as an effective force against corruption.

The main **advantages** of first-stop shops is that they are an effective way of bringing together all relevant information and approval procedures in one place, thus making it easier for investors to obtain information that is already available, but not necessarily accessible; they offer a good way for governments to be able to identify unnecessary complexity and inconsistency in regulations, and thus offer a good point at which to identify ways to make regulations and procedures more investor-friendly; and they offer a good mix of active and passive channels.

The **disadvantages** lie in the cost, and in actually implementing the concept successfully. The cost of setting up an effective first-stop shop can be quite large, especially if an economy is overregulated. In some cases, the one-stop or first-stop shop just becomes yet another place that the investor has to approach.

### (f)   Coordination of relevant authorities in responding to queries

Instead of setting up a one-stop or first-stop shop, it may sometimes be more effective simply to seek to coordinate informally (e.g., by means of guidelines and checklists, and occasional departmental meetings) existing agencies so that they do not provide inconsistent or misleading information to SME investors. A coordinating SME agency may play a useful role in doing this. The advantage in doing it this way is that it may be cheaper than first-stop shops (as it does not require a separate office and staff) and that it is focused more on SMEs, whereas one-stop investment shops have to meet all investors' needs.

### (g)   Role of business associations:  networking systems

Business and industry associations (such as chambers of commerce, bilateral/multilateral chambers of commerce and friendship societies etc.) can offer effective channels for the dissemination of information to potential SME investors. For example, a country might seek to establish or encourage and support a bilateral chamber of commerce or a link with existing chambers of commerce in another country (e.g., an Australia-Viet Nam Chamber of Commerce). To illustrate, Technonet Asia, an initiative of the German Federation of Small Business, has worked as a means of encouraging greater participation of and cooperation between government, chambers of commerce and business in Asia in matters related to SMEs. SME investment can then be encouraged by providing existing members with relevant information (brochures, videotapes, guest speakers etc.) and encouraging them to encourage in turn other SMEs to consider investment or trade.

The main **advantage** of such an approach is that it is very cost-effective, and that it puts government closely in contact with SME investors and potential investors, so that it is easier to monitor and meet their needs.

### (h)   Role of trading companies and facilitators

Trading companies assist investment by SMEs in a number of ways -- for example, by setting up trade links between domestic companies and companies abroad, by identifying business investment opportunities for other companies, by playing a part in subcontracting networks between large companies and SMEs, and by building investment parks. Traditionally, trading companies have been particularly important in the case of FDI from Japan. Malaysia is in the process of establishing its own national trading company.

Facilitators are specific consultants (usually SMEs themselves) that act to facilitate trade and investment activity in some or all of the following ways:

- providing special expertise in the internationalization of specific products or markets;

- offering a package of internationalization services (market research, export agency, freight forwarding, risk management, legal advice and services, financing etc.) to a client;

- extending the value chain of SMEs into international locations;

- working closely with clients to ensure that the link between production and customers is maintained, and that an SME supplier can develop in order to meet changing customer needs; and

- orchestrating or coordinating with other SMEs to offer customers around the world a competitive product or range of products.

Both trading companies and facilitators can play an important and useful role in encouraging SME trade and investment. *The first step* in getting them to do so is to identify and establish contact with appropriate trading companies and other firms to see if they have an interest in working with the government. *The second step* is to maintain a dialogue with them during the development of SME strategic plans. *The third step* is to provide them with suitable information on a regular basis, and to seek their advice on what information is required by their clients.

The main **advantages** of using these organizations are that by working with trading companies and facilitators, it is possible for governments to disseminate more effectively information to potential SME investors; much of the cost of getting the information to investors is borne by the private sector, not by the government; the facilitators and trading companies take on a more active role in actually encouraging appropriate SME FDI and trade; and because the SME investors have access to the advisory services and assistance of trading companies and facilitators, they are less likely to face problems or to fail in their endeavours. The **disadvantages** are that trading companies and facilitators have the interests of their own clients as their primary commitment. This may sometimes be inconsistent with what are seen as the national interests of some governments.

*(i)    Chambers of commerce publications and other trade publications*

Most chambers of commerce are now becoming more internationalized and most also have regular magazines or publications for their members. Most members are SMEs, but most SMEs will not necessarily have thought about trading or investing in a developing country. Simply by being exposed to a germ of an idea it is possible to start off a thought process that ultimately leads to investment. Similarly, there are numerous trade magazines, produced by governments or by private-sector publishers, that target specific business audiences and specialize in specific industries or aspects of trade. Finally, there are more generalist publications that often attract business readers (such as in-flight airline magazines). Simply making people aware of business, trade and investment opportunities is an important step. This can be done by providing editorial and advertising content to publishers of suitable magazines. Providing material that is useful and likely to be used usually requires a professional approach that understands the technical needs of magazine publishers and is attuned to their readers' needs. It is sometimes difficult to get this skill in government media units or departments.

The **advantages** of relying on these channels are that it is a highly cost-effective way of reaching a much broader audience (chance is an important initial aspect of many SMEs' internationalization), and can be especially effective if it is done in conjunction with other events or promotions, such as trade shows, trade missions or other newsworthy events. The **disadvantages** are that since use of these channels is not very targeted and is at the mercy of publishers and their editorial intervention, results may take a considerable time to emerge and it may thus be hard to justify continuing to allocate funds to it given that the cost of having a professional media unit or consultant to develop the material can be quite expensive.

### (j)    Web sites

Internet web sites are increasingly being used as a relatively cheap channel for the dissemination of information. The web page might provide information on business opportunities, contact points for firms seeking investment or trade, government policies, access to statistics on industries and the economy, summaries of government regulations relating to trade and investment, visa requirements, business and cultural customs, contact points and assistance available to investors, international bilateral chamber of commerce contacts, international agreements and conventions acceded to, future events (trade shows, conferences etc.) etc.

The **advantage** of web sites is that they allow very wide dissemination of information at zero marginal cost no matter how many people access the information. Since for many SMEs, "chance" is a key aspect of internationalization, increasing accessibility increases the number of potential SMEs that may, partly by chance, come across relevant information that may ultimately lead them to trade or invest. The **disadvantages** include high set-up and maintenance costs, since information has to be in electronic form, and has to be converted to a form that is web-readable; although this is becoming easier to do, it is still expensive to establish a web page. The real cost comes in regularly updating the information, which will have to be done anyway in an information age. The penetration of Internet technology is still relatively low amongst SMEs, especially in developing Asia (as well as Japan). This will change, but it means that some very relevant target markets in Asia are not really very accessible by the web at present; the sheer overload of the web makes it difficult to find relevant information, even if potential investors know roughly what they are looking for. "Entry points" or "key sites" are becoming more important as a means of overcoming this problem, and being linked to such a site is an important part of any web-based information strategy.

### (k)    Key entry sites:  international agencies

Some international agencies are moving to provide electronic "entry points" for firms seeking to invest and trade. The two most notable ones are UNCTAD's Tradepoint system and the MIGA's IPAnet. These are both electronic systems which allow a firm to search electronically for information about business and trade opportunities, economic conditions, regulations etc. in a wide range of countries. The electronic systems are then supported by networks of facilitators (finance providers, customs brokers etc.) who can assist with the actual deals. These systems are still in their infancy, but like the rest of the Internet, they are expanding rapidly. The UNCTAD system is not designed so much for investors as for trade (but trade is often a precursor of investment). The MIGA system is geared more to investors, but not specifically to SMEs. APEC also offers a home page, which is hot-linked to other APEC-related pages. For example, it is possible to obtain access to the pages of statistics agencies in various APEC member countries, to review the APEC investment statistics, and to access the individual action plans for trade and investment liberalization.

The **advantage** is that these electronic means offer a very cost-effective channel for making information available to potential SME investors. The use of entry points increases the accessibility to sites offered by smaller developing countries and, to some extent, overcomes the problem of information overload on the web. The **disadvantage** is that these means require information to be in electronic form and, increasingly, they require fairly sophisticated web-page design. The set-up costs of this are decreasing, but they are still high, and the cost of maintaining and regularly upgrading and reviewing the information provided is often quite large. Many SMEs in Asia do not yet have access to the web, though this may be changing quickly.

### (l) Technology-exchange programmes

Technology-exchange programmes offer a matching of lists of firms that are seeking technology with those that are willing to offer it. Since technology is often a critical element in FDI, and since a technology licence or agreement is often an alternative option to an equity or position, especially for an SME, these exchange programmes are often a starting point for SME FDI. In APEC, for example, an attempt has been made to establish ACTETSME (the APEC Centre for Technology Exchange and Training for SMEs) in the Philippines.

### (m) International forums and conferences

International forums and conferences offer government officials and, sometimes, SME managers the opportunity to meet and establish contacts. Also, it is sometimes possible to set up display stands, or to disseminate information to key officials and decision makers more effectively by targeting selective conferences and forums. Attendance at some international forums is limited by diplomatic considerations.

### (n) Other national trade-promotion bodies

National trade promotion agencies (such as JETRO in Japan, KOTRA in the Republic of Korea and AusTrade in Australia) have established databases of potential clients. Although, their main purpose was originally to promote exports from their home base, most are increasingly becoming interested in promoting investment opportunities abroad as well as in the home country. These organizations thus offer an effective way of targeting information specifically at potential investors. The first step is to liaise with relevant organizations to identify common points of interest, and to explore which of their clients are likely to be interested in FDI. It is then a matter of providing the national trade promotion agency with information packages (brochures, videos, web addresses, combined with seminars, trade missions etc.) to pass on to relevant SMEs in their databases.

## D. Encouraging linkages between SMEs across borders

## 1. Rationale

More than half of SME FDI involves some sort of partnership or alliance between the investor and the recipient. In other words, the investor abroad looks first for an existing SME to work with or invest in, rather than setting up an entirely new enterprise from the beginning. In Part One it was shown that, according to UNCTAD's survey, being approached by a partner from abroad was very important to the internationalization of about 60 per cent of SMEs in developing countries, and being approached by a customer from abroad was very important to nearly 70 per cent of them (chapter III). When there are suitable domestic firms able to form partnerships with investors abroad, FDI is much more likely to occur. It was also noted that a large part of finding a suitable partner is a matter of chance, and that it is one of the aspects of SME FDI where governments can play a role in making it easier and less risky to match up with a suitable partner. Around 30 per cent of SME investors from abroad were found to have problems in finding suitable partners (chapter III).

As noted in Part Two, governments can contribute in four main ways to the building of linkages across borders by SMEs: by creating a pool of internationally oriented domestic SMEs and managers that are both able and willing to make linkages; by facilitating the introduction processes (e.g., through matchmaking conferences and electronic means); by assisting in the formalization process (e.g., by simplifying regulations pertaining to corporate ownership, assisting potential partners to gain access to due diligence services, financial and legal services etc.); and by developing conflict-resolution services and encouraging transparent legal and regulatory systems for use by those SMEs that are involved in disputes.

## 2.  Practical measures and examples

### (a)  Matchmaking conferences

Matchmaking conferences bring together investors and potential recipients at a conference or trade show. These are usually best organized multilaterally, so that firms seeking partners are brought together from a range of different countries. They are also usually best focused on a limited number of fairly specific industries. In APEC, a series of matchmaking conferences for SMEs have been held in association with the annual SME ministerial meetings. For firms to derive much real benefit, a considerable amount of planning is required:

*The first step* is to identify areas and industries of common interest to which a sufficient number of SMEs are likely to be attracted. The usual process is to work at the government-to-government level, in cooperation with chambers of commerce and industry associations.

*The second step* is to target specific firms in each country and invite their participation. Lead times for this are long -- six to twelve months of planning is often needed, simply because many SMEs need time to make arrangements to travel and to reschedule their business activities and undertake some research.

*The third step* is to arrange some pre-introductions so that SME managers can contact each other in advance. This usually makes meetings more fruitful when they do occur.
*The remaining steps* are those associated with conference organization. This is usually left to professional conference organizers.

The main **advantages** of matchmaking conferences are that they lead to face-to-face meetings between interested SME executives. The main **disadvantages** are that they are only effective if considerable pre-conference planning has been undertaken, if SMEs attending are ready and prepared to discuss investment opportunities, and if they are not too expensive for SMEs to attend.

### (b)    Electronic matchmaking and introduction services

Electronic matchmaking services have blossomed in recent years with the growth of the Internet; as already mentioned, UNISPHERE, IBEX and GBOC are all designed with SMEs in mind (chapter VII).  Accessing these is simply a matter of having the necessary hardware (essentially a computer and modem) and web or e-mail software.  The cost of this is usually in the order of only a few thousand dollars.   Access and assistance can be provided through a central point, for example by government offices or chambers of commerce, where SMEs themselves do not have access to Internet services.  The main steps to be followed by governments seeking to use such services to attract SME FDI are:

*First*, it is necessary to appraise the potential relevance to domestic SMEs of Internet exchange programmes, since many are not geared to SMEs in developing countries.

*Second*, to the extent that it is relevant, it is necessary to develop some capability in Internet technology in government, so as to be able to advise SME clients.  This can form part of a broader information strategy dealt with in the first step.

*Third*, it is necessary to alert relevant SMEs to the potential opportunities and addresses, and to provide access points to SMEs without the necessary technology.

*Fourth*, there is a case for exploring ways of reducing the risks associated with business partnering. This is a difficult area for governments to control effectively; but finding suitable partners is a major challenge for SMEs.  The main problem is that SME partners have to be able to be trusted.  It is difficult for an SME abroad to assess whether someone can be trusted.  In using chambers of commerce networks or matchmaking conferences, there is a *de facto* procedure which checks the suitability of the SMEs being invited to participate.  This is not as easy to do using electronic networks, and the process leaves itself open to misuse by the small proportion of people who are willing to fraudulently exploit SMEs from abroad.  Unfortunately, even if this makes up only a small proportion of cases, it can tend to destroy the efforts of the entire country and give it a reputation for being an unreliable investment destination.  Consideration may thus be given to encouraging or even requiring any matchmaking agreements to be "mentored" via a reputable agent (e.g., the board of investment); establishing a register of "angels"-- older or more experienced business people -- to help mentor and advise potential partners; and establishing a "warning list" of people or firms that have behaved improperly towards foreign investors.

The main **advantage** of these services is that the cost of accessing them is very low.  The main **disadvantage** is that they offer only an introduction, and are not necessarily oriented towards FDI, or FDI in developing countries.  Although, increasingly, many offer support services of consultants, financial providers etc., the electronic introduction is really not enough to build a genuine business relationship.  It is necessary to have follow-up and personal meetings.

### (c)    Using chambers of commerce and other facilitators

Chambers of commerce and other facilitators (accountants, trade brokers etc.) can assist in bringing SME managers together and in promoting business-matching opportunities through their own databases and publications.  They can also assist in identifying suitable SMEs to join bilateral friendship arrangements, trade missions etc. Governments seeking to use these resources to encourage linkages between SMEs across borders and to encourage suitable SME FDI need to establish liaison mechanisms with appropriate organizations at home and abroad. For example, as part of regular meetings which are often held with representatives from chambers of commerce, government officials may also seek to add SME FDI facilitation to the agenda. This, in turn, may lead to cooperative programmes between chambers of commerce and governments that formalize this process. The main **advantage** of such programmes is that they are driven by personal contacts and trust, so that they tend to offer more reliable means of making introductions and building up strong linkages. The **disadvantage** is that they are more time-consuming and less likely to reach as wide an audience as the electronic mechanisms.

### (d) Clustering or networking

Clustering or networking programmes are an innovation that have emerged out of Italy and the Nordic countries. The principle is to encourage the development of clusters of firms, so that they become able to compete better internationally as a cluster.[2] In some government programmes, a cluster manager is subsidized by government, and works with the cluster of firms to identify where there are synergies and where additional firms need to be brought to the cluster to give it necessary capabilities, and to help manage the development of new markets and products. In Taiwan Province of China this clustering process has been quite important in building up international competitiveness. Part of the role of the cluster manager is in identifying market opportunities abroad, and potential investment partners.

The main **advantage** of such programmes in SME development is that they are often suited to encouraging craft industries and other smaller SMEs that would not ordinarily be suited to FDI or to international competition. FDI is only a small part of the more general thrust of such programmes of activity, but it can be very useful in allowing a cluster access to training, finance, technology and markets abroad. The **disadvantages** are the expense of running clustering programmes, and the difficulties in finding suitable people to act as network coordinators.

### (e) SME subcontracting and trading companies

Many SME linkages across borders are part of subcontracting networks, either directly with a large company, such as a trading company or a major customer, or with other SMEs that in turn subcontract to a larger company. These linkages bring domestic SMEs into international subcontracting networks. Singapore and Malaysia have used this avenue as a means of developing their domestic SMEs and encouraging FDI in them. To use this as a means of increasing FDI to domestic SMEs requires that the domestic SMEs have the capability to be internationally competitive. However, this capability is difficult to achieve without investment in technology and management skills. Therefore, this requires a programme of activities that may encompass any or all of the following elements:

- industry development plans and initiatives that seek to attract particular industries to a country or location;

- potential supplier databases, so that inquiries from large companies abroad as to which domestic firms can meet subcontracting requirements can be dealt with quickly;

- targeted programmes to identify and assist the expansion of domestic SMEs with the potential to achieve the standards expected of international subcontractors;

- technical advice and training in quality control;[3] and

- joint government and private-sector training programmes at industry or even firm-specific levels for SME managers and staff.

### (f)  Franchising and licensing

Franchising is a fast-growing form of non-equity international linkages. It is generally characterized by a form of licensing agreement that allows a franchisee to use a brand name with some degree of exclusivity, and to be provided with support by the franchisor or investor. The support typically takes the form of a business format and plan, training and technology, product development, promotions and advertising or procurement. Fees are usually paid from the franchisee to the franchisor, and there is usually no foreign equity. However, franchising involves training of domestic staff and managers of the franchisor firms in international business practices. There is thus a significant potential for training and technology transfer. Franchising is thus a useful way of expanding the skill base of the domestic SME sector and making it more internationally oriented.

Governments usually play only a small role in encouraging franchise activity, at most developing a code of franchising practice or a franchise-industry association. They can, however, help to develop information packages for potential franchisees on their rights and obligations, and develop advisory services to assist potential franchisees in evaluating franchise deals.

### (g)  Regulation of networks, alliances and resolution of disputes

Building linkages with SMEs abroad is an effective way of encouraging SME FDI. However, many of these linkages start as informal arrangements, and almost all are built on trust. Most are also built on anticipated personal gains. Problems arise when the trust is broken, when the gains do not materialize, and when there are disputes over who has contributed what to the gains. Unravelling complicated and informal business linkages is an inevitable part of the internationalization of economic activity, including SME FDI.

It is obviously better to avoid problems in the first place by means of advice and advisory services, mentoring and regulatory review and simplification so that it is easier to formalize agreements. However, some problems still have to be expected, especially for governments that wish to make significant use of the potential offered by SME FDI. Procedures to solve disputes and reconcile parties are required. Administrative and legal systems in most developing countries are not geared to addressing the problem. Options for doing this are discussed in section G below.

## E.  Providing appropriate incentives

### 1.  Rationale

Offering incentives is the fastest way for most governments to attract FDI, including SME FDI, although it is not always the best way. The incentives offered may be fiscal (i.e., the forgoing of taxable revenues); monetary (i.e., direct grants and payments); or other (involving provision of infrastructure or other forms of assistance in non-monetary form). Incentives can be available to all investors, or targeted at specific investors.

The main rationales for offering incentives are that (UNCTAD, 1995, p. 289 ff; 1996, p. 9 ff):

- They can correct a market failure, as, for instance, where there are public external benefits associated with FDI that cannot be captured by the investor. For example, if SME FDI leads to management training, it can generate external benefits that the investor may not be able to recover. The problem with this argument is that if they are not properly implemented, incentives may make the situation worse, not better, by leading to rent-seeking behaviour -- potential investors invest more with a view to getting the short-term benefits associated with an incentive rather than engaging in longer-term investment in productive activity.

- They offer a second-best solution to a problem which is difficult to eliminate, for example that other competing destinations offer incentives, or that administrative inefficiencies, such as corruption, impose unnecessary expenses or risks on the investor. The problem here is that, at a global level, the incentives have a zero effect, and lead to a lose-lose situation: if all countries provide incentives, they can get into a bidding war that does not lead to any net increase in investment. Similarly, it makes more sense to correct the problem (e.g., reducing corruption) than it does to pay investors an incentive to ignore it.

- They help overcome a "hump" and allow the economy or industry to capture dynamic benefits. This is a revised form of the infant-industry argument. For example, by encouraging the development of SMEs with computer-programming capabilities it may be possible for a country to develop an industrial base in its computer industry that has comparative and competitive advantages *vis-à-vis* other countries. The problem here is both with the implementation (and the rent seeking) and with the risk of bidding wars.

Almost all countries offer some incentives to potential investors (UNCTAD, 1995). Incentives can play a useful role in the strategic development of SME FDI. The issue is not whether to use incentives or not, or whether incentives are good or bad n the issue is that countries using incentives need to take steps to ensure that the benefits of using incentives outweigh the costs. Governments using incentives need to be aware of these costs, relative to the benefits, and of ways to design and administer the incentives so as to derive the greatest net benefits. Ensuring that the benefits outweigh the costs of incentives is not easy, and several factors need to be taken account in attempting to do so:

**First**, the benefits may be limited. Most studies show that incentives play only a limited role in FDI decisions (UNCTAD, 1996, p. 41). Evidence from Part One indicates that tax incentives are perhaps a little more important for SMEs than for larger firms, but they are still only part of a broader package of things which influence locational decisions (chapter III). For example, unless there are business opportunities, tax concessions are unlikely to offer much to investors. The point is that the benefits associated with increasing incentives may be relatively limited, and it may be better to concentrate on other, more important aspects.

**Second**, the benefits may be lost or diminished in the associated administrative process. Administration of incentives creates another layer of officials, approval processes and regulations that may open up possibilities for corruption and rent-seeking behaviour. This may easily have the effect of defeating the benefits associated with an incentive. As discussed in Part One, corruption is cited as a major problem by over 50 per cent of SMEs engaged in FDI in developing Asian countries (chapter III).

**Third**, the costs of incentives are difficult to predict. Incentives have both direct costs and hidden costs. The direct costs are usually associated with the revenue forgone, and the direct costs of the monetary payments are reasonably easy to quantify *ex post*, but *ex ante* it may be difficult to predict what the costs are likely to be. However, the more successful incentives are in attracting investment, the more they cost. The indirect costs, or hidden costs, are more difficult both to predict and to quantify *ex post*. For example, giving resource-access rights to foreign investors may have quite low direct costs, but the economic and political costs may be enormous in adverse circumstances. Since predicting the costs is difficult, governments need to put in place effective means to manage the costs and liabilities created by incentives. If the liabilities and costs rise above acceptable levels, the programme needs to be reviewed or discontinued. Incentives can also be packaged as "carrots and sticks". For example, incentives (such as a training subsidy or an exclusive right to a domestic market) may be provided if a firm maintains a certain target level of exports. The hidden costs of this sort of package are often extremely difficult to estimate.

Although it is technically possible to target incentives specifically at encouraging SME FDI, it is administratively complex and cumbersome to do so. Encouraging SME FDI by means of incentives is more a matter of knowing what the likely advantages and disadvantages of different types of incentives are: some types of incentives are better suited to SMEs, and some less so, as discussed below.

## 2. Practical measures and examples

### (a) Fiscal incentives

Fiscal incentives involve governments' forgoing taxable revenue, examples of which are provided below. In most developed countries there has been a move away from fiscal incentives in favour of more specific financial incentives (UNCTAD, 1995). This is presumably because fiscal incentives usually require changes to legislation or the regulations associated with legislation, and because they are difficult to phase out. They are also less flexible, and less easy to target at specific investors. However, in developing countries there seems to have been increased use of fiscal incentives, because they do not require allocation of funds in the budget, and they are thus politically and financially easier to implement.

The main practical consideration is to identify whether the tax system as a whole is competitive with that offered in other destinations, particularly with respect to SMEs. This requires the ability to monitor regularly the competitiveness of a country *vis-à-vis* other competing destinations as a whole, and with respect to specific types of firms. If the tax system is uncompetitive, there may be a case for reviewing it, or for making some temporary incentives available to overcome disadvantages. Similarly, if there is a strong strategic case for encouraging specific types of SMEs, there may be a case for assessing the impact of particular incentives.

#### i. Tax reductions

These are reductions in the rates of tax levied on foreign investors. These can apply to taxes on profits, sales, imports, value added, and to social security obligations. Where a country has tax rates that are significantly above those in other competing FDI destinations, tax reductions can be a useful measure. Some tax regimes put SMEs at a competitive disadvantage, especially in the way they are implemented. For example, if tax payments must be made in advance, this tends to disadvantage smaller fast-growing firms financing on cash flow.

### ii. Tax holidays

Tax holidays allow taxes on investors to be waived for several years after setting up. This makes it easier for investors to fund their expansion on cash flow, and is useful when finance is limited, a situation that is often relevant to SME ventures. In these circumstances it is arguable that tax holidays should be available to any legitimate business. The problem with tax holidays for SMEs is the temptation simply to open up and close down businesses. They can be a useful incentive when investors need to invest heavily in capital infrastructure and most of that is sunk, but in these cases accelerated write-off is probably better, as discussed below.

### iii. Accelerated write-offs, investment allowances and specific deductions

Accelerated write-offs mean that depreciation of capital equipment is permitted at a higher rate than normal, for tax purposes. This is attractive to firms that have to engage in significant sunk capital expenditure to get a project going. It has the benefit that, unless a firm is engaged in capital expenditure, it does not get the tax benefit, although it is sometimes possible to circumvent this by "selling" the benefit to otherwise ineligible firms. Similarly, investment allowances mean that a proportion of capital expenditure can be written off in the first year or so, and then the losses held over or sold to another firm.

Specific deductions allow firms to deduct a higher proportion than usual of expenses associated with specific types of expenditure, such as training or product development for tax purposes. They are useful in encouraging investors to relocate some types of activity to the host economy. For example, they may assist further product development and the sharing of higher value-added activities across borders by SMEs.

### (b) Financial incentives

Financial incentives mean that governments directly subsidize investor activity. In most developing countries, as there are budgetary constraints, these incentives are not used frequently. Whether to adopt financial incentives to encourage SME FDI depends on the assessment as regards the following:

- What impediments exist that might restrict SME FDI?
- What alternatives are available, other than financial incentives, to address the impediments?
- Will the incentives lead to any additionality? Will the money spent actually lead to any change in FDI activity, or will it simply increase the profitability of FDI activity that would have taken place anyway?
- Will the incentives attract rent-seeking investors; that is, will firms be attracted to undertaking activities (such as finding an overseas partner to elicit FDI) not because an investment activity will be productive, but just because they will be able to access a grant?
- What will it cost a SME to apply for incentives? Depending on how they are designed, the administrative procedures necessary for applying for a grant or a subsidized loan

can require a significant amount of management time. This can be very unproductive, and may discourage SMEs from applying.

- Will large firms be the main beneficiaries? Large firms are often better equipped to find out what assistance packages are available, and can employ consultants and lobbyists to maximize the chances of successfully applying for a grant or subsidy. As a result, SMEs may tend to be disadvantaged and not benefit much from such programmes.
- What are the administrative costs of distinguishing between suitable and unsuitable applicants?
- What are the incentives likely to cost under different scenarios of projected use? Usually, incentives programmes are initiated under the budget, which almost invariably does not match reality. It is sensible to use several scenarios in projecting expected budget commitments, or to limit the budget allocations in some way (such as by a rationing process or lottery for available funds).
- Will it be difficult to wind the incentives back in future?

Some examples of financial incentives follow.

### i. *Specific grants or subsidies*

Specific grants or subsidies may be provided for the installation of infrastructure (such as roads or generating equipment) or worker training. There is some case for doing this when the private sector investor can carry out the provision of necessary infrastructure or training more efficiently and at lower cost than the government itself can. However, if this is the case, there is sometimes a better argument for build-own-operate-and-transfer arrangements than for specific grants or subsidies.

### ii. *Preferential loans*

Preferential loans are subsidized loans, or loans made more accessible to certain types of investor or investment. In the broader context of industrial development strategies, this sort of loan activity can make some sense, especially if the government acts as an underwriter to secure lower-cost finance than would otherwise be available to smaller firms. In the longer term it makes more sense to try to improve the efficiency of financial markets.

### iii. *Equity participation*

The government may assist foreign ventures by taking an equity stake and injecting capital into the venture. In some cases this may actually be more of a disincentive than an incentive, depending on the conditions of participation and how the equity injection is actually funded and valued.

### (c) *Other incentives*

Other incentives cover a wide range of hybrid measures that generally involve an indirect subsidy to the investor. It is often difficult to assess the hidden costs of such measures, and they are both economically and politically dangerous to use. The practical procedures for appraising the suitability of other incentives is essentially the same as for financial incentives, with the additional proviso that hidden costs need special attention.

### i.   Resource-access guarantees

The supply of certain critical inputs (power, water, labour, raw materials etc.) may be granted to foreign investors on a priority basis. This can be useful where FDI is important in developing industrial capability, for example where the development of export competitiveness is central to development as a whole, and where this is otherwise threatened by unbalanced and unpredictable input supplies. In some cases, a resource guarantee consists in allowing imports to overcome shortages, where quotas would otherwise prohibit imports. There is an obvious danger that, in adverse conditions, resource guarantees may lead to a total squeezing out of indigenous firms from critical inputs, and allow profiteering by foreign investors.

### ii.   Protective tariffs and quotas

Foreign investors may be given undertakings that import competition will be restricted by tariffs and quotas. Whilst this approach may lead to increased FDI by some firms, it may only do so at a significant cost to the community in increased prices and in reduced international competitiveness. Whilst it is usually unlikely that tariffs are used as protective devices for SMEs, they are sometimes used to protect larger investors, who then in turn purchase from domestic SMEs at higher prices than would otherwise be possible. The danger is that this increases costs, decreases competitiveness and limits the potential market. In the longer term this inhibits FDI and development. It almost always makes more sense to use a subsidy instead of protective tariffs, because this makes the cost of the tariff more explicit and reduces protective measures to increase international competitiveness.

### iii.   Rent holidays and peppercorn leases

Rent holidays and peppercorn leases offer foreign investors access to government-owned facilities (e.g., foreign trade zones, foreign access zones, industrial parks) rent-free or at a nominal rent for a period of time. This can be a useful incentive for some SMEs to invest in these areas. As firms do not necessarily have to be the first investor into a location or market, limiting the incentive to the first few firms to invest can be considered.

### iv.   Foreign exchange rights

It may be an incentive to waive or modify restrictions on foreign exchange for foreign investors. Exchange restrictions are usually used to conserve foreign currency reserves. In the longer term, foreign exchange controls are a major impediment to FDI and trade, and it is better to seek ways to achieve convertibility.

### v.   Import rights and profit-repatriation rights

Where import controls are imposed (usually to conserve foreign currency reserves), foreign investors may be permitted to import machinery or raw materials that would otherwise be prohibited or restricted. As such restrictions (like foreign exchange restrictions) are an impediment to FDI, it is better to seek ways to liberalize them as quickly and as transparently as possible. Conferring profit-repatriation rights means that some foreign investors may be exempt from some existing profit-repatriation restrictions or withholding taxes for a period.

### (d)    Targeting incentives

To derive the greatest net benefit from providing incentives usually requires that they be targeted at the areas or enterprises where they will have most effect or impact. Deciding which areas should be targeted is part of the broader strategic planning process as discussed in chapter IX. There are two broad ways in which SME FDI incentives can be targeted:

- *Only allowing eligible SMEs (or certain types of SMEs) to access the incentive.* At a practical level, this is difficult to do because it requires some operational definition of what is an eligible SME and what is not. The result is to have very specific definitions for specific circumstances. For example, an SME might be defined as having fewer than 20 employees and less than $10 million turnover to be eligible for one sort of incentive, but as having fewer than 200 employees and less than $100 million turnover for another incentive. This sort of procedure is fairly widely used (e.g., in Japan and the Republic of Korea) for access to services and incentives for domestic SMEs. The result is administratively cumbersome, and lends itself to artificial restructuring by companies in order to comply with the requirements. The advantage is that, in principle, the benefits of incentives can be targeted more precisely.

- *Designing the incentive so that it is available to any firm, but is more likely to be of benefit for SMEs.* For example, an incentive of a subsidy may be available in relatively small amounts (say, tens of thousands of dollars) to any firm engaged in training the staff of a local partner. The small size of the subsidy may make it less attractive to larger firms. This approach can be administratively simpler. The disadvantage of this is that, as it is imprecise as to who will receive the benefits, it is difficult to determine in advance what the incentive programme will cost.

#### i.    Special industry/region concessions

Targeting the development of particular industries or regions is one way of encouraging SMEs. Some developing regions are more likely to benefit from SME investment, but less likely to be the recipients of SME FDI than large cities or more developed regions. By attaching a package of incentives to particular industries or regions, it is sometimes possible to encourage SME FDI.

#### ii.    Subcontracting and supply-industry incentives

Targeting supply-industry SMEs is a logical component of strategic plans for SME development. Countries such as Singapore have tended to target this through large firms. A package of incentives may be made available to large firms to encourage them to provide technology, quality control, and management training to local SMEs.

#### iii.    Special SME-only industries

Some countries (Indonesia, Philippines, Republic of Korea) have in the past restricted FDI in certain industries (such as agriculture, national crafts and retailing) by declaring them to be industries reserved only for domestic firms or domestic SMEs. The rationale is to limit potential competition from large foreign firms in industries that are politically sensitive and employ large numbers of people (but may be inefficient). Whilst politically expedient, the policy limits development, and it may be better to use networking or clustering policies in combination with other support mechanisms.

*iv.    Export promotion and import-substitution programmes*

Encouraging the development of export capability and international competitiveness is another target area of interest to governments, and encouraging SME FDI is one way of doing this. As noted in Part One, SMEs are more likely than large firms to see exports as a key element of their FDI strategy (chapter IV).

## F.    Providing investors with access to support services and infrastructure

### 1.    Rationale

"Investors" in this section refers to both SMEs investing from abroad and the SMEs they invest in, and "support services" refers to a broad range of different programmes of support offered to SMEs in the areas of finance, human resource development, technology transfer etc. Providing SMEs with access to support services has been a central feature of the development of most of the leading economies in Asia; Japan, the Republic of Korea, Singapore and Taiwan Province of China all have extensive portfolios of programmes to support SMEs. These have already been described in Part Two. The usual rationale is that, by making support available to them, SMEs are better able to overcome temporary problems, and are thus able to fulfil their potential. For most developing countries comprehensive support programmes for all domestic SMEs may be difficult to provide. However, there is some point in providing limited support services for SMEs engaged in FDI. It may seem somewhat odd and unfair to provide support services to foreign firms when resources are not available to support all the local SMEs that might need assistance; however, there is some logic in this. As noted in Part One, the entrepreneurial engine is driven by a relatively small number of fast-growing firms. Over half of SME FDI involves partnerships or foreign equity participation in domestic firms. Firms that receive or engage in FDI are more likely to be growth-oriented and to be major contributors to the entrepreneurial engine. They are likely to face some problems that inhibit their growth potential, but they are not likely to need comprehensive support services. For example, they may be inhibited because of local regulations, or because their expansion is constrained by a lack of suitably trained staff. By providing suitable limited-support mechanisms for SMEs receiving FDI, or to foreign SMEs engaged in FDI, governments are effectively investing in the entrepreneurial engine.

The main practical issues to consider in developing support mechanisms for SMEs engaged in FDI are:

- **First**, to identify the areas in which SME investors may benefit from support services, and compare these with existing services available. This is best done by monitoring impediments to SME investment; methods for doing this systematically are examined in section G.

- **Second**, to assess the resources available to provide additional services. Providing resources only to assist firms from abroad and/or their local partners is obviously not as desirable as more general programmes, but it may be a cost-effective element in attracting SME FDI, and also provides a way of getting some general support service programmes started.

- **Third**, to seek ways to fund programmes. This means looking at options for cost recovery and cost sharing with the SMEs that use the services. Similarly, in some cases, cooperative programmes can be established with foreign governments, chambers of commerce or industry associations from abroad, or larger foreign firms. This helps share the set-up costs.

- **Fourth**, to examine ways in which services provided to SME investors can be made available at marginal cost to other indigenous SMEs. For example, training programmes or advisory services, once established, might be made available to other, local SMEs.

## 2. Practical measures and examples

### (a) *Central agency coordination: one-stop or first-stop shops*

The concept of establishing a central coordinating agency to coordinate SME strategy is a common feature of SME programmes in Asia. In developing countries, it may take time to establish such an agency, even though being able to respond to problems faced by investors is a key element of providing effective support. It may thus make some sense to establish a one-stop or first-stop shop as an interim coordinating point.

### (b) *Cooperative programmes designed to develop appropriate skills or intangible infrastructure*

The lack of suitably trained technicians or of middle managers is sometimes an impediment to the growth of SMEs investing from abroad, even if they have access to foreign equity capital. Programmes aimed at developing skills or providing other intangible infrastructure, such as advisory services, can therefore help overall development. Such programmes can be set up by governments, in cooperation with universities, training institutes, chambers of commerce, international industrial associations and large firms.

### (c) *Industrial zones, foreign trade zones, technology parks and incubators*

To provide physical infrastructure (roads, electricity, communications, housing etc.) and intangible infrastructure (training, security etc.) to all SMEs is expensive. Access to it is often an important consideration in attracting some types of FDI. One policy option is to provide only access to key physical infrastructure to a relatively limited number of firms, such as investors from abroad and their local partners. This limits the cost, and can make cost recovery of the infrastructure investment easier. Foreign trade zones, industrial zones, technology parks and incubators can all be developed in this way. These facilities can also be developed in cooperation with foreign companies (such as the major trading companies) or with foreign governments. For example, Singapore has established industrial parks in Bangalore (India) and in Suzhou (China) to encourage its firms to invest abroad.

### (d) *Credit guarantee and financial systems*

SMEs engaging in investing in SMEs often need some form of credit guarantee for their investments. The process of investment may involve their raising capital abroad to invest in the host country. They might then seek to raise additional capital in the host country, as a natural hedge against currency volatility. International credit guarantee agencies are now more willing to provide guarantee arrangements to local financial providers, as a package deal. This requires, however, that the government of the host country cooperates in the process, and that there is some supervisory process. The development of such arrangements can be effected at relatively little cost to the host country, but it can offer significant support to some types of SME investors.

## G. Addressing specific impediments and barriers to SME FDI

### 1. Rationale

Impediments are factors that stop SMEs from investing in the first place, or make it harder for them to expand and grow once they have invested. Evidence from Part One suggests that there are many such factors. By addressing the impediments and enhancing factors which help SMEs to invest, it may be possible to increase the investment and economic activity of existing investors, and to attract new SME investors. As noted, the biggest problem area is that of impediments created by governments themselves.

There are three main practical issues:

- How to identify and monitor the relative importance of different impediments. Some impediments are more serious than others. Because there are many SMEs and because they are affected in different ways, it is necessary to have some form of systematic monitoring that allows impediments to be identified and ranked in order of importance relative to their impact on development.

- How to act on impediments. Many impediments are a symptom of a more fundamental problem. For example, corruption is a major impediment to many SMEs, but it is often a symptom of more fundamental issues, such as a lack of resources for paying public-sector staff. Dealing with the fundamental issues may not always be possible, at least in the short term. Some pragmatic temporary solutions or actions are suggested below for the most significant impediments.

- How to help SMEs address impediments themselves. Different SMEs are affected in different ways; while for some an impediment may be quite significant, while for others it may only be a minor nuisance. Helping SMEs know how to address some impediments may be easier than dealing with the impediment themselves.

### 2. Practical measures and examples

*(a)    Mechanisms to identify impediments*

The main practical steps in setting up systems to monitor factors impeding the growth of SME FDI are:

- A commitment and strategic intent to use FDI, and especially SME FDI, as a means of development. This is important where it is necessary to make structural and organizational changes.

- Establishing channels to allow regular communication with investors and potential investors about their concerns and the impediments facing them.  These channels may be both formal and informal, and may involve the use of government agencies and non-government organizations.

- Establishing a review process that can appraise information about impediments and systematically assess the significance of impediments for the development potential.  This review process can be entirely within the government, or it can be a more open and consultative process.

### i.    *User-friendly boards of investment and agencies dealing with SME investors*

SMEs engaged in FDI usually have the boards of investment as their first main contact point with a government.  Boards of investment are responsible for reviewing, approving and, usually, also monitoring investment applications.  As such, they are often seen as an impediment, because they delay the investment process and insist on administrative compliance with procedures that do not assist the investor (and that may do little to assist development either).  There is no necessary reason why boards of investment cannot be made more investor-friendly, although to do so requires some rethinking of their role and procedures.  The practical steps involved in making more effective use of the resources tied up in boards of investment are as follows:

- **First**, to redefine the role and objectives of the boards of investment to be more investor-oriented.  An investor-friendly board of investment has as its objective the facilitation of development through FDI.  As such, it may still seek administrative compliance, but this becomes secondary to the more fundamental issue of encouraging investors, investment and their contribution to development.  An alternative administrative solution is to turn the board of investment into a first-stop shop for investors, so that it becomes subordinate to a facilitation process.

- **Second**, to modify administrative and monitoring procedures.  Boards of investment concerned with administrative compliance often collect a great deal of information, both at the time of the investment and then in each reporting period, which can be as frequent as monthly intervals.  Most of this information goes unused, and it is not designed to help governments monitor impediments or ways to improve the investment climate.  By rethinking the reporting processes it is possible to encourage investors to identify problem areas.  In some cases, it is even worth appointing "client managers" who can periodically contact investors to discuss issues and problems with them, and pass the information back up the line for action.

- **Third**, to have regular and systematic reviews of problems and impediments.  This is part of the ongoing SME strategic planning process, and is probably best done by a central SME agency.

### ii.    *Chambers of commerce*

Chambers of commerce also offer a channel for SME investors to convey to government concerns about issues and impediments.  As their heads often have regular meetings with government officials, it is easy to add an agenda item on SME FDI concerns.  For these meetings to be useful, however, chambers have to have direct access to SME investors. To obtain such access, the government may need to liaise and provide chambers with updated lists of investors. In addition, governments may consider providing chambers with some resources and assistance in carrying out surveys or reviews of impediments and other issues concerning investors. Most chambers are under-resourced and rely heavily on voluntary work, especially in developing countries. Independent surveying helps to allow investors to retain anonymity, and is more likely to provide accurate information.

### iii. International notification systems

International or bilateral chambers of commerce also offer channels for investors and potential investors to raise concerns. To take advantage of these channels, governments need to establish regular liaison and communication, and to invite such organizations to assist in identifying factors that unnecessarily impede SME FDI.

### (b) Common impediments limiting SME FDI

Common impediments to SME FDI were identified in Part One. The main issues and some suggestions as to how they may be dealt with are set out below.

### i. Corruption

Corruption is seen as the single most important problem for SME investors, not so much because of the cost of it as because of the unpredictability associated with it. It tends to be a more significant problem for medium-sized investors than for small investors. Corruption is usually associated with gaining the necessary approvals, or with subsequently meeting the conditions associated with approvals. Eliminating corruption is a long-term process of simplifying regulations, developing transparent legal and regulatory systems, imposing penalties on corrupt officials, and increasing public service pay rates. In the short term, it may be possible to reduce significantly the undesirable aspects of corruption for SMEs by restructuring FDI approval procedures to be more user-friendly; giving one-stop or first-stop shops the authority to act on behalf of SME investors in securing necessary approvals; imposing strict anti-corruption guidelines on the staff of the one-stop shops; and allowing one-stop shops to charge SME investors for the services provided with respect to gaining the necessary approvals, but requiring that the charges be transparent and clearly related to the services and approvals required.

As noted in section B above, many SME managers would not object to paying charges if there was more certainty and less unpredictability in the system. This does not mean that the charges would have no upper limit; at some stage, they would start to make the destination uncompetitive.

### ii. Approval procedures and documentation

Approval procedures can reduce flexibility, and impose unnecessary transaction costs and delays on investors. For example, in some countries, approval for FDI is tied very specifically to a particular activity. If the investor receives approval to invest in the manufacture of shoes, but finds that the market is not there and that manufacturing leather furniture for export is more likely to be successful, it is necessary to go back and seek approval for the change. In most cases, the approval procedure adds nothing to the development process, but it very much impedes the ability of SMEs to compete in a flexible way. Complicated approval procedures also open up opportunities for corruption.

However, approval procedures can also be quite helpful, especially if they are adapted to be more investor-friendly.

### iii.    Minimum investment requirements

Some countries require a minimum amount of investment to be made by a foreign investor. The rationale for this is partly to protect local SMEs from foreign firms that establish small affiliates. It may also derive from an administrative reason: boards of investment may not want to process small amounts as time and resources spent for them may be roughly the same as those for large amounts. Such regulations discourage SME FDI. The regulations are ineffective anyway -- SMEs wishing to invest small amounts simply find unofficial ways of doing the same thing, but are then more exposed to corruption. Abolishing the regulation is the simplest and easiest way of dealing with the problem. Alternatively, for amounts of less than a certain minimum amount, the requirement for approval may be eliminated, although small investors may still have to lodge a formal notification. Restructuring the functions of boards of investment to be more investor-friendly is one way of dealing with the problem.

### iv.    Foreign exchange regulations and rates

Some countries impose foreign exchange regulations that either limit the amount of currency that can be converted, or regulate the rates at which it can be converted. This is cited as a particular impediment where official conversion rates differ significantly from parity rates or market rates. Exchange rate regulations also pose problems when the local finance and banking industry is not well developed. The lack of a financial market prompts firms to raise finance abroad, thus exposing them to exchange rate risks. For SMEs it is harder and more expensive to hedge risks by use of futures or swaps. Exchange rate fluctuations also pose problems for SME investors because of the unpredictability and the costs of hedging against fluctuations.

In the longer term, these exchange rate issues can be addressed only by currency convertibility, by developing financial markets and institutions, and by responsible monetary and fiscal management of the macro economy. Currency realignment is always going to cause some short-term pain, but it will usually encourage more FDI in the longer term. In the shorter term, credit-guarantee arrangements can assist SME investors in dealing with fluctuations and realignments.

### v.    Telecommunications

Reliable and reasonably priced telecommunication services are important to many SMEs investing across borders. Managers of international SMEs rely on telecommunications (telephone, mobile telephone, fax, Internet) to keep track of their operations, communicate with staff and partners, place orders, transmit plans and documents, etc. In other words, telecommunications are central to the operation of a competitive international small business. The main criticism of telecommunications offered in developing countries relates to:

- Restrictions on access, especially to the Internet. Although the Internet poses some social problems for some governments, it needs to be realized that many small business use it extensively as a form of management communication, and that it offers some very significant benefits in terms of access to markets and information.

- The price of the services. The creation of monopoly suppliers of telecommunication services has often led to very high charges for services, especially services for international use. This can be a significant impediment to smaller businesses.

- The reliability of services. In some developing countries, services are still unreliable, even though technology is now making it easier and cheaper to provide reliable and accessible telephone and data services without incurring major infrastructure investment costs.

Resolving these impediments requires that governments assess the regulatory and technological options available to them in the light of a globalized economy, and in the light of their need to attract SME FDI.

### vi.    Disputes and dispute settlement procedures:  cultural factors

Disputes, and the difficulties in resolving disputes, can be a problem for some SMEs. Disputes are typically with staff or organized labour (e.g., over pay or conditions); local partners (e.g., over rights to assets or profits); suppliers (e.g., over ability to supply on time); and government (e.g., over the enforcement of regulations). There are a number of things that governments can do. The first step is to try to help SMEs to avoid disputes in the first place. In many cases, labour disputes are due to lack of understanding of cultural factors, or a lack of awareness of local labour practices; disputes with partners or suppliers can be partly due to the lack of an effective system for the registration of agreements, and of title to land or other property, or more simply the lack of cultural understanding; and disputes with government can be the result of imprecision in the codification of laws or regulations, or ambiguities in the interpretation of the law.

Once a dispute has occurred, the procedure for settling it becomes important. The government might:

- assist by providing skilled mediators to advise both sides and help them come to an agreement;
- provide training programmes for the judiciary to assist them in understanding and resolving fairly disputes that involve international firms, especially SMEs;
- work towards more precise codification of regulations that are causing problems, or issue guidelines on the interpretation of certain regulations and acts; and
- set up separate specialist administrative tribunals to handle disputes faced by foreign investors.

### vii.    Visas and entry requirements

The inability to get visas for key staff, or delays and inconvenience in obtaining them, impedes some investors. This is a particular nuisance to SME managers, because they tend to bear the administrative burden in these areas themselves, rather than having staff to do it, and they are less likely to have access to the special treatment offered to larger investors. Many countries no longer require visas for short-stay arrangements. For example, business-visa arrangements in APEC now often allow special entry channels to be used to save business people from queuing at immigration counters. APEC has been even discussing the abolition of the visa requirement for business travellers in the region.

*viii. Access to skilled staff and managers*

Skilled staff, such as technicians or middle managers, are often important to the growth of firms. FDI is often seen as a means of gaining access to skilled staff and technology. In the longer term, local enterprises cannot continue to rely on FDI as the sole source of training for sustained growth. Governments can play a role by encouraging the establishment of training centres and programmes (see section F above).

*ix. Unfair competition*

Unfair competition is regarded as a major problem by about one-third of SME investors surveyed (chapter III). This includes:

- state-owned enterprises, or their foreign partners getting special favourable treatment, e.g., in terms of access to supplies or markets;

- corrupt officials interpreting laws or regulations in discriminatory ways, for example as a result of competitors bribing them;

- significantly higher charges, or sometimes bribes, being levied on foreign investors relative to local companies; and

- unfair or unethical competitive practices (such as copying trademarks or patented products, using false and misleading advertising, or even industrial sabotage) that are difficult to combat because of a lack of effective competition and consumer protection laws.

Addressing unfair competition is a matter of knowing where and why it occurs. Sometimes it can be resolved simply on a case-by-case basis, but where the issue is more systemic it may require a review of regulations and government practices. In some cases, unfair competition is attributable to incentives offered to some firms.

*(c) Helping SMEs to address impediments*

In some cases SMEs involved in FDI can be helped to address impediments themselves. These relate, for example, to:

- *Management practices and cultural factors.* SME managers often cite difficulties in applying the work practices and management systems that they use at home to their operations in host countries. By encouraging new investors to discuss and learn from earlier successful (or even unsuccessful) investors it is possible to remodel these practices so as to take into account cultural differences and local conditions.

- *Business partners and matching.* A common problem facing SME investors is finding a business partner that they can trust. Encouraging SMEs to take advantage of the networks and sources of information that exist can help them to search for and identify reliable partners.

- *Approval processes.* Sometimes SME managers fail to take the necessary time to understand local conditions and requirements, and become frustrated when the approval process is drawn out or their applications are sent back for revisions. Helping SMEs to plan realistically and understand the approval processes, and showing them how to meet the requirements, can reduce frustrations and the temptation to bribe officials to overlook inadequacies in the application or to accelerate the approval process.

## Notes

[1] For example, an economy wishing to attract investment in the electronics or agribusiness industry might invite delegations from abroad to visit a specific region or industry to review investment prospects.

[2] For example, while individually a woodworker, a fabric maker and a leather worker may not have much in common, there may be a market for fabricating shop fittings for an international market.

[3] In Singapore, for example, such advice and training are provided as part of government programmes at the Productivity and Standards Board.

# CHAPTER XI

## MAKING USE OF INTERNATIONAL COOPERATION TO PROMOTE SME FDI IN DEVELOPING COUNTRIES

The issues of how home countries and international organizations can facilitate the flow of SME FDI to developing countries were examined in Part Two (chapter VIII). This chapter briefly revisits those issues and suggests practical avenues by means of which governments in developing countries can work with international organizations and other governments to encourage SME FDI as a means of development.

### A. International cooperation

International cooperation is becoming more important in the delivery of SME support programmes and infrastructure. It may be in the form of technical and financial assistance directly from governments or international agencies, or indirectly through intermediate agencies, or even jointly with the private sector. Examples are the development of industrial parks and associated infrastructure suited to SME needs; training programmes offered to SME managers from developing countries; sharing of experience on SME policy and programme development; international cooperation on credit-guarantee facilities for SMEs; and technical assistance in setting up advisory and consulting services for SMEs.

The practical steps needed to take advantage of the opportunities offered by international cooperation are:

- Regular monitoring of the availability of relevant programmes and projects. For example, major international organizations such as the Asian Development Bank make available forward notice of types of projects. The European Union has the European Community

Investment Partners scheme (ECIP), whose objective is to encourage FDI by European Union SMEs in countries throughout Asia as well as Latin America, the Mediterranean and South Africa (UNCTAD and European Commission, 1996). Governments in developed countries publicize thorough select channels the availability of technical assistance and training programmes.

- Development of SME strategy and identification of priority areas for SME development. It is easier to attract interest from international agencies and governments if the government in the developing country has defined and researched its needs clearly, and can demonstrate the potential benefits accruing from cooperation and technical assistance.

- Liaison with governments in more developed economies, and with international agencies, on the possibility of accessing existing programmes or of designing specific cooperation initiatives.

## B. Codes of investment and market access

Compliance with international codes or agreements on investment and trade are important aspects of the internationalization of economies, and play a role in a country's ability to attract FDI, both from SMEs and from larger firms. SMEs generally benefit from the liberalization and certainty that the adoption of general codes offers. This means that it is important for governments to monitor the changes being recommended or suggested in forums such as the WTO, APEC and OECD, even though they may not be active participants in the processes of those organizations. It is also important to endeavour to set clear milestones and targets for moving towards the adoption of investment and other international codes, so that investors can plan ahead.

## C. Networking, information systems and global commerce

Global commerce offers quite considerable opportunities, especially to SME development, but it also poses some threats. The enormous explosion of information, and the opportunities for trade and investment that this brings, are unavoidable. At a practical level, this requires governments to develop plans regarding how they will cooperate with international matchmaking services and conferences (such as IBEX and the Global Business Opportunities Convention), and with information providers such as the UNCTAD's Trade Point system and MIGA's IPAnet system. Such plans need to address which providers, key entry points etc. the government wishes to deal with; the information to be provided to the endorsed providers; and the extent to which the government will take steps to facilitate access to those services by local SMEs or, conversely, the restrictions and impediments to be attached to access.

## D. Multilateral cooperation to identify and reduce barriers to SME FDI

Identifying and reducing barriers to SME FDI is partly a matter of gleaning input from decision makers and investors outside the country. As shown in Part One, SME investors tend to share control of decision-making with local partners, preferring joint ventures to fully owned affiliates (chapter IV). Accessing decision makers and potential investors in other countries requires some cooperation with agencies and organizations responsible for SMEs abroad.

The main practical steps required are to:

- identify where most SME FDI is coming from, or likely to come from;
- encourage the setting up and operation of bilateral chambers of commerce and friendship associations with SMEs in those locations;
- identify the main organizations (both government and industry) that are responsible for SMEs in those locations; and
- hold regular meetings between government and representatives of those chambers of commerce and other SME organizations to identify opportunities and impediments to SME investment. Where appropriate, government-to-government discussions need to be held.

## E. Monitoring of competitiveness in attracting SME FDI

There is an increasing need for developing countries to be able to monitor their attractiveness to foreign investors (relative to other competing destinations) on a systematic and ongoing basis. As noted in Part Two, what is needed is a systematic comparison of "objective" factors (such as economic fundamentals, government regulations and incentives) and monitoring of investor sentiments (that requires surveying of investors). The problem facing any given country is that collecting and updating such information from other countries on a systematic basis is expensive, duplicates their efforts and is not necessarily all that accurate. It makes more sense for a single international agency, such as UNCTAD, UNIDO or MIGA, to cooperate with countries to develop a standard format and reporting procedure. That way, each participating country would have to provide information on only its own economy on a regular basis. This could then be consolidated, and supplemented with additional information from other sources (e.g., from rating agencies). The consolidated tables could then be made available to governments and to investors alike via the web and other publication channels.

What is first required is for governments to agree to provide information in a comparable format. For example, information might be collected on:

- Economic fundamentals -- information which allows comparison of broad economic performance indicators (e.g., GDP, economic growth, GDP per capita, inflation, interest rates, government deficit, current account deficit, exchange rates, reserves).

- Comparative costs on a standardized basket relevant to business (e.g., office rental in major cities, warehouse costs, factory costs, telephone costs, unskilled labour costs).

- Risks (e.g., country risk ratings provided by investment agencies; other risks, e.g., crime rates affecting business people).

- Policy targets and performance at a general level (e.g., targeted growth of GDP and other targets for key indicators).

- Taxes and business regulations generally (e.g., taxes on profit and income, withholding tax, incorporation requirements).

- Regulations, policies and incentives as they relate to foreign investment, both at general levels and at specific industry or provincial level (e.g., transparency, most-favoured-nation treatment, national treatment, repatriation and convertibility of profits and investment, entry and stay of personnel, tax treatment, performance requirements, incentives available and other measures).

Ultimately, the delivery of such a service depends on funding for it, and this will require support from interested countries.

# REFERENCES

Asia-Pacific Economic Cooperation (APEC) (1994). *The APEC Survey on Small and Medium Enterprises 1994* (Singapore: APEC Secretariat).

Chrisman, James and F. Katrishen (1994). "The economic impact of Small Business Development Centre Counselling Activities in the United States: 1990-1991", *Journal of Business Venturing*, 9, pp. 271-280.

Fujita, Masataka (1998). *The Transnational Activities of Small and Medium-Sized Enterprises* (New York and Dordrecht: Kluwer Academic Publishers).

Hall, Chris (1996). *Report of the APEC Symposium on HRD for SMEs* (Taipei: China Productivity Centre).

International Monetary Fund (IMF) (1993). *Balance of Payments Manual*, fifth edition (Washington, D.C.: IMF).

Kaiser, Robert (1996). "The role of credit guarantee systems in assisting the development of SMEs and international trade", paper presented at the APEC Seminar on Credit Guarantee Systems, Taipei, Taiwan Province of China, 17-19 September.

Lecraw, Donald (1996). "Comparative analysis of investment incentives in Asia and the Pacific", paper presented at the Workshop on Location Asia Pacific, organized by UNCTAD, Manila, 26-28 September.

Organisation for Economic Co-operation and Development (OECD) (1997). *Globalisation and Small and Medium Enterprises,* Volume 1: *Synthesis Report* (Paris: OECD).

Pacific Economic Cooperation Council (PECC) (1995). *Survey of Impediments to Trade and Investment in the APEC Region* (Singapore: PECC Secretariat).

Singapore, Economic Development Board (1993). *Growing with Enterprise: A National Effort* (Singapore: Economic Development Board).

Tan, Jek Min (1996). "Training and consulting services in Singapore", in Chris Hall *Report of the APEC Symposium on HRD for SMEs* (Taipei: China Productivity Centre), pp. VI-K.

United Nations Conference on Trade and Development (UNCTAD) (1993). *Small and Medium-sized Transnational Corporations: Role, Impact and Policy Implications* (Geneva and New York: United Nations), United Nations publication, Sales No. E.93.II.A.15.

_____ (1995). *Incentives and Foreign Direct Investment* (Geneva and New York: United Nations), United Nations publication, Sales No. E.96.II.A.6.

_____ (1995a). *World Investment Report 1995: Transnational Corporations and Competitiveness* (New York and Geneva: United Nations), United Nations publication, Sales No. E.95.II.A.9.

_____ (1996). *World Investment Report 1996: Investment, Trade and International Policy Arrangements* (New York and Geneva: United Nations), United Nations publication, Sales No. E.96.II.A.14.

_____ (1996a). *International Investment Instruments: A Compendium:* Volume II: *Regional Instruments* (New York and Geneva: United Nations), United Nations publication, Sales No. E.96.II.A.10.

_____ (1997). *World Investment Report 1997: Transnational Corporations, Market Structure and Competition Policy* (New York and Geneva: United Nations), United Nations publication, Sales No. E.97.II.D.10.

_____ and European Commission (1996). *Investing in Asia's Dynamism: European Union Direct Investment in Asia* (Luxembourg: Office for Official Publications of the European Communities).

Van Elkan, Rachel (1995). "Singapore's development strategy" in *Singapore: A Case Study in Rapid Development*, IMF Occasional Paper 119 (February).

World Bank (1993). *The East Asian Miracle: Economic Growth and Public Policy* (Oxford: Oxford University Press).

Zheng, Ching Long (1992). "Industrial land development and the growth of small and medium sized firms in Taiwan", paper presented at the Seminar on the Development Experience of Small and Medium Enterprises, Taiwan Institute of Economic Research, International Economic Cooperation Fund, Ministry of Economic Affairs, Taipei.

# ANNEX

# NOTE ON SURVEY METHODOLOGY

The methodology used for this *Handbook* involved the use of questionnaires and case studies of firms engaged in or receiving foreign direct investment (FDI).

## Questionnaire surveys

Questionnaire surveys of small and medium-sized enterprises (SMEs) *receiving* FDI were carried out in Myanmar, Viet Nam and the Philippines. Surveys of SMEs *engaging* in FDI were carried out in the Republic of Korea, Singapore and Taiwan Province of China. The questionnaire used in each of these cases, respectively, is reproduced below. In Taiwan Province of China and the Republic of Korea, the questionnaire was translated into the local language. In all other countries, the questionnaire in English was used.

The survey questionnaire had three main aims:

- to provide a reasonably robust estimate of the relative contribution of SME FDI to development, directly and indirectly. This is relative to larger firms (or to total development, investment etc.) and also relative to other economies that may be more successful;

- to identify specific impediments and policies of assistance, especially government programmes. This was also followed up in case studies; and

- to be able to analyze SME FDI in terms of major characteristics or patterns (country of origin, type of firms, type of investment, type of market etc.).

Identifying the target population of SMEs was not easy. Among the countries surveyed, only the Republic of Korea keeps any record of FDI by size of firm. Only there was it possible to get some measure of the population from which the sample was being drawn. For this reason, the sampling could not be done in a systematic way. The approach adopted was to target "small package" FDI, that is FDI approvals of less than $1 million. This biased the selection to smaller firms, but still included some larger ones. In Myanmar, as fairly detailed lists of all investors are available and the numbers are relatively small, it was possible to target more precisely. In the Philippines, assistance was provided by the Chamber of Commerce of the Philippines Foundation, Inc., in order to supplement data from the Board of Investment.

The specific steps involved in the questionnaire surveys were as follows:

1.    Consultants liaised with and obtained from the board of investment, or other sources as appropriate, lists of local firms that had received foreign investment in the three years immediately preceding the survey. The information was obtained in electronic format and contained the following information wherever possible:

- • name, fax number, telephone number and address of the local firm;
- • name, fax number, telephone number and address of the foreign firm making the investment;
- • contact name of the manager in the local firm;
- • date of approval or application for approval of the investment;
- • amount of investment sought or approved; and
- • industry category.

2.    Liaison was undertaken with the department of industry or other appropriate bodies on the content of economy-specific questions about impediments and programmes of assistance. These were then included in the questionnaire version specific to that economy.

3.    In conjunction with UNCTAD, consultants liaised with the board of investment or department of industry as appropriate, to obtain a supporting letter for the questionnaire.

4.    In liaison with UNCTAD, consultants selected a sample of about 300-500 firms on the basis that they had received relatively small amounts of FDI. This selection procedure meant that some larger firms were also selected. These larger firms then acted as a trial group or control group.

5.    The consultant mailed or faxed a covering letter seeking cooperation in the survey, the supporting letter and the questionnaire to the targeted firms.

6.    A limited telephone follow-up and survey of non-returns or partial returns, to encourage complete returns and establish the reasons for non-return, was undertaken where possible.

For the survey on SME investors, similar steps were followed. In the Republic of Korea, it was relatively easy to identify such investors as SME FDI has been recorded by the Bank of Korea. In Singapore it was not possible to obtain lists of firms engaged in FDI, and so assistance was sought from the Singapore National Employers Federation, which cooperated by surveying its member base. Similarly, in Taiwan Province of China identification of a target group was carried out on the basis of cooperation between the Chung Hua Research Institute and the relevant government authorities.

Response rates were typically less than 10 per cent of the forms sent out.

Total returns obtained from host countries were as follows:

|  | returns |
|---|---|
| Myanmar | 16 |
| Viet Nam | 37 |
| Philippines | 25 |
| **Total from recipients** | **78** |

Thirty-four out of the 78 fell into the category of SME-SME (i.e., FDI by a SME in a SME). The rest were cases of SME-LE (i.e., FDI by an SME in a large firm). The home economies of FDI among these 78 respondents are, in order of magnitude, Singapore (10 respondents), Western Europe (10), Japan (9), the United States (6), Taiwan Province of China (6), the Republic of Korea (3) and other (14). Twenty respondents did not disclose the nationality of the foreign investors.

The distribution of the responses from the investor firms surveyed was as follows:

|  | returns |
|---|---|
| Republic of Korea | 40 |
| Singapore | 21 |
| Taiwan Province of China | 25 |
| **Total from investors** | **86** |

## Case studies

The main point of the case studies of SME FDI undertaken in selected countries was to:

- examine in greater depth the issues facing SMEs involved in FDI, and especially their suggestions for improving policy; and

- provide examples of SMEs engaged in FDI, in order to supplement the information gathered in the questionnaires.

The format used for the case studies was broadly as follows, although variations were necessary at times:

- Brief description and history of company and industry, especially its business development (e.g., what does it make or provide? when did it start business? how fast is it growing?).

- How and why it has internationalized? (e.g., what type of FDI and resource flows has it engaged in, why did it adopt the strategy it has?).

- What problems has it faced in developing its business? (e.g., are the problems mostly internal to the firm (such as management) or are they problems that governments can do something about (such as reducing regulations, tackling corruption)?).

- In what ways has it contributed to the economy and economic development? (e.g., by investment, training, new product development, R & D).

- What is stopping it from developing more? (e.g., realistically, how much more might it be able to grow and contribute to the economy if problems were reduced, and what suggestions are there that might be useful to governments?)

## Questionnaire for the survey on SMEs receiving FDI

*Please tell us about the nature of your international activity*

| | *...equity investment including reinvested earnings from abroad and loans from related companies* | *...long term loans from unrelated organisations abroad* | *...technology from abroad (eg licenses, or patents from companies abroad)* | *...training from abroad (eg specialist advisers)* |
|---|---|---|---|---|
| 1. In the last five years have you received from abroad... | [ ] yes  [ ] no if no, please ignore the rest of this column | [ ] yes  [ ] no if no, please ignore the rest of this column | [ ] yes  [ ] no if no, please ignore the rest of this column | [ ] yes  [ ] no if no, please ignore the rest of this column |
| 2. How important would you say that this has been to the development of your company? | [ ] very important<br>[ ] important<br>[ ] some importance<br>[ ] no importance<br>[ ] negative effect<br>[ ] not sure | [ ] very important<br>[ ] important<br>[ ] some importance<br>[ ] no importance<br>[ ] negative effect<br>[ ] not sure | [ ] very important<br>[ ] important<br>[ ] some importance<br>[ ] no importance<br>[ ] negative effect<br>[ ] not sure | [ ] very important<br>[ ] important<br>[ ] some importance<br>[ ] no importance<br>[ ] negative effect<br>[ ] not sure |
| 3. From which countries or regions was it mostly sourced? (if more than one please rank them e.g., 1, 2 etc.) | [ ] USA<br>[ ] Japan<br>[ ] Taiwan Prov. China<br>[ ] Korea (Rep. of)<br>[ ] Singapore<br>[ ] Europe<br>[ ] other please specify | [ ] USA<br>[ ] Japan<br>[ ] Taiwan Prov. China<br>[ ] Korea (Rep. of)<br>[ ] Singapore<br>[ ] Europe<br>[ ] other please specify | [ ] USA<br>[ ] Japan<br>[ ] Taiwan Prov. China<br>[ ] Korea (Rep. of)<br>[ ] Singapore<br>[ ] Europe<br>[ ] other please specify | [ ] USA<br>[ ] Japan<br>[ ] TaiwanProv. China<br>[ ] Korea (Rep. of)<br>[ ] Singapore<br>[ ] Europe<br>[ ] other please specify |
| 4. What was the relation to your firm of the organisation abroad providing the funds, technology etc.? | [ ] parent company<br>[ ] group member<br>[ ] alliance partner<br>[ ] joint venturer<br>[ ] trading co. | [ ] another company<br>[ ] government agent<br>[ ] international aid<br>[ ] bank, finance co.<br>[ ] unrelated investor<br>[ ] government agent<br>[ ] consultant<br>[ ] contractor | [ ] parent company<br>[ ] group member<br>[ ] alliance partner<br>[ ] joint venturer<br>[ ] unrelated investor<br>[ ] government agent<br>[ ] consultant<br>[ ] contractor | [ ] parent company<br>[ ] group member<br>[ ] alliance partner<br>[ ] joint venturer |
| 5. What was the approximate size of the foreign organisation providing the funds, technology etc? | Please write the approximate number of employees (eg 500)<br><br>.......... | Please write the approximate number of employees (eg 500)<br><br>.......... | Please write the approximate number of employees (eg 500)<br><br>.......... | Please write the approximate number of employees (eg 500)<br><br>.......... |
| 6. What were the funds, technology or training mostly used for? (please rank 1, 2, etc if more than one) | [ ] plant equipment<br>[ ] buildings<br>[ ] working capital<br>[ ] stock/inventory<br>[ ] technology | [ ] plant equipment<br>[ ] buildings<br>[ ] working capital<br>[ ] stock/inventory<br>[ ] technology | [ ] new products<br>[ ] new process<br>[ ] product improving<br>[ ] process improving<br>[ ] unskilled staff | [ ] management<br>[ ] marketing<br>[ ] technical<br>[ ] skilled staff |
| 7. In each year what was the approximate....<br>1995<br>1994<br>1993<br>1992<br>1991 | ..amount invested in you from abroad<br>$US......................<br>$US......................<br>$US......................<br>$US......................<br>$US...................... | ..amount lent to you from abroad<br>$US......................<br>$US......................<br>$US......................<br>$US......................<br>$US...................... | ..value of technology from abroad<br>$US......................<br>$US......................<br>$US......................<br>$US......................<br>$US...................... | ..value of training from abroad<br>$US......................<br>$US......................<br>$US......................<br>$US......................<br>$US...................... |
| 8. Approximately how much was this as ...<br>1995<br>1994<br>1993<br>1992<br>1991 | ...a % of all investment funds<br>..................%<br>..................%<br>..................%<br>..................%<br>..................% | ..a % of all loan funds<br>..................%<br>..................%<br>..................%<br>..................%<br>..................% | .. a % of technology expenditure<br>..................%<br>..................%<br>..................%<br>..................%<br>..................% | ..a % of all training expenditure<br>..................%<br>..................%<br>..................%<br>..................%<br>..................% |

*Please tell us about your company..*

9. In which year was your firm established (eg 1989) _____

10. In which year did you first commence international activity (including importing or exporting) _____

---

11. What best describes your firm?
(please tick as many as appropriate)

[ ] profit centre or division of a larger firm
[ ] independently owned and operated

[ ] wholly owned subsidiary of a local parent firm
[ ] wholly owned subsidiary of parent firm abroad
[ ] partly owned subsidiary of a local parent firm
[ ] member of joint venture with local firm
[ ] member of joint venture with a firm abroad

---

12. What industry best describes your firm?
[ ] Mining
[ ] Construction
[ ] Wholesale trade
[ ] Retail trade
[ ] Transport and storage

[ ] Finance, property and business services
[ ] Communications
[ ] Recreation and personal services
[ ] Heavy manufacturing (eg chemicals, metals etc)
[ ] Light manufacturing (eg textiles, food etc)

---

13. Please describe briefly what you make or sell (eg producer of fabricated metal parts, retailer of perishable food)

---

| 14. Relative to the market, where does your firm stand in terms of ... | well below average | below average | average average | above average | well above average |
|---|---|---|---|---|---|
| ...technology? | [ ] | [ ] | [ ] | [ ] | [ ] |
| ..competitiveness? | [ ] | [ ] | [ ] | [ ] | [ ] |
| ..quality? | [ ] | [ ] | [ ] | [ ] | [ ] |
| ..innovativeness? | [ ] | [ ] | [ ] | [ ] | [ ] |
| ..meeting customer needs? | [ ] | [ ] | [ ] | [ ] | [ ] |
| ..ability to export? | [ ] | [ ] | [ ] | [ ] | [ ] |

---

| 15. In each year what was your approximate.. | capitalisation | number of employees (eg 120) | wages and salaries | sales or turnover | non labour supplies locally sourced | non labour supplies from abroad |
|---|---|---|---|---|---|---|
| 1995 | $US.............. | .......... | $US............ | $US........... | $US.............. | $US.............. |
| 1994 | $US.............. | .......... | $US............ | $US........... | $US.............. | $US.............. |
| 1991 | $US.............. | .......... | $US............ | $US........... | $US.............. | $US.............. |

---

| 16. Approximately what proportion of your sales revenue is from abroad? | .... directly as sales to end user customers abroad | to a local affiliate which then sells abroad | to a local unaffiliated company which sells abroad | to an unaffiliated company abroad | to an affiliated or parent company abroad | Approximate value of all sales abroad |
|---|---|---|---|---|---|---|
| 1995 | ..........% | ..........% | ..........% | ..........% | ..........% | $US.............. |
| 1994 | ..........% | ..........% | ..........% | ..........% | ..........% | $US.............. |
| 1991 | ..........% | ..........% | ..........% | ..........% | ..........% | $US.............. |

---

| 17. How are management functions allocated between your firm and firms abroad? | all local | mostly local | about equal | mostly abroad | all abroad |
|---|---|---|---|---|---|
| Strategic management decisions | [ ] | [ ] | [ ] | [ ] | [ ] |
| Financing decisions | [ ] | [ ] | [ ] | [ ] | [ ] |
| Product design decisions | [ ] | [ ] | [ ] | [ ] | [ ] |
| Marketing advertising decisions | [ ] | [ ] | [ ] | [ ] | [ ] |
| Information and research | [ ] | [ ] | [ ] | [ ] | [ ] |

*Have you experienced any special difficulties, or found anything especially helpful, in developing your business?*

| 18. Please indicate the importance of the following as problems or as being of assistance to your business development | not applicable | very major problem | problem | neither a help or a problem | helpful | very helpful |
|---|---|---|---|---|---|---|
| Availability of skilled staff locally | [ ] | [ ] | [ ] | [ ] | [ ] | [ ] |
| Availability of skilled staff abroad | [ ] | [ ] | [ ] | [ ] | [ ] | [ ] |
| Access to technology | [ ] | [ ] | [ ] | [ ] | [ ] | [ ] |
| Finding suitable distributors | [ ] | [ ] | [ ] | [ ] | [ ] | [ ] |
| Availability of reasonably priced finance | [ ] | [ ] | [ ] | [ ] | [ ] | [ ] |
| Specific restrictions on access to market | [ ] | [ ] | [ ] | [ ] | [ ] | [ ] |
| Specific tariffs/ quotas | [ ] | [ ] | [ ] | [ ] | [ ] | [ ] |
| Unfair competition | [ ] | [ ] | [ ] | [ ] | [ ] | [ ] |
| Distribution systems | [ ] | [ ] | [ ] | [ ] | [ ] | [ ] |
| General business regulations | [ ] | [ ] | [ ] | [ ] | [ ] | [ ] |
| Approval procedures for investment | [ ] | [ ] | [ ] | [ ] | [ ] | [ ] |
| Approval procedures for construction | [ ] | [ ] | [ ] | [ ] | [ ] | [ ] |
| Local content requirements | [ ] | [ ] | [ ] | [ ] | [ ] | [ ] |
| Corruption in minor officials | [ ] | [ ] | [ ] | [ ] | [ ] | [ ] |
| Corruption at senior official levels | [ ] | [ ] | [ ] | [ ] | [ ] | [ ] |
| Infrastructure - telecommunications | [ ] | [ ] | [ ] | [ ] | [ ] | [ ] |
| Infrastructure - roads/transport | [ ] | [ ] | [ ] | [ ] | [ ] | [ ] |
| Dispute settlement mechanisms | [ ] | [ ] | [ ] | [ ] | [ ] | [ ] |
| Legal system | [ ] | [ ] | [ ] | [ ] | [ ] | [ ] |
| Labour restrictions | [ ] | [ ] | [ ] | [ ] | [ ] | [ ] |
| Attitude of workers | [ ] | [ ] | [ ] | [ ] | [ ] | [ ] |
| Cultural differences across borders | [ ] | [ ] | [ ] | [ ] | [ ] | [ ] |
| Market liberalisation agreements (eg APEC) | [ ] | [ ] | [ ] | [ ] | [ ] | [ ] |
| Business parks/technology parks | [ ] | [ ] | [ ] | [ ] | [ ] | [ ] |
| Business matching services | [ ] | [ ] | [ ] | [ ] | [ ] | [ ] |
| Access to low cost labour | [ ] | [ ] | [ ] | [ ] | [ ] | [ ] |
| Government management training programs | [ ] | [ ] | [ ] | [ ] | [ ] | [ ] |
| Government business advisory services | [ ] | [ ] | [ ] | [ ] | [ ] | [ ] |
| Government sponsored trade missions | [ ] | [ ] | [ ] | [ ] | [ ] | [ ] |
| Market intelligence and information | [ ] | [ ] | [ ] | [ ] | [ ] | [ ] |
| Services from Chambers of Commerce | [ ] | [ ] | [ ] | [ ] | [ ] | [ ] |
| Required 10% of procurement from SMIs | [ ] | [ ] | [ ] | [ ] | [ ] | [ ] |
| Inconsistencies in regulations | [ ] | [ ] | [ ] | [ ] | [ ] | [ ] |
| Affiliation with a transnational corporation | [ ] | [ ] | [ ] | [ ] | [ ] | [ ] |
| Finding suitable partners in Indonesia | [ ] | [ ] | [ ] | [ ] | [ ] | [ ] |

19. If any thing has been a major problem, could you briefly indicate what if anything you think might realistically be done to reduce the problem? If necessary please make further comments on the last page.

20. If any things have been very helpful, could you please briefly indicate *why* they have been helpful? If necessary please make further comments on the last page.

*Please tell us about your firm's strategy, and plans for the future.......*

| 21. How important *now* (ie 1996) are the following factors in your reasons for pursuing and maintaining linkages with firms abroad? | not applicable | not important | important | very important | 22. *Five years ago* (ie 1991) was this factor more or less important than it is now? less | same | more |
|---|---|---|---|---|---|---|---|
| Lack of opportunities for growth at home | [ ] | [ ] | [ ] | [ ] | [ ] | [ ] | [ ] |
| Lack of access to finance at home | [ ] | [ ] | [ ] | [ ] | [ ] | [ ] | [ ] |
| Lack of access to technology at home | [ ] | [ ] | [ ] | [ ] | [ ] | [ ] | [ ] |
| Rising production costs in home market | [ ] | [ ] | [ ] | [ ] | [ ] | [ ] | [ ] |
| Increased competition in home market | [ ] | [ ] | [ ] | [ ] | [ ] | [ ] | [ ] |
| Erosion of home market share | [ ] | [ ] | [ ] | [ ] | [ ] | [ ] | [ ] |
| Volatility and risk diversification | [ ] | [ ] | [ ] | [ ] | [ ] | [ ] | [ ] |
| Access to skilled labour from abroad | [ ] | [ ] | [ ] | [ ] | [ ] | [ ] | [ ] |
| Access to management skill from abroad | [ ] | [ ] | [ ] | [ ] | [ ] | [ ] | [ ] |
| Lower costs of production | [ ] | [ ] | [ ] | [ ] | [ ] | [ ] | [ ] |
| Larger market growth opportunities | [ ] | [ ] | [ ] | [ ] | [ ] | [ ] | [ ] |
| Tax incentives for investment from abroad | [ ] | [ ] | [ ] | [ ] | [ ] | [ ] | [ ] |
| Access to special materials | [ ] | [ ] | [ ] | [ ] | [ ] | [ ] | [ ] |
| Overcome protective restrictions | [ ] | [ ] | [ ] | [ ] | [ ] | [ ] | [ ] |
| Advantage from local market knowledge | [ ] | [ ] | [ ] | [ ] | [ ] | [ ] | [ ] |
| Technical or product lead advantages | [ ] | [ ] | [ ] | [ ] | [ ] | [ ] | [ ] |
| International experience of managers | [ ] | [ ] | [ ] | [ ] | [ ] | [ ] | [ ] |
| Information about opportunities abroad | [ ] | [ ] | [ ] | [ ] | [ ] | [ ] | [ ] |
| Careful planning and market research | [ ] | [ ] | [ ] | [ ] | [ ] | [ ] | [ ] |
| Chance encounters  (eg with clients) | [ ] | [ ] | [ ] | [ ] | [ ] | [ ] | [ ] |
| Approached by customer from abroad | [ ] | [ ] | [ ] | [ ] | [ ] | [ ] | [ ] |
| Approached by partner from abroad | [ ] | [ ] | [ ] | [ ] | [ ] | [ ] | [ ] |
| Saw opportunity and took it | [ ] | [ ] | [ ] | [ ] | [ ] | [ ] | [ ] |

| 23.  How important are the following to your strategic business development? | not applicable | not important | some importance | important | very important |
|---|---|---|---|---|---|
| Linkages with overseas firms | [ ] | [ ] | [ ] | [ ] | [ ] |
| Increasing exports or foreign earnings | [ ] | [ ] | [ ] | [ ] | [ ] |
| Increased use of local suppliers | [ ] | [ ] | [ ] | [ ] | [ ] |
| Training of local unskilled staff | [ ] | [ ] | [ ] | [ ] | [ ] |
| Training of local managers | [ ] | [ ] | [ ] | [ ] | [ ] |
| Adapting products to meet local market | [ ] | [ ] | [ ] | [ ] | [ ] |
| Providing new products/services | [ ] | [ ] | [ ] | [ ] | [ ] |
| Improving quality of product/services | [ ] | [ ] | [ ] | [ ] | [ ] |
| Adapting technology to local needs | [ ] | [ ] | [ ] | [ ] | [ ] |
| Good relations with government | [ ] | [ ] | [ ] | [ ] | [ ] |

24.  Please write the approximate percentage change you expect under realistic conditions over the next three years (eg +25%, or -10%, or 0% for no change) in each of the following...

25.  Under *ideal* conditions (ie if all impediments were removed). Please write the percentage change (eg +25%, or -10%, or 0%)

| | not applicable | Percentage change | | |
|---|---|---|---|---|
| sales or turnover | [ ] | .........% per annum | | .........% per annum |
| exports | [ ] | .........% per annum | | .........% per annum |
| employment | [ ] | .........% per annum | | .........% per annum |
| imports | [ ] | .........% per annum | | .........% per annum |
| investment in plant equipment | [ ] | .........% per annum | | .........% per annum |
| research and development | [ ] | .........% per annum | | .........% per annum |
| training activity | [ ] | .........% per annum | | .........% per annum |

## Questionnaire for the survey on SME investors

*Please tell us about your firm's international activities....*

| 1. In the last five years has your firm engaged in... | *...equity investment abroad, reinvestment of earnings, or direct loans to affiliates ?*<br>[ ] yes    [ ] no<br>if *no* please ignore q 2 to 4 in this column | *...long term loans made abroad to non affiliated companies?*<br>[ ] yes    [ ] no<br>if *no* please ignore q 2 to 4 in this column | *...technology sent abroad? (eg licenses, or patents)*<br>[ ] yes    [ ] no<br>if *no* please ignore q 2 to 4 in this column | *...training abroad (eg specialist advisers)*<br>[ ] yes    [ ] no<br>if *no* please ignore q 2 to 4 in this column |
|---|---|---|---|---|
| 2. How important would you say that this has been to the success and development of your company? | [ ] very important<br>[ ] important<br>[ ] some importance<br>[ ] no importance<br>[ ] negative effect<br>[ ] not sure | [ ] very important<br>[ ] important<br>[ ] some importance<br>[ ] no importance<br>[ ] negative effect<br>[ ] not sure | [ ] very important<br>[ ] important<br>[ ] some importance<br>[ ] no importance<br>[ ] negative effect<br>[ ] not sure | [ ] very important<br>[ ] important<br>[ ] some importance<br>[ ] no importance<br>[ ] negative effect<br>[ ] not sure |
| 3. In each year what was the approximate.. in... 1995 1994 1993 1992 1991 | ..amount invested abroad by you<br>$S.....................<br>$S.....................<br>$S.....................<br>$S.....................<br>$S..................... | ..amount lent abroad by you<br>$S.....................<br>$S.....................<br>$S.....................<br>$S.....................<br>$S..................... | ..value of technology transferred abroad<br>$S.....................<br>$S.....................<br>$S.....................<br>$S.....................<br>$S..................... | ..value of training made abroad<br>$S.....................<br>$S.....................<br>$S.....................<br>$S.....................<br>$S..................... |
| 4. What were the amounts in question 3 as an approximate % of all your expenditure on... in... 1995 1994 1993 1992 1991 | ..equity investments and loans to affiliates<br>.......%<br>.......%<br>.......%<br>.......%<br>.......% | ..loans to non affiliates<br>.......%<br>.......%<br>.......%<br>.......% | ..technology<br>.......%<br>.......%<br>.......%<br>.......%<br>.......% | .. training<br>.......%<br>.......%<br>.......%<br>.......%<br>.......% |

| 5. Please tell us in about which year you commenced each of the international activities in the following economies or regions (if none leave blank) | import from | export to | appoint local agent | form alliance or partner-ship with local firm | transfer or license technology | establish local office or production plant |
|---|---|---|---|---|---|---|
| | 1975 | 1980 | 1983 | | 1994 | 1993 |
| Myanmar | | | | | | |
| Viet Nam | | | | | | |
| Philippines | | | | | | |
| People's Republic of China | | | | | | |
| Thailand | | | | | | |
| Indonesia | | | | | | |
| Malaysia | | | | | | |
| Cambodia | | | | | | |
| Other SE Asia | | | | | | |
| Japan | | | | | | |
| Republic of Korea | | | | | | |
| Taiwan Province of China | | | | | | |
| India | | | | | | |
| Bangladesh | | | | | | |
| Sri Lanka | | | | | | |
| Other Asia/middle east | | | | | | |
| North America | | | | | | |
| South and Latin America | | | | | | |
| Europe | | | | | | |
| Central and Eastern Europe | | | | | | |
| Africa | | | | | | |
| Oceania Pacific | | | | | | |

*Please tell us about your company...*

6. In which year was your firm established (eg. 1989) _____

7. In which year did you first commence international activity (including importing or exporting) _____

8. What best describes your firm (please tick as many as appropriate)
   [  ] profit centre or division of a larger firm
   [  ] independently owned and operated
   [  ] parent firm with subsidiaries abroad
   [  ] member of a group of firms, one of which is a larger multinational firm
   [  ] member of joint venture or alliance with a firm, or firms, abroad

9. What industry best describes your firm?
   [  ] Mining
   [  ] Construction
   [  ] Wholesale trade
   [  ] Retail trade
   [  ] Transport and storage
   [  ] Finance, property and business services
   [  ] Communications
   [  ] Tourism, recreation and personal services
   [  ] Heavy manufacturing (eg chemicals, metals etc)
   [  ] Light manufacturing (eg textiles, computers, etc)

10. Please describe briefly what you make or sell (eg  fabricated metal parts,  retailer of perishable food, etc )

11. Please describe your company relative to the market in terms of..

| | well below average | below average | average | above average | well above average |
|---|---|---|---|---|---|
| ..technology | [ ] | [ ] | [ ] | [ ] | [ ] |
| ..competitiveness | [ ] | [ ] | [ ] | [ ] | [ ] |
| ..quality | [ ] | [ ] | [ ] | [ ] | [ ] |
| ..innovativeness | [ ] | [ ] | [ ] | [ ] | [ ] |
| ..meeting customer needs | [ ] | [ ] | [ ] | [ ] | [ ] |
| ..ability to export | [ ] | [ ] | [ ] | [ ] | [ ] |

12. For just your firm, what was the approximate

| | capitalisation | number of employees (e.g. 120) | wages and salaries | sales or turnover | non labour supplies locally sourced | non labour supplies from abroad |
|---|---|---|---|---|---|---|
| 1995 | $S.............. | .......... | $S.............. | $S.............. | $S.............. | $S.............. |
| 1994 | $S.............. | .......... | $S.............. | $S.............. | $S.............. | $S.............. |
| 1993 | $S.............. | .......... | $S.............. | $S.............. | $S.............. | $S.............. |
| 1992 | $S.............. | .......... | $S.............. | $S.............. | $S.............. | $S.............. |
| 1991 | $S.............. | .......... | $S.............. | $S.............. | $S.............. | $S.............. |

13. For the group of firms (including those abroad) what was the approximate

| | capitalisation | number of employees (e.g. 1500) | wages and salaries | sales or turnover | non labour supplies locally sourced | non labour supplies from subsidiaries or partners abroad |
|---|---|---|---|---|---|---|
| 1995 | $S.............. | .......... | $S.............. | $S.............. | $S.............. | $S.............. |
| 1994 | $S.............. | .......... | $S.............. | $S.............. | $S.............. | $S.............. |
| 1993 | $S.............. | .......... | $S.............. | $S.............. | $S.............. | $S.............. |
| 1992 | $S.............. | .......... | $S.............. | $S.............. | $S.............. | $S.............. |
| 1991 | $S.............. | .......... | $S.............. | $S.............. | $S.............. | $S.............. |

14. How are management functions and decisions allocated between your firm and firms abroad?

| | all local | mostly local | about equal | mostly abroad | all abroad |
|---|---|---|---|---|---|
| Strategic management decisions | [ ] | [ ] | [ ] | [ ] | [ ] |
| Financing decisions | [ ] | [ ] | [ ] | [ ] | [ ] |
| Product design decisions | [ ] | [ ] | [ ] | [ ] | [ ] |
| Marketing advertising decisions | [ ] | [ ] | [ ] | [ ] | [ ] |
| Information and research | [ ] | [ ] | [ ] | [ ] | [ ] |

*Have you experienced any difficulties, or found anything especially helpful, in developing your business internationally?*

| 15. Please indicate the importance of the following as problems, or as being of assistance to your business development | not applicable | very major problem | regular problem | neither a help nor a problem | helpful | very helpful |
|---|---|---|---|---|---|---|
| availability of local skilled staff | [ ] | [ ] | [ ] | [ ] | [ ] | [ ] |
| access to technology | [ ] | [ ] | [ ] | [ ] | [ ] | [ ] |
| finding suitable distributors | [ ] | [ ] | [ ] | [ ] | [ ] | [ ] |
| availability of reasonably priced finance | [ ] | [ ] | [ ] | [ ] | [ ] | [ ] |
| market access | [ ] | [ ] | [ ] | [ ] | [ ] | [ ] |
| tariffs/ quotas | [ ] | [ ] | [ ] | [ ] | [ ] | [ ] |
| unfair competition | [ ] | [ ] | [ ] | [ ] | [ ] | [ ] |
| local distribution systems | [ ] | [ ] | [ ] | [ ] | [ ] | [ ] |
| general business regulations | [ ] | [ ] | [ ] | [ ] | [ ] | [ ] |
| approval procedures for investment | [ ] | [ ] | [ ] | [ ] | [ ] | [ ] |
| approval procedures for construction | [ ] | [ ] | [ ] | [ ] | [ ] | [ ] |
| local content requirements | [ ] | [ ] | [ ] | [ ] | [ ] | [ ] |
| official corruption | [ ] | [ ] | [ ] | [ ] | [ ] | [ ] |
| infrastructure - telecommunications | [ ] | [ ] | [ ] | [ ] | [ ] | [ ] |
| Infrastructure - roads/transport | [ ] | [ ] | [ ] | [ ] | [ ] | [ ] |
| dispute settlement mechanisms | [ ] | [ ] | [ ] | [ ] | [ ] | [ ] |
| local legal system | [ ] | [ ] | [ ] | [ ] | [ ] | [ ] |
| labour restrictions | [ ] | [ ] | [ ] | [ ] | [ ] | [ ] |
| attitude of workers | [ ] | [ ] | [ ] | [ ] | [ ] | [ ] |
| cost of imports | [ ] | [ ] | [ ] | [ ] | [ ] | [ ] |
| cultural differences | [ ] | [ ] | [ ] | [ ] | [ ] | [ ] |
| general moves to market liberalisation | [ ] | [ ] | [ ] | [ ] | [ ] | [ ] |
| access to partners abroad | [ ] | [ ] | [ ] | [ ] | [ ] | [ ] |
| access to technology abroad | [ ] | [ ] | [ ] | [ ] | [ ] | [ ] |
| business parks/technology parks | [ ] | [ ] | [ ] | [ ] | [ ] | [ ] |
| access to capital | [ ] | [ ] | [ ] | [ ] | [ ] | [ ] |
| access to labour | [ ] | [ ] | [ ] | [ ] | [ ] | [ ] |
| information services | [ ] | [ ] | [ ] | [ ] | [ ] | [ ] |
| business matching services | [ ] | [ ] | [ ] | [ ] | [ ] | [ ] |
| chamber of commerce services | [ ] | [ ] | [ ] | [ ] | [ ] | [ ] |
| selection of about ten items from specific programs and problems identified in recipient questionnaire, e.g. | | | | | | |
| program A | [ ] | [ ] | [ ] | [ ] | [ ] | [ ] |
| program B etc. | [ ] | [ ] | [ ] | [ ] | [ ] | [ ] |
| local content requirements | [ ] | [ ] | [ ] | [ ] | [ ] | [ ] |
| minimum export requirements | [ ] | [ ] | [ ] | [ ] | [ ] | [ ] |
| import restrictions | [ ] | [ ] | [ ] | [ ] | [ ] | [ ] |
| local partner requirements | [ ] | [ ] | [ ] | [ ] | [ ] | [ ] |
| reporting requirements etc. | [ ] | [ ] | [ ] | [ ] | [ ] | [ ] |
| ownership limits | [ ] | [ ] | [ ] | [ ] | [ ] | [ ] |
| export obligations | [ ] | [ ] | [ ] | [ ] | [ ] | [ ] |
| foreign currency restrictions/ remittance limits | [ ] | [ ] | [ ] | [ ] | [ ] | [ ] |
| tax concessions, incentives | [ ] | [ ] | [ ] | [ ] | [ ] | [ ] |

16. If any things have been a major problem, could you briefly indicate what if anything you think might realistically be done to reduce the problem? If necessary please make further comments on the last page.

17. If any things have been very helpful, could you please briefly indicate why they been helpful? If necessary, please make further comments on the last page.

*Please tell us about your firm's strategy and plans for the future*

| | 18. How important *now* (ie 1996) are the following factors in your reasons for pursuing and maintaining linkages with firms abroad? | | | | 19. *Five years ago* (ie 1990) was this factor more or less important than it is now? | | |
|---|---|---|---|---|---|---|---|
| | not applicable | not important | important | very important | less | same | more |
| lack of opportunities for growth at home | [ ] | [ ] | [ ] | [ ] | [ ] | [ ] | [ ] |
| rising costs in home market | [ ] | [ ] | [ ] | [ ] | [ ] | [ ] | [ ] |
| increased competition in home market | [ ] | [ ] | [ ] | [ ] | [ ] | [ ] | [ ] |
| erosion of home market share | [ ] | [ ] | [ ] | [ ] | [ ] | [ ] | [ ] |
| volatility and risk diversification | [ ] | [ ] | [ ] | [ ] | [ ] | [ ] | [ ] |
| access to skilled labour abroad | [ ] | [ ] | [ ] | [ ] | [ ] | [ ] | [ ] |
| lower costs of production abroad | [ ] | [ ] | [ ] | [ ] | [ ] | [ ] | [ ] |
| larger market growth opportunities | [ ] | [ ] | [ ] | [ ] | [ ] | [ ] | [ ] |
| special tax incentives offered abroad | [ ] | [ ] | [ ] | [ ] | [ ] | [ ] | [ ] |
| access to special materials | [ ] | [ ] | [ ] | [ ] | [ ] | [ ] | [ ] |
| to overcome protective restrictions | [ ] | [ ] | [ ] | [ ] | [ ] | [ ] | [ ] |
| competitive advantage from knowledge | [ ] | [ ] | [ ] | [ ] | [ ] | [ ] | [ ] |
| less risk from alliances than going alone | [ ] | [ ] | [ ] | [ ] | [ ] | [ ] | [ ] |
| technical or product lead advantages | [ ] | [ ] | [ ] | [ ] | [ ] | [ ] | [ ] |
| international experience of managers | [ ] | [ ] | [ ] | [ ] | [ ] | [ ] | [ ] |
| information about opportunities abroad | [ ] | [ ] | [ ] | [ ] | [ ] | [ ] | [ ] |
| careful planning and market research | [ ] | [ ] | [ ] | [ ] | [ ] | [ ] | [ ] |
| chance encounters | [ ] | [ ] | [ ] | [ ] | [ ] | [ ] | [ ] |
| approached by overseas customer | [ ] | [ ] | [ ] | [ ] | [ ] | [ ] | [ ] |
| approached by overseas partner | [ ] | [ ] | [ ] | [ ] | [ ] | [ ] | [ ] |
| saw opportunity and took it | [ ] | [ ] | [ ] | [ ] | [ ] | [ ] | [ ] |

| Approximately what change do you expect to make over the next three years (1996-1999) to each of the following? | not applicable | 20. Under *realistic* conditions. Please write the percentage change (eg, -25%, or -10%, or 0% for no change). | 21. Under *ideal* conditions (ie if all impediments were removed). Please write the percentage change (eg +25%, or -10%, or 0%. |
|---|---|---|---|
| sales or turnover | [ ] | % per annum | % per annum |
| exports | [ ] | % per annum | % per annum |
| employment | [ ] | % per annum | % per annum |
| imports | [ ] | % per annum | % per annum |
| investment abroad | [ ] | % per annum | % per annum |
| investment locally | [ ] | % per annum | % per annum |
| research and development | [ ] | % per annum | % per annum |
| training activity | [ ] | % per annum | % per annum |
| locally/abroad | [ ] | % per annum | % per annum |

| 22. What is your approximate total investment commitment (loans, plus equity) to date in each of these economies? (if nothing, write nil) | People's Republic of China $US.......... | Myanmar $US.............. | Bangladesh $US.............. | Viet Nam $US........... | Philippines $US........... | Indonesia $US.......... |
|---|---|---|---|---|---|---|

| 23. Are you *now* considering increasing your international activity (investment etc) in any of these economies? | [ ] yes [ ] no | [ ] yes [ ] no | [ ] yes [ ] no | [ ] yes [ ] no | [ ] yes [ ] no | [ ] yes [ ] no |
|---|---|---|---|---|---|---|

| 24. If the problems you cited in question 15 were removed, would you be likely to increase your investment activity in the next three years? | [ ] yes a lot [ ] yes some [ ] no [ ] not sure | [ ] yes a lot [ ] yes some [ ] no [ ] not sure | [ ] yes a lot [ ] yes some [ ] no [ ] not sure | [ ] yes a lot [ ] yes some [ ] no [ ] not sure | [ ] yes a lot [ ] yes some [ ] no [ ] not sure | [ ] yes a lot [ ] yes some [ ] no [ ] not sure |
|---|---|---|---|---|---|---|

| 25. Could you please rank these economies from 1 - 6 in terms of attractiveness for your firm to invest in? | rank = | rank = | rank = | rank = | rank = | rank = |
|---|---|---|---|---|---|---|

# Selected UNCTAD publications on
# Transnational Corporations and Foreign Direct Investment

## A. Individual studies

*World Investment Report 1997: Transnational Corporations, Market Structure and Competition Policy*. 420 p. Sales No. E.96.II.D.10. $45.

*International Investment: Towards the Year 2001*. 81 p. Sales No. GV.E.97.0.5. $35. (Joint publication with Invest in France Mission and Arthur Andersen, in collaboration with DATAR.)

*World Investment Directory. Volume VI: West Asia 1996*. 192 p. Sales No. E.97.II.A.2. $35.

*World Investment Directory. Volume V: Africa 1996*. 508 p. Sales No. E.97.II.A.1. $75.

*Sharing Asia's Dynamism: Asian Direct Investment in the European Union*. 162 p. Sales No. E.97.II.D.1. $26.

*Transnational Corporations and World Development*. 656 pp. ISBN 0-415-08560-8 (hardback), 0-415-08561-6 (paperback). £65 (hardback), £20.99 (paperback).

*Companies without Borders: Transnational Corporations in the 1990s*. 224 pp. ISBN 0-415-12526-X. £47.50.

*The New Globalism and Developing Countries*. 336 pp. ISBN 92-808-0944-X. $25.

*Investing in Asia's Dynamism: European Union Direct Investment in Asia*. 124 p. ISBN 92-827-7675-1. ECU 14. (Joint publication with the European Commission.)

*World Investment Report 1996: Investment, Trade and International Policy Arrangements*. 332 p. Sales No. E.96.II.A.14. $45.

*World Investment Report 1996: Investment, Trade and International Policy Arrangements. An Overview*. 51 p. Free-of-charge.

*International Investment Instruments: A Compendium*. Sales No. E.96.IIA.12 (the set). $125.

*World Investment Report 1995: Transnational Corporations and Competitiveness*. 491 p. Sales No. E.95.II.A.9. $45.

*World Investment Report 1995: Transnational Corporations and Competitiveness. An Overview*. 51 p. Free-of-charge.

*Small and Medium-sized Transnational Corporations: Executive Summary and Report on the Osaka Conference*. 60 p. UNCTAD/DTCI/6. Free-of-charge.

*World Investment Report 1994: Transnational Corporations, Employment and the Workplace*. 482 p. Sales No. E.94.II.A.14. $45.

*World Investment Report 1994: Transnational Corporations, Employment and the Workplace. An Executive Summary*. 34 p. Free-of-charge.

*World Investment Directory. Volume IV: Latin America and the Caribbean*. 478 p. Sales No. E.94.II.A.10. $65.

*Liberalizing International Transactions in Services: A Handbook*. 182 p. Sales No. E.94.II.A.11. $45. (Joint publication with the World Bank.)

*Accounting, Valuation and Privatization*. 190 p. Sales No. E.94.II.A.3. $25.

*Environmental Management in Transnational Corporations: Report on the Benchmark Corporate Environment Suvey*. 278 p. Sales No. E.94.II.A.2. $29.95.

*Management Consulting: A Survey of the Industry and Its Largest Firms*. 100 p. Sales No. E.93.II.A.17. $25.

*Transnational Corporations: A Selective Bibliography, 1991-1992*. 736 p. Sales No. E.93.II.A.16. $75. (English/French.)

*Small and Medium-sized Transnational Corporations: Role, Impact and Policy Implications*. 242 p. Sales No. E.93.II.A.15. $35.

*World Investment Report 1993: Transnational Corporations and Integrated International Production*. 290 p. Sales No. E.93.II.A.14. $45.

*World Investment Report 1993: Transnational Corporations and Integrated International Production. An Executive Summary*. 31 p. ST/CTC/159. Free-of-charge.

*Foreign Investment and Trade Linkages in Developing Countries*. 108 p. Sales No. E.93.II.A.12. $18.

*World Investment Directory 1992. Volume III: Developed Countries*. 532 p. Sales No. E.93.II.A.9. $75.

*Transnational Corporations from Developing Countries: Impact on Their Home Countries*. 116 p. Sales No. E.93.II.A.8. $15.

*Debt-Equity Swaps and Development*. 150 p. Sales No. E.93.II.A.7. $35.

*From the Common Market to EC 92: Regional Economic Integration in the European Community and Transnational Corporations*. 134 p. Sales No. E.93.II.A.2. $25.

*World Investment Directory 1992. Volume II: Central and Eastern Europe*. 432 p. Sales No. E.93.II.A.1. $65. (Joint publication with ECE.) $65.

*World Investment Report 1992: Transnational Corporations as Engines of Growth: An Executive Summary*. 30 p. Sales No. E.92.II.A.24. Free-of-charge.

*World Investment Report 1992: Transnational Corporations as Engines of Growth*. 356 p. Sales No. E.92.II.A.19. $45.

*World Investment Directory 1992. Volume I: Asia and the Pacific*. 356 p. Sales No. E.92.II.A.11. $65.

# B. Serial publications

**Current Studies, Series A**

No. 30. *Incentives and Foreign Direct Investment*. 98 p. Sales No. E.96.II.A.6. $30. (English/French.)

No. 29. *Foreign Direct Investment, Trade, Aid and Migration*. 100 p. Sales No. E.96.II.A.8. $25.

No. 28. *Foreign Direct Investment in Africa*. 119 p. Sales No. E.95.II.A.6. $25

No. 27. *The Tradability of Banking Services: Impact and Implications*. 195 p. Sales No. E.94.II.A.12. $50.

No. 26. *Explaining and Forecasting Regional Flows of Foreign Direct Investment*. 58 p. Sales No. E.94.II.A.5. $25.

No. 25. *International Tradability in Insurance Services*. 54 p. Sales No. E.93.II.A.11. $20.

No. 24. *Intellectual Property Rights and Foreign Direct Investment*. 108 p. Sales No. E.93.II.A.10. $20.

No. 23. *The Transnationalization of Service Industries: An Empirical Analysis of the Determinants of Foreign Direct Investment by Transnational Service Corporations*. 62 p. Sales No. E.93.II.A.3. $15.00.

No. 22. *Transnational Banks and the External Indebtedness of Developing Countries: Impact of Regulatory Changes*. 48 p. Sales No. E.92.II.A.10. $12.

No. 20. *Foreign Direct Investment, Debt and Home Country Policies*. 50 p. Sales No. E.90.II.A.16. $12.

No. 19. *New Issues in the Uruguay Round of Multilateral Trade Negotiations*. 52 p. Sales No. E.90.II.A.15. $12.50.

No. 18. *Foreign Direct Investment and Industrial Restructuring in Mexico*. 114 p. Sales No. E.92.II.A.9. $12.

*The United Nations Library on Transnational Corporations*. (Published by Routledge on behalf of the United Nations.)

**Set A** (Boxed set of 4 volumes. ISBN 0-415-08554-3. £350):

Volume One: *The Theory of Transnational Corporations*. 464 p.

Volume Two: *Transnational Corporations: A Historical Perspective*. 464 p.

Volume Three: *Transnational Corporations and Economic Development*. 448 p.

Volume Four: *Transnational Corporations and Business Strategy*. 416 p.

**Set B** (Boxed set of 4 volumes. ISBN 0-415-08555-1. £350):

Volume Five: *International Financial Management*. 400 p.

Volume Six: *Organization of Transnational Corporations*. 400 p.

Volume Seven: *Governments and Transnational Corporations*. 352 p.

Volume Eight: *Transnational Corporations and International Trade and Payments*. 320 p.

**Set C** (Boxed set of 4 volumes. ISBN 0-415-08556-X. £350):

Volume Nine: *Transnational Corporations and Regional Economic Integration*. 331 p.

Volume Ten: *Transnational Corporations and the Exploitation of Natural Resources*. 397 p.

Volume Eleven: *Transnational Corporations and Industrialization*. 425 p.

Volume Twelve: *Transnational Corporations in Services*. 437 p.

**Set D** (Boxed set of 4 volumes. ISBN 0-415-08557-8. £350):

Volume Thirteen: *Cooperative Forms of Transnational Corporation Activity*. 419 p.

Volume Fourteen: *Transnational Corporations: Transfer Pricing and Taxation*. 330 p.

Volume Fifteen: *Transnational Corporations: Market Structure and Industrial Performance*. 383 p.

Volume Sixteen: *Transnational Corporations and Human Resources*. 429 p.

**Set E** (Boxed set of 4 volumes. ISBN 0-415-08558-6. £350):

Volume Seventeen: *Transnational Corporations and Innovatory Activities*. 447 p.

Volume Eighteen: *Transnational Corporations and Technology Transfer to Developing Countries*. 486 p.

Volume Nineteen: *Transnational Corporations and National Law*. 322 p.

Volume Twenty: *Transnational Corporations: The International Legal Framework*. 545 p.

*Transnational Corporations* (formerly *The CTC Reporter*).

Published three times a year. Annual subscription price: $35; individual issues $15.

*Transnationals*, a quarterly newsletter, is available free of charge.

United Nations publications may be obtained from bookstores and distributors throughout the world. Please consult your bookstore or write to:

### United Nations Publications

| | | |
|---|---|---|
| Sales Section | OR | Sales Section |
| Room DC2-0853 | | United Nations Office at Geneva |
| United Nations Secretariat | | Palais des Nations |
| New York, N.Y. 10017 | | CH-1211 Geneva 10 |
| U.S.A. | | Switzerland |
| Tel: (1-212) 963-8302 or (800) 253-9646 | | Tel: (41-22) 917-1234 |
| Fax: (1-212) 963-3489 | | Fax: (41-22) 917-0123 |
| E-mail: publications@un.org | | E-mail: unpubli@unog.ch |

All prices are quoted in United States dollars.

For further information on the work of the UNCTAD Division on Investment, Technology and Enterprise Development, please address inquiries to:

United Nations Conference on Trade and Development
Division on Investment, Technology and Enterprise Development
Palais des Nations, Room E-9123
CH-1211 Geneva 10
Switzerland

Telephone:     (41-22) 907-5707
Telefax:       (41-22) 907-0194

# QUESTIONNAIRE

## Handbook on Foreign Direct Investment by Small and Medium-sized Enterprises: Lessons from Asia
Sales No. E.98.II.D.4.

In order to improve the quality and relevance of the work of the UNCTAD Division on Investment, Technology and Enterprise Development, it would be useful to receive the views of readers on this and other similar publications. It would therefore be greatly appreciated if you could complete the following questionnaire and return to:

*Readership Survey*
*UNCTAD Division on Investment, Technology and Enterprise Development*
*United Nations Office at Geneva*
*Palais des Nations*
*Room E-9123*
*CH-1211 Geneva 10*
*Switzerland*

1.  Name and address of respondent (optional):

    _____
    _____
    _____
    _____

2.  Which of the following best describes your area of work?

    | | | | |
    |---|---|---|---|
    | Government | ☐ | Public enterprise | ☐ |
    | Private enterprise institution | ☐ | Academic or research | ☐ |
    | International organization | ☐ | Media | ☐ |
    | Not-for-profit organization | ☐ | Other (specify) _____ | |

3.  In which country do you work? _____

4.  What is your assessment of the contents of this publication?

    | | | | |
    |---|---|---|---|
    | Excellent | ☐ | Adequate | ☐ |
    | Good | ☐ | Poor | ☐ |

5.  How useful is this publication to your work?

    Very useful ☐          Of some use ☐          Irrelevant ☐

6.  Please indicate the three things you liked best about this publication:

    _____

    _____

    _____

7.  Please indicate the three things you liked least about this publication:

    _____

    _____

    _____

8.  If you have read more than the present publication of the UNCTAD Division on Investment, Technology and Enterprise Development, what is your overall assessment of them?

    Consistently good ☐          Usually good, but with some exceptions ☐

    Generally mediocre ☐          Poor ☐

9.  On average, how useful are these publications to you in your work?

    Very useful ☐          Of some use ☐          Irrelevant ☐

10. Are you a regular recipient of *Transnational Corporations* (formerly *The CTC Reporter*), the Division's tri-annual refereed journal?

    Yes ☐          No ☐

    If not, please check here if you would like to receive a sample
    copy sent to the name and address you have given above ☐

Printed in France
GE.98-50400–April 1998–5,520

UNCTAD/ITE/IIT/6

United Nations publication
Sales No. E.98.II.D.4

ISBN 92-1-112425-5